Dishonesty is the Second-Best Policy

David Mitchell is a comedian, actor, writer and the polysyllabic member of Mitchell and Webb. He won BAFTAs for *Peep Show* and *That Mitchell and Webb Look* and has also starred in *Jam & Jerusalem*, *Ambassadors*, *Back* and as Will Shakespeare in Ben Elton's *Upstart Crow*. He writes for the *Observer*, chairs *The Unbelievable Truth*, is a team captain on *Would I Lie to You?* and can't drive.

DAVID MITCHELL

DISHONESTY IS THE
SECOND-BEST POLICY

AND OTHER RULES
TO LIVE BY

First published by Guardian Faber in 2019
Guardian Faber is an imprint of Faber & Faber Ltd,
Bloomsbury House, 74–77 Great Russell Street,
London WC1B 3DA

Guardian is a registered trade mark of
Guardian News & Media Ltd,
Kings Place, 90 York Way, London N1 9GU

This paperback edition published in 2020

Typeset by Ian Bahrami
Printed and bound by CPI Group (UK) Ltd, Croydon CR0 4YY

A CIP record for this book
is available from the British Library

ISBN 978-1-78335-198-5

To Barbara

CONTENTS

INTRODUCTION

The Best Two Policies

Some honesty to begin with: "Dishonesty is the second-best policy" is a phrase coined by the late American comedian George Carlin. So I didn't come up with it. Although, in complete honesty again, I really believe I thought of it independently. I don't think I'd ever heard it before I thought it. The sensation when it came into my head was of invention, not remembrance, and unless you're an advertising "creative" it's not easy to confuse the two.

But there's no denying that George Carlin thought of it before I did. And indeed died before I thought of it. And thought of it before he died. And also before I died. At time of writing, I have not yet died. George Carlin is ahead of me on so many fronts.

As a comedian myself, I should probably have been more aware of George Carlin. The fact that I was in a position to think I'd invented one of his famous quotations is a damning indictment of my ignorance. Or rather of my knowledge. It's a triumph for my ignorance. A big public victory all over the cover of a book. Take that, my knowledge!

I am now imagining my Knowledge and my Ignorance as two forces within me battling for each other's eclipse: one striving to make me omniscient, the other seeking the complete evacuation of my brain. A bit like a hoarder versus someone who favours the minimalist school of interior design.

Oh dear, now I've implied that the acquisition of knowledge is the cerebral equivalent of living in a weird and stinking house stacked to the ceiling with newspapers and labelled jars of wee. That's not at all the sort of message I should be sending out to the kids. And the truth is that I'd much prefer to live in an obsessive's smelly paper labyrinth than a trendy, echoing home containing widely spaced-out, uncomfortable chairs and a solitary orchid.

So having, as it seemed to me, invented the phrase "Dishonesty is the second-best policy", it felt like an apposite reflection on an era frequently referred to as "post-truth". I thought it might make a good title for this collection of columns, written for the *Observer* between 2014 and 2019. And then I thought, "That feels like the sort of phrase someone might've come up with already." And so I Googled it to check, and that's when George Carlin burst posthumously into my life. Incidentally, William the Conqueror also burst posthumously. At his funeral, so they say. Some claim he actually exploded. I don't know how Ignorance missed all that. The brain Hoover must be losing its suck.

Obviously, people have always lied – so we shouldn't get too excited about our own society, as if it's done something which, while admittedly bad, is devilishly inventive, like feeding Christians to lions or devising whisky. Lying is as old as the hills. Older than ones made of landfill, which I suppose are lying about being hills.

Personally, I lie quite often, mainly about whether I am free to attend social events. It's all because the phrase "I can come but I don't want to" seems not to be permitted. There's no way of dressing that sentiment up so that it's socially acceptable. I'll have a go, though:

"It's so kind of you to invite me and I am sincerely grateful for the thought but, on that day, I know I will be tired and would prefer to stay at home, and I very much doubt that you'd really want me to come if I really don't want to myself, so if it's OK, I won't."

You see? Won't do. At best, you'd get some sort of diagnosis. And you'd hurt the inviter's feelings. And the inviter would think less of you – that's the real kicker.

So there's nothing for it but "Thanks so much – I'd love to come, but sadly I've got to [insert lie here]." It's the only way of availing yourself of your liberty not to attend without breaking social convention. If you believe in freedom and you don't want people to think you're a dick – and the vast majority of us fall into this category – you've got to lie, and lie well.

It's a bit crazy really. As a consequence, we live in a world in which ostensibly everyone wants to go to everything they're invited to. They *always* want to, but sometimes they just can't. The notion of people not wanting to go to parties that they're actually free to attend is not openly acknowledged by our society. It's like prostitution in the Victorian age: it's happening everywhere, but everyone pretends it isn't.

In the case of the party-invitation-response convention, that means there is no language for effectively expressing sincere gratitude for an invitation to an event that you genuinely would like to go to but genuinely can't. All the phrases you might use for expressing that have been stolen by lying excuse-makers like me. Some societies, in this kind of fix, would develop a helpful etiquette: "I'm so sorry but I can't make it" would mean "I don't want to come but you're not allowed to hate me," while "I'm so sorry but I *really* can't make it" would express genuine gratitude and regret.

But that's not how we roll these days. The "really" would be instantly co-opted by the insincere brigade to make their lies more believable and reduce their reputational jeopardy, just as every politically correct term for mental illness ever devised, from cretin onwards, has been co-opted as a term of abuse.

The Truth Won't Out

Lying is probably the inevitable consequence of being able to communicate. Language is an amazing tool, one that's not available to most organisms, but I reckon as soon as you have the power to pass on the truth, it's going to occur to you not to. Some of those bee dances and whale calls are almost certainly bullshit.

So I suppose it makes sense that the advent of the most powerful communication technology ever devised – the internet and the smartphone – should have caused an exponential rise in dishonesty. We should have expected it; we just got distracted by all the hyperbolic chat about the "democratisation of truth" from people who, if they were being totally honest themselves, would admit that they're in it primarily for the gadgets.

I'm fond of saying that the internet and its smartphone delivery system are a more disastrous human invention than nuclear weapons. And it's certainly arguable at this point in history. Though I admit that's largely because there's never been a full-scale nuclear war.

So broadly speaking, if I'm right, it's good news! One of the many things a full-scale nuclear war would blast away is the arguability of my claim. All of which makes me a sort of doom-mongering optimist. I'm saying that maybe there won't ever be a big nuclear war, which leaves the field clear for smartphones to wreak their slightly less dramatic form of havoc in a way that will eclipse the harm done, so far, by nuclear bombs. Hooray!

One of the advantages of nuclear weapons, as disastrous things to invent go, is that they were immediately obviously a disastrous thing to invent. Nobody's going to be fooled for a second into thinking they're going to democratise anything, except possibly death, which is pretty democratised already.

4

Conversely, the smartphone/internet combination is in the cigarettes and plastic straws school of disastrous invention. Not because it's also tubular – neither the internet nor any mobile phones are, to my knowledge, tubular – but because it initially seemed harmless and fun. The cancer and scourge-of-marine-life issues only raised their heads later, in stinging rebuke of the initial invention's triviality and superfluousness.

To be fair to smartphones (and I always like to be fair to inanimate objects), they never seemed trivial in the same way as plastic straws. They seemed like they'd be useful. And they are useful. It's very useful to be able to communicate instantly and globally, to be able to find things out, buy things and be entertained by things without having to move, or while moving around doing something else which currently can't be achieved online, such as gardening or attending funerals.

It's extremely useful to be able to do all that. The only fly in the utility ointment is that *everyone* can do it. Frankly, that spoils it. If you were the only person with smartphone powers – able to shop, watch TV, write and receive correspondence, make phone calls, access more data than the Library of Congress wherever you were – that would be brilliant. So labour saving! You'd never have to go to work. But when everyone can do it, it effectively means you never *leave* work – if you're lucky enough to be in work, that is, which, if your area of expertise involves shops, restaurants, pubs or any of the old media, you're much less likely to be post-internet. And that's a particularly rough deal because you've also got several extra monthly bills to pay in order to remain a normal citizen: mobile, broadband, cable TV, maybe a bit of Netflix or Amazon Prime, and rental of space in a "cloud" as well. Well, it all adds to the GDP, I suppose, and conceals the fact that society is coming to bits.

The trouble is that all that – paying every month for a new invisible thing that means you can never literally and metaphorically switch off, and which has undermined economic norms that have existed for millennia – is the fucking least of it. It's the mere tip of the technological iceberg along which the good ship *Life-As-We-Know-It* is scraping its hull.

We haven't even got to the grooming, the dramatic reversal of the decades-long decline in child abuse, the increasing impossibility of distinguishing truth from lies, the financial degradation of the old-media investigative institutions that used to provide that truth, the bullying, the abuse, the threats of murder and rape, and the incalculable long-term effects of social media, bristling as it is with virtue-signalling, selfies and revenge porn, on all of our brains, particularly those of young people, who have grown up with this technology in its current raw, unregulated form. Plus, people don't keep appointments any more because they just text and say they're running late. It's all fucking terrible! Who knows what the ultimate outcome of all this will be but, anecdotally at least, it doesn't look like happiness.

Most insidious of all is the effect on truth. Suddenly it feels so flimsy. My whole view of existence is predicated on the notion that, in the end, the truth will out. Possibly long after the protagonists of any controversy have died, but eventually, and for the eternal knowledge of posterity.

That's how you get taught history at school. Tudor propagandists added a hunched back to Richard III's portrait, but we now know he only had scoliosis. The crucial phrase is "we now know". But what if the blizzard of words and imagery that the internet generates about everything, often manipulated by malign interest groups, makes the truth impossible ever to discern? It's in that haystack somewhere, but it's just one of the pieces of hay. Suddenly the whole of human existence is like an episode of *Poirot* in which the murder remains unsolved.

And it's not just the bare-faced lying that scares me but all the subjectivity. In the online world, which has become such a high percentage of many people's experience of existence, almost everything we see has been curated for us: the adverts that appear, the political claims that are made, the people we interact with, the products that are suggested to us when we search for something and the news that we're told about. It's all been tailored according to what we're likely to respond to. No two people see the same thing.

Even the BBC News website is at it. It's taken to asking me if I want to "change nation". Considering the Brexit situation, I bloody do. Sadly, the only options are England, Scotland, Wales and Northern Ireland, which is a bit of a samey range if you ask me. But it's not really offering to change my nationality; it's telling me that it will report stories from where I live, or where I'm most interested in, more prominently. I hate that. I just want to look at the BBC News website. I want to see the same one as everyone else, just like I would if I'd bought a newspaper in a shop.

I can seek out the subjects I particularly want to find out about by myself. I want to be able to find them, but I don't want them pushed towards me. The level of interest an algorithm thinks I'm likely to show in any given news report is not a meaningful gauge of how important it actually is. If I only want to read stories about, say, cricket, I'll go to a cricket website or buy a cricket magazine. I don't want all my news feeds to suddenly start banging on exclusively about cricket because some machine has worked out I'm into it, thereby giving me the illusion that the most important global events are all cricket-related.

No wonder we talk about our online echo chambers, where everyone seems to agree with each other and any transgression from a range of approved views is jumped upon and the transgressor shamed. Social media corrals people into interacting solely with those who share their viewpoint more effectively than the court of Versailles in the last days of the Bourbons.

This already dangerous situation is exacerbated by the fact that the only news, adverts or products that each echo chamber will get to see are specifically designed to attract the attention of its members – and so inevitably to confirm them in their opinions and prejudices. How else can the censorious and admonitory extreme political correctness of some university campuses coexist in the same world as the unabashed rise of crypto-fascism?

The fact is that, virtually speaking, they don't exist in the same world. There is no unified reality, and that really might be a disaster. Objective truth may always have been unattainable, but that doesn't mean it isn't worth striving for.

If we all just settle into small, mutually ignorant online support groups exchanging comforting half-truths, then civilisation is in for a rough ride. No one will know what is really going on, and working out what is really going on has, for most of history, been humankind's main purpose. Losing that is a high price to pay for being able to order pizza without speaking to anyone.

Chivalry Is Dead

Look, I'm not Amish. I understand that humans are driven to invent things, that technology, in general, becomes more advanced over time, and, again in general, I'm in favour of that. Maybe we were happier as hunter-gatherers, but it's too late to go back to doing that now, as there are roughly seven billion more people on the planet than that lifestyle could support. So even if starting to farm and live in towns was a big mistake, there's no going back. We might as well double down on the cock-up (as they say in porn) and develop crop rotation and the yoke and the seed drill and the steam engine and, as it turns out, nuclear weapons, asbestos, porn and Twitter.

So I'm not cross with the people who invented this stuff. It's what humans do – you might as well get cross with beavers for building dams. Our brains got us into this and, if anything will get us out of it, it's our brains. All the more reason to hope that they haven't been fundamentally warped and brutalised by over-exposure to Instagram.

It's not fair to blame inventors and, in fact, I don't think it's very constructive, in general, to blame people. I mean, it's enjoyable and it's often deserved. Nobody is going to take away my righteous contempt for David Cameron, for example. My unshakeable view is that he hugely damaged the country with his mixture of self-interest and being-wrong-about-everything, but the more important question is: how was such a second-rate scoundrel in a position to do what he did? There must have been failings in the system.

I also think this about another figure often singled out for personal blame: businessman Sir (at time of writing) Philip Green. I'd genuinely hate him to lose his knighthood, because the fact that he's got one is such an illuminating case study of the self-defeating way our society dishes out rewards.

In theory, knighthoods are supposed to go to people who do good things – who are successful and good. But who, for an instant, ever thought Sir Philip Green was good – that he was a really good man? Here I'm just talking about the activities of the businesses he runs, not the allegations of bullying and sexual misconduct. Even assuming that they're all groundless, which would surprise me but is theoretically possible, who ever thought that he was a decent chap or a nice guy? I mean, he might have been successful, but he clearly never gave a damn about the country or society. He just wanted to make money.

That's OK with me – we live in a capitalist system, so that's what we should expect lots of people to want – but what was the knighthood for? He gets to keep the money, doesn't he? Do we worry that, without the added promise of a chivalric award, he wouldn't have bothered to dedicate his life to his own enrichment, and so our economy would have suffered? I'm pretty sure he'd have done it anyway. And, as a side note, we might have been better off if he hadn't.

But blaming him misses the point. Circumstances existed in which he was able to practise business as he did – ie with minimum collateral benefit to the community – and was honoured by our sovereign for doing it. Blaming him is like blaming the burglar if you leave your house unlocked. It's morally coherent but not particularly helpful. If that burglar hadn't stolen your stuff, another burglar probably would've done it. The root of the problem is not the personality of the burglar, but the circumstances in which the burglar can prosper.

For the avoidance of being sued, I am not suggesting any illegality in Sir Philip Green's business practices. What I'm saying is that an environment where those practices are completely legal – and indeed honoured in the same way as the Arthurian Lancelot's legendary heroism – is the metaphorical unlocked house. If it wasn't him (and of course it isn't just him), it would be someone else. Publicly admonishing him is just a distraction.

That doesn't mean it isn't instructive to analyse him. He was born in 1952 and grew up in post-war welfare state Britain. The country was, at that time, becoming fairer at a dramatic rate. That's not to say that it ever became fair, or that it was fairer then than it is now. 2019 Britain, for all its inequities, is a better place than, say, 1959 Britain. But it doesn't come close to matching 50s and 60s Britain's rate of improvement. Things are probably getting worse today, whereas in those decades, in terms of social justice, they were clearly improving. The strictures of the Victorian class system were, if not completely disappearing, taking a massive beating. Social mobility was, admittedly from a very low base, sharply on the rise.

This engendered in many of us a notion of Britain as a relatively just place where centuries-old wrongs were being righted, and this notion has outlasted the real improvements on which it was based. That's the problem with Green and his ilk. They are acting as if the system were fair and able to contain their unfettered self-interest. In a properly fair and well-run society, if people stay within the rules and are successful, they will end up doing good, even if they don't mean to and don't care. The system will incentivise societally beneficial behaviour. For too long we have flattered ourselves that we live in such a society, and in consequence the rich and the powerful have been let off the moral hook.

The recent focus on Green as a villain shows that something is changing, but not in the right way. Blaming him personally is effectively calling for a return to a sort of benevolent paternalism, a sense of *noblesse oblige*. That's what the Victorians had instead of social justice, and it's a shit system. If your local lord of the manor is a nice guy, like in *Downton Abbey*, life is unfair, but you don't starve – but that's as good as it gets, unless you're born into the ruling kleptocracy.

By all means slag off Green, but the solution to the problem he symbolises is not to embarrass him into being nicer, and seeing that as the solution is harmful. He is nothing more than an index of the failures of the system. By putting the onus on him, we're calling for a return to a society of toffs and philanthropists where, instead of a welfare state, you get crumbs from the rich man's table. Green is like a sort of reverse canary: while he's still prosperously chirruping on his perch, we know for sure that we're in the midst of something poisonous.

My Solution to Everything

Everyone says this is a divisive age, so in that spirit let's do some dividing! Let's divide all other ages into two: there are the ages where things are getting better and the ages where they're getting worse. It's not always easy to tell which sort of age you're in but it's bound to be one of the two. (Unless things are just staying the same, I suppose, but I reckon that would be quite a brief age. More of an instant, a momentary teeter, so we can disregard it.)

What sort of age is this age then, other than a divisive one? Is it an improver or a worsener? I'm afraid I think it's a worsener – for Britain anyway – and I didn't think that until recently. So maybe it wasn't the case until recently? It's possible that, in my lifetime, we've gone from an age where things were generally getting better to one where they're generally getting worse. I refuse to blame myself, which may be part of the problem.

This conviction is my justification for all the moaning (and Remoaning) in this book. Britain in 2019 is not a terrible place, historically speaking, to live. But if it is a place that is getting worse, and was recently a place that was getting better, that is a bit of a shame. Moral and economic decline isn't the end of the world (though of course it could lead to it): roughly half the people who have ever lived have done so in declining civilisations, and this one is declining from quite a high point, with freedom of speech, public order and lots of hot and cold running water. But this shift from improvement to deterioration is going to have a marked psychological impact on the community. It's really depressing, basically. Things getting inexorably worse, even if they're not by any objective historical measure that bad, is liable to make existence itself feel a bit pointless.

One of the most worrying symptoms of the current malaise is that people often ask me what I think is going on. I am just a comedian who writes a humorous newspaper column, and am therefore the wrong person to ask. But I suspect the people who ask me didn't ask me first – which means they got unsatisfactory answers from those who might actually know. So now they're asking me out of desperation. Next stop: the dog. Or maybe they've already asked the dog. Why should I expect to be asked before the dog?

Perhaps they're just trying to make conversation. I am quite an awkward person to talk to, after all. But I still reckon there is a lot of bewilderment around: about Brexit, about climate change, about identity politics, about political extremism, about *Strictly*. I mean, why are the judges so horrible to the celebrities? No wonder they can no longer attract contestants people have heard of.

Maybe I'm wrong. Maybe everything's great, and it's just that I'm 45. I've never been 45 before – perhaps the world always seems like it's declining to 45-year-olds simply because they are. It's a bit of a coincidence that I'm coming to this conclusion just as the fact that I've passed the midpoint of my likely existence hits home. Perhaps I'm just feeling apocalyptic because I've realised I'm not immortal?

But maybe I'm right and things are going wrong. And, if so, I know exactly what to do to fix them. Genuinely. I reckon the following would do it – or at least cause a marked upturn. Ready? It's nothing to do with Jesus, crystals or any secret conspiracy, I promise. It's on the dry side, to be frank, but I reckon it would be worth a shot:

- Introduce proportional representation so that the two-party grip on power is broken.
- Pay MPs loads more, while simultaneously putting enormous constraints on their extra-parliamentary activities, not just while they're MPs but for the rest of their lives, in order to undermine the malign influence of lobbyists.
- Put a tax on carbon so that commercial activities carry a financial cost equivalent to their environmental one. Some say we need to totally restructure our economy to deal with climate change, but I reckon channelling capitalism is a better plan than attempting to replace it. If we want people to find ways of emitting less carbon to save the planet, let's harness the

awesome power, dedication and inventiveness of the human urge to dodge tax.

I'm afraid I don't know what to do about the internet except wish it didn't exist. But maybe that might help in itself. At least we'd stop having to celebrate it as if the stratospheric enrichment of a bunch of Californians who go to work in flip-flops was some sort of boon for humanity.

But, basically, do all that and I'm pretty sure the country, and the world, would become a better place. I reckon it would reverse the worsening. Apologies if you think it's presumptuous of a comedian to offer this sort of trite manifesto, but I figure it's the least I can do if I'm going to keep on moaning. And my resolve to do that is unshakeable.

The only big problem I can see with My Solution to Everything is that I have absolutely no idea how to make society do all of it – or, actually, any of it. I think they're policies that would work, but there's absolutely no way of making them happen politically. Knowing what to do but having no idea of how to do it is worthless – like a penguin who's invented fire. "Rub two sticks together! It'll really warm us up!" he says to the other penguins, who look at their flippers and look at the endless snow. And then one of them says: "I don't think that's going to happen."

I suppose I could always try convincing people that it's the right thing to do by using reasoned argument and then it might happen by democratic will. And there'll be other jokes later in the book.

The subjects covered include (in no particular order) TV, board games, advertising, Boris Johnson, Nurofen, religion, farting, cinema, corporate greed, champagne, fashion, art, smoking and roads with rude names. I have put them in groups and an order, but your statutory rights are unaffected. Read this book however you like. Mix it up, dip in or read all the preposi-tions first – it's up to you. You do not, strictly speaking, have to read it at all – but I would be rather hurt if you didn't. I mean, come on – you've got this far.

Despite all the hand-wringing above, this collection of col-umns is as often glass-half-full as glass-half-empty. There's still plenty of lovely liquid in our national metaphorical glass (though I'm hoping it's metaphorical Pyrex rather than metaphorical crys-tal as I'm putting quite a lot of metaphorical pressure on it in this sentence), but however much is currently in it, I'm pretty sure it's being emptied, not filled.

1

Popular and Unpopular Culture

A look at some high arts, such as opera, some
slightly less high arts, such as photography, and some
other stuff that you may or may not think of as arts,
so let's just call them non-sciences.

Let's start by addressing a properly big question: what are things?

You know, things? Pens and tomatoes and motorcycles and daffodils. And I don't just mean objects: also chess and Valentine's Day and ants and poetry and Somalia. They're all things.

A newspaper is a thing, and so is the *Observer* newspaper, and so is the particular edition of the *Observer* that published this. But an individual copy of that issue of the *Observer* is also a thing – and a different thing from the institution of the newspaper itself, or the concept of a day's individual edition, but somehow linked. But then you might be reading this on a phone (a thing) or computer (a thing), either way via the medium (a thing? A person? A lady with a turban?) of the *Guardian* website (which is also a thing). Or in a copy (a thing) of a book (a thing) in which this thing (a column) has also been published.

I have a feeling I'm stumbling along a path already trodden by those more learned and with more time on their hands than I. I vaguely remember listening to an episode of *In Our Time* in which some hapless boffins had to explain all the knots Bertrand Russell had got himself into trying to prove that numbers were a thing, while Melvyn Bragg got so cross and bored you could actually hear his irritated glare.

So, things: it's a broad church. Or they're a broad church. And a broad church is, as well as a metaphor (itself a thing) for things, also a thing. Such as might have a magnificent tower or spire, perfect for bell-ringing. And the practice of bell-ringing is also, of course, a thing.

But what sort of thing? Now we're getting down to it. Well, it is not, currently, a sport. (A sport is a type of thing.) But Robert Lewis, editor of *The Ringing World*, says it should be. Because he thinks it is. I mean, he thinks it should be classified as a sport, which must surely mean he believes it already is one. He can't think that the classification alone would be enough to make it one, like a fairy godmother's wand. He's not hitching mice to a pumpkin and calling himself princess.

"Ringing is . . . a healthy mental and physical workout," Lewis says. "We would like many more people to have the opportunity to try it and identification as a sport could help achieve that." I wonder why it would help. It would put me off. Because books about it would be in a different section of the library? Next to old *Wisden*s and the novelisation of *Rocky*? Funding probably, isn't it. It's always bloody funding. That's *definitely* a thing.

Anyway, in this case the fairy godmother, or rather the organisation in charge of saying "It's no good putting that in a pie, it's got an axle," is Sport England. It decides what's a sport and recently told the game of bridge it wasn't one because it didn't entail a "physical activity". It's a lot stricter than Card Game England, which let in Twister on the basis that it's "all played on a single large card".

I reckon bell-ringing's case is fairly persuasive. It's clearly a physically strenuous activity that requires skill, and there are hotly, indeed sweatily, contested competitions between different bell-ringers. Shooting, darts, quoits, angling, yoga and ballooning are official sports, so why not?

The main reason is that its governing body, the Central Council of Church Bell Ringers, doesn't want to apply. "The primary object of the council is to promote and foster the ringing of bells for Christian prayer, worship and celebration," it said. "We enjoy and rely on an excellent relationship with various church bodies and we would not wish to risk prejudicing this." What a weird difference of opinion among the campanologists. They don't disagree over what bell-ringing involves, what they should all actually do – just over how the activity is classified.

This reminded me of the fuss surrounding the nomination of *The Martian* for best comedy at the Golden Globes, an award it then won. Many felt that not only was the film not funny, something which wouldn't necessarily make it stand out among comedies, but it wasn't even meant to be. A post-structuralist might argue that the film-makers' intentions were irrelevant. Others considered them cynical and accused *The Martian*'s producers of muscling in on the comparatively cushy comedy category in order to grab an easy award and add to the pre-Oscars buzz surrounding their film, without having to take on heavy hitters like *The Revenant* in the more competitive best self-important-three-hour-slog category.

But how could an unfunny film be judged the winner of the comedy category? I suppose the judges must have liked it better than the films with jokes. They can't have thought it a better comedy; just a better film, a better thing. It's like a bacon sandwich winning the "tastiest apple" award at a farm show. Comedies aren't as easily defined as sandwiches and apples. I'm sure there's some deliberate humour in *The Martian*, so maybe that means it is a comedy. And the award, after all, is for best comedy, not funniest comedy. Maybe all that funny stuff in the other films made the Hollywood Foreign Press Association feel cheap.

But all of these problems stem from trying to divide things into meaningful groups: sports, calls to prayer, comedies, tragedies, films, YouTube clips. What is a call to prayer but a noisy sport without a scoring system? What is a drama but an unbelievably long comedy without any jokes? What is an awards ceremony but a strange and inefficient distribution system for vulgar knick-knacks? Well, some would say it's a comedy, some a drama, some, what with all the getting up and down, a sport. And it's certainly a call to prayer for many nominees.

A spoon is just a very ineffective fork with a single blunted tine. A fork is only a spoon with annoying holes that inhibit soup consumption. What is soup but a liquid mousse? And isn't steak and chips just a very hearty, lumpy consommé? Or a hot and greasy weapon? Or a work of modern art? Or a weirdly meaty non-dairy cheese?

So does the big question I posed have an answer? No. But actually "No" is an answer. And a word. And a thing.

* * *

Apparently some people are capable of lucid dreaming. In a dream, they can control what's going on – direct the actions of themselves and others in ways that please, excite, arouse or interest them. That would be my worst nightmare. Worse than my worst nightmare to date, which, though terrifying, was at least not of my own conscious (while unconscious) invention.

I'd rather be tormented by ghouls, have to take my A-levels again while wearing Speedos, appear on stage in an incredibly lifelike Donald Trump mask which I can't remove even with a razor, fall off a cliff edge into impenetrable darkness or offend my mother-in-law by weeing and weeing and weeing in her face (these are just a few from last night) than be in control of it all. I hate being in control – it means that, when things are horrible, it's my fault. And things are going to be horrible – that's a given.

Another reason the prospect of steering dreams makes me glum is that deciding what happens in things that aren't really happening is part of my job. So the thought of having to continue to do it even while asleep is exhausting. I'd rather unconsciously process planning applications, issue parking tickets or work out VAT. But perhaps a planning officer, traffic warden or accountant would be refreshed by getting to show-run their own inert imaginings of living in a gold palace, eating their way out of a maze made of cake, having sex with a film star or whatever else constitutes a lucid dreamer's dream dream.

Don't get me wrong: deciding what happens in things that aren't really happening is nice work if you can get it – indoors and the money can be decent – I just couldn't do it in my sleep. I've been involved in making many TV programmes depicting events that almost certainly didn't occur. The hope is that people will find watching what happens sufficiently entertaining that they won't mind that it didn't (just as, I suppose, the tedium of watching football highlights must be mitigated for some by the fact that it did).

Of course, with something like that, you can never be completely sure it's going to work. Which leads to a lot of fretting and analysing, and dozens of discussions of how things should be: "Should the scene end like this or like that?" "Should we say it this way or that way?" "Should we use this hat or that hat?" Even after the scripts have been redrafted for the tenth time, it's all still an agony of small decisions, like people always complain when they're planning their wedding, though, in that instance, the only people they really have to please are themselves.

But there are nice moments when you can let yourself off that decision hook and film things in a way that allows you to "decide in the edit". It's a wonderful phrase. We don't have to work out what's best now, all tired and stressed; we can defer the decision to "the edit" – the promised land of future wisdom where the right course of action will become clear.

With that in mind, I found the news that Netflix is planning a new kind of TV show, in which viewers get to decide key plot decisions for themselves, incredibly relaxing. It's been described as the TV equivalent of those "Choose Your Own Adventure" and "Fighting Fantasy" books that were big in the 80s. In this utopian vision, programme-makers wouldn't just get to defer difficult decisions to the edit, but to their viewers' very living rooms. "You bloody decide!" we'll be able to say. "We'll shoot it both ways and you pick. And if you hate it, it's your fault!"

This would be a return to people making their own entertainment, but instead of singing "D'Ye Ken John Peel?" to the wheezing of an accordion, they get to assemble their own classic comedy and drama from a bewildering array of scenes with glitteringly high production values laid out for them by the world's wealthiest online broadcaster. Just don't lose the remote.

This plan is brilliant in two ways. First, it is the sort of thing people will always say they want, like New Coke. If you survey people or herd them into focus groups and ask them if they'd like more control over a thing, they'll invariably say yes. It feels lame to say anything else, particularly if you're the sort of person who ends up doing surveys and taking part in focus groups. By doing that, you're already signalling a desire to affect things, to make your view count. The chances of such a person saying "No thanks – I'd rather the people who made the programmes decided the story" are never going to hit the 50% required to generate negative feedback about this crackpot scheme. So it's guaranteed a positive buzz.

And second, by announcing this, Netflix must know it will further put the wind up other, more conventional broadcasters. There'll be a worried meeting at the BBC about the technical limitations of the red button, Channel 4 will start examining logos for their version and having meetings with execs from Tinder in the hope they'll pay for it, and ITV will buy the rights to *The Warlock of Firetop Mountain*. It's brilliant propaganda, like a country at war starting rumours of a new super-weapon. Suddenly their enemies' resources start being wasted on trying to compete with a phantasm.

The only downside is that no one will want it. It's like 3D, which every generation of film-makers makes another fruitless attempt at getting cinema-goers excited about. I'd be amazed if lower-tech versions of Netflix's notion haven't been pitched every eight to 15 years since the dawn of TV. And, in the current technological context, the idea falls perfectly equidistantly between the two stools of fiction and video games. It has the strengths of neither and the weaknesses of both. The fact that people enjoy both hot baths and rollercoasters doesn't make the two experiences ripe for merger.

People like stories. Not as much as they like food or shelter, but a lot. And a good story is held together by one question: what happens next? It's a question for the audience to ask and the storyteller to answer. It's something an entertained audience wants to find out, not decide. There's no suspense if the denouement is of your own devising.

* * *

Nowadays the BBC seems to get attacked by everyone, but back in March 2016 it was left to the Conservative government to do most of the kicking . . .

There's a new word in the lexicon of media bullshit: it is "distinctiveness". A report, commissioned by the Department for Culture, Media and Sport and published last week, argues that "greater distinctiveness" in the BBC's output will allow its commercial rivals to make an extra £115m a year.

That seems pretty great, doesn't it? The BBC's output gets massively more "distinctive", which sounds like absolutely unanswerably superb news, and at the same time commercial broadcasters make millions of extra pounds. How hugely splendid all round. Hooray.

So what is this "distinctiveness" that we're all going to be enjoying? What are distinctive things? Well, I'm immediately thinking of the taste of chicken liver, the sound of James Mason's voice, the design tradition of Citroën cars until the late 80s, the smell of pipe smoke, the style of Raymond Chandler's prose. Those are all thoroughly attractive attributes, and I can't wait for the BBC's TV and radio programmes to sort of somehow start having more of that kind of thing about them.

And, in other related brilliantness, ITV, Sky, Heart FM et al. will have lots more money – which obviously isn't distinctive at all, a certain uniformity being an unavoidable drawback of any currency, but is still nice to have, and they can always choose to use it to buy lovely distinctive things, like sci-fi chess sets, pool showers made out of telephone boxes, toby jugs and clown shoes. So that's great too.

Unfortunately, the distinctiveness of a Hitchcock movie, a Lowry painting or a Cole Porter lyric doesn't seem to be the sort the report is getting at, because that's a kind people really like. That would be entirely counterproductive to its stated aims. By "distinctiveness", the report means that the BBC should deliberately target smaller and more niche audiences, in order to allow the commercial sector to take the bigger ones. Its distinctive flavour would be less like chicken liver and more like calves' brains. Because that would be fairer on the marketplace.

This repellent tang is to be achieved in broadly three ways: the corporation should generate more content in less populist, and indeed less popular, genres; it should schedule programmes less aggressively; and it should take more risks in commissioning new ones. So Radio 1 should be more like Radio 1Xtra, broadcasting more obscure music and talking. The news website should ditch entertainment and soft news stories in favour of in-depth analysis. And BBC1 should do arts documentaries in primetime, make more new programmes and stop using *Strictly Come Dancing* as a stick with which to beat *The X Factor*.

These aren't terrible ideas. Aggressive scheduling is annoying. I'm sure many viewers, as well as ITV's shareholders, take the view that, if the BBC were to rise above the fray and schedule *Strictly Come Dancing* at a time that doesn't clash with *The X Factor*, it would be serving the public better. And the notion of more primetime arts, science and history programming, more analytical journalism and more risk-taking new commissions is metaphorical music to ears that scorn Radio 2's literal kind.

But these ideas have not been arrived at in order to improve the BBC, but specifically to make it do less well. The report doesn't advocate highbrow content *despite* the fact that it might not be popular, but *because* of it. If a new BBC1 documentary about Turgenev for seven o'clock on Saturday nights turned out to be a runaway ratings winner, then that too should be axed and replaced by something else.

The report's authors advocate greater risk-taking specifically in the hope that such risks do not pay off. For them, the only risk is that they do. If the distinctiveness they claim is vital were actually to be enjoyed by more people than the corporation's current output, then ITV, Sky and Channel 5 would be complaining about that and the culture secretary would have to commission a report calling for more blandness, less risk-taking and more audience-despising primetime bilge.

This puts the BBC in an almost impossible position. How can a broadcasting institution be expected deliberately to perform less well than it's capable of? To put shows on at a certain time, when it knows more people would watch them at another time? To stop making its most popular programmes and not merely take risks on new shows that might not be so popular, but on ones that had *better bloody not be* or there'll be hell to pay in Whitehall? This is like telling a boxer to throw a fight and make it look realistic. And what's to be the corporation's reward – its equivalent of a bookie's massive bribe? At most, to limp through charter renewal with comparatively little further pummelling. For now.

The BBC is under unprecedented political pressure, its morale is low and those who work for it and run it are understandably asking the question: what do we have to do to assuage our critics, to be allowed to continue? This report's answer can be summed up in one word: fail. Fundamentally, that is the requirement. "More distinctive" is just a way its authors have found of saying "less successful", but which they think will nevertheless sound vaguely positive to media wankers who flatter themselves that they're creative. Idiots with clever-sounding jobs can nod along with the uncontroversial-seeming concept of distinctiveness and are very unlikely to bother working out what it actually means.

It will be a fight to get rid of the BBC. Of the nearly 200,000 people who responded to a government consultation also published last week, 81% said the BBC was serving its audience "well or very well". People still like it, they still consume its services more than any other broadcaster's, and so, crucially, they would miss it. This report is in favour of reducing its audience – but, according to Mark Oliver, one of the study's authors, it "would still leave BBC reach at a level that would be sufficient to maintain support for the licence".

Maybe it would. For now. But this report makes the strategy of those commercially or ideologically opposed to the BBC startlingly clear. An overt challenge to the corporation's existence remains politically unfeasible – the public would miss it too much. The first step, then, is to turn it into something that fewer people would miss – and eventually, over time, to make it so distinctive that hardly anyone likes it at all.

* * *

My parents are the owners of what I'm pretty sure is a bad painting of Neath Abbey. I can't be completely certain because I know nothing about painting and I've never seen Neath Abbey. But it doesn't look much like anything I have seen, so I'm willing to believe it looks like Neath Abbey. Though not that it looks exactly like Neath Abbey – it's not credible to me that any medieval ruin (Neath Abbey is a medieval ruin) could, in real life, so closely resemble a vertical plane of dried paint.

My best shot at an objective conclusion about it is that someone of above average painting skill for a human, but below average for a professional artist, has rendered on canvas some shapes which, if you knew Neath Abbey, would remind you of it but wouldn't come close to fooling you that you were really looking at it.

These are deep waters, I realise. Ignorant about art though I am, I've still heard the whole thing about some paintings not having to look exactly like their subjects, or anything at all, to be deemed good. I get that – it's not photography. Everything's valid in a certain sort of way. Unless it isn't.

Because, of course, there is another category: paintings that don't look exactly like their subjects, but were meant to. They look wrong, but not in a Picasso two-eyes-on-the-same-side-of-the-nose way that pushes through into being applauded. They're a narrower miss: nowhere near the triple 20, but it's hit the board, so the thrower can't get away with claiming he wasn't playing darts in the first place. I reckon that's what we're dealing with here.

The artist, by the way, is long dead. I don't know his name, but the story in our family is that, about 100 years ago, he gave the painting as payment of a bar bill to an ancestor of my mother's who ran a pub. He obviously didn't owe very much.

27

For all that, I love it. It's large, dark and old, and it's got a thick gilt frame. It's extremely painting-like. It's a big old painting and, deep in my middle-class soul, I know there's nothing better for making a room seem posh than a big old painting on the wall.

So I was interested to see it reported that big old paintings are falling out of favour. Sir Nicholas Penny, former director of the National Gallery, wrote in the *London Review of Books* that art investors and collectors are suffering from "a sort of collective intoxication" with contemporary art and that institutions founded to house "old art" were now "determined to welcome" new works.

It appears the market for top-end modern artworks is booming because, Penny says, they're being "bought as investments, more than has ever previously been the case; they are deemed to constitute a secure 'alternative asset class'". This trend is receiving "strong institutional endorsement from the museums that hope to receive, or at least to borrow, some of this art" and is further enhanced by "a background of popular enthusiasm". This last point is illustrated by the fact that visitor numbers for Tate Modern are much higher than for its elder sister, Tate Britain.

Now he comes to mention it, I think I've noticed this going on. Everything seems increasingly modern arty. It goes with that clean and spacious interior design style that magazines and hotels are so insistent on. All glass and marble and exposed brick. Big expanses of floor or wall, perfect for some interesting "piece": perhaps a giant pair of neon lips, or a floor-to-ceiling shiny acrylic rendition of part of the word "February", or half a Fiat Uno with Marilyn Monroe's head bobbing through the sunroof on a spring.

I'm probably letting myself down with these dated or inexact references. Maybe it isn't Marilyn Monroe any more, though vaguely Monroeish imagery seems to have been a resilient feature of this kind of clobber ever since Warhol kicked it all off.

So perhaps I mean tall nobbly taupe sticks, or giant aluminium fish, or a huge, voluptuously lashed eye with a tiny golden ear at the very centre of the pupil, or a giant hunk of cheese marked "chalk", or a small watercolour of the front at Sidmouth with a swastika daubed on it in dog shit.

I'm not being fair, but I'm not really talking about the art, which I don't understand and never will. I'm talking about the "modern art" domestic look, as opposed to the "old pictures" domestic look. For these purposes, I lump Constable in with the Neath Abbey bar bill guy, and whoever incontrovertibly does modern art well with whoever incontrovertibly does it badly (and if there's no consensus about who's in which camp, please don't tell me as I'll find it frustrating).

You see, to me, modern art usually looks vulgar. Not in a gallery, where it looks appropriate – I mean at home. I don't much like it – I think it's jarring and is often an attempt on the part of its owner to project both taste and originality. In my view, you have to pick one. Going for the double is hubristic, and the physical manifestation of that hubris is a horrible living room you're pretending to like. Get some bookshelves up and a bunch of old paintings, maybe a little table covered in family photos and knick-knacks – that'll be much nicer.

I'm now just shouting at hippies to get a haircut, and of course people can do whatever they want with their homes (and who cares about my approval anyway? I like a bad old painting of Neath Abbey), but I'm finding it liberating to admit all this. My whole life, the culture has been pushing various versions of a "designed" environment in which it is advocated that we should live. To me, it always looks broadly the same, from the 1950s to the present day – all part of a massive and relentless reaction to the dark clutteredness of the Victorian era.

I like clutter, and I don't think that's unusual. But I think the appeal of old, comfy stuff is one of those feelings people mistrust in themselves. They think they're supposed to want to "de-clutter", so they dutifully replace their shelf of dusty and chipped porcelain dogs with a single grey bowl of silver pebbles. And they tell themselves that's much better.

Meanwhile, the gallery sends another lorry load of gilt frames into storage so it can clear a whole wing for self-referential Perspex.

* * *

The presenters of the BBC's new TV version of arts programme *Front Row* have already sparked controversy. Before I get into it (or rather, after I've got into it but now I'm going back and putting this in at the start), I should say that one of those pre-senters is my brother-in-law, Giles Coren. Which means you're even freer than usual to ignore everything I say because of bias. If so, I applaud the choice – go on your way with my blessing, helping yourself to a history GCSE on your way out.

The controversy is about theatre, one of the art forms the new show will be covering. In an interview with the *Radio Times*, all three presenters made remarks about it that annoyed people. Amol Rajan said he didn't get to the theatre as much as he'd like to because of his young baby, but that his "favourite place is Shakespeare's Globe and I love musical theatre. I went to New York a couple of years ago and saw Andrew Lloyd Webber's *School of Rock*".

Nikki Bedi said she likes a "fresh new piece of theatre", but "film is my passion". She added: "I resent going to the theatre and not having an interval for two hours and 45 minutes. I want more intervals. I like tight, fast-paced, creative theatre that moves away from tradition."

Giles also mentioned his young family as a reason for not hav-ing seen many plays recently and said he found theatre stressful because "I just worry about the poor bastards forgetting their lines". When asked how theatre-going could be improved, he said: "The seats! Why is it that in the theatre the seats are never as comfortable as the cinema? . . . I'd also like easier access to the loo."

So what's your reaction? "Those unforgiveable philistines should never be presenting a programme about the arts!"? Or "Bloody hell, the currency of controversy is pretty devalued! Isn't that what everyone thinks about the theatre?"

Unsurprisingly, the theatre world is solidly in the former camp. Dominic Cavendish, theatre critic of the *Daily Telegraph*, said he was "almost speechless", but rallied impressively to add: "What is the BBC doing, given the world-envied pre-eminence of our theatre culture, handing over the invaluable job of informing the TV-viewing public about what's on stage, what's good, what's not and why, to a *Come Dine With Me* melange of lightweights who between them seem to have quite liked going to Shakespeare's Globe and *School of Rock* IN NEW YORK!"

Mark Shenton, of the *Stage*, said it was "dispiriting" that the presenters were "so casually dismissive of theatre", rejecting Coren's worry about actors remembering lines as "spurious", as it's something "they're paid to do, and mostly succeed at". And *WhatsOnStage*'s Sarah Crompton lamented "the way in which everybody thought it was acceptable to talk that way about theatre".

Everybody really didn't. Online the outrage was splattered around like Kensington Gore at the end of *Hamlet*. Artistic directors, theatre critics, playwrights and rival arts journalists all had a pop at how "entitled" and "underqualified" the presenters are, how they apparently wouldn't be so dismissive of football or novels, and how terrible the BBC is for employing them. Playwright Dan Rebellato tweeted, "Dear @bbc when you need people to talk about theatre, don't send these idiots, send me. At least I know what I'm talking about," while arts blogger Victoria Sadler got in with "Hey @BBCFrontRow I think I can help. I actually go to the theatre & have great opinions."

I'm not quite sure what a "great opinion" is. Is it the opinion that something's great? If so, I bet the theatre world would love her to get the job. Or is it a correct opinion? In which case it'll be that the seats are uncomfortable. Because they are. "Oh, come on!" you may be thinking. "If the seats are so bad, how come it's so easy to fall asleep?" That's a poser.

At this point, I should make clear that some of the most joyous and energising experiences of my life have been in the theatre. I love theatres and I love shows. But the part of theatre I like most is being on stage. I find that enormous fun. You're all dressed up with something to say and loads of people are watching and, with a fair wind, they might laugh and clap. That is, in my view, lovely.

I've never been so keen on watching. Don't get me wrong, some shows are brilliant, but some are awful. I feel I should be supportive of theatre because (and I don't mean this to sound kinky), since I like being watched, it's only fair that I should watch other people now and again. But I don't enjoy it anywhere near as much as prancing around myself, and I would be amazed if my view isn't (possibly secretly) shared by most performers.

So I'm a bit squeamish about this show-off community, of which I'm proud to be a member, getting on its high horse about how grateful people should be to pay up and be showed off to, and insisting other media be reverential about how magical it all is. I'm not sure theatre criticism should be the preserve of, as Dan Rebellato suggests, those who know what they're talking about. Because that really just means insiders, people who see a lot of theatre and therefore don't necessarily react to it like a normal punter. Theatre is not for experts; it's supposed to be for everyone.

So when three intelligent, well-informed broadcasters mildly imply that theatre isn't a huge part of their lives, that shows can go on a bit, that the seats are uncomfortable and it's nice to have a few songs, I think that's fair enough. It hardly disqualifies them from broadcasting on the subject – they've expressed views held by many. And, when the theatre world is immediately furious and calls those critics sneering lightweights, one suspects they've touched a nerve.

No one would deny that some theatre shows are boring. There's no shame in that for those involved in the productions if they've done their best. They attempted something difficult, so it's a noble failure. But it's a failure. And it's only going to happen more often if theatreland's knee-jerk response to a bored audience member in a back-breaking seat is to scream at them to show some respect.

* * *

A winning photograph in the Wildlife Photographer of the Year 2017 competition has been disqualified because the animal in the picture turned out to be dead. That's according to the people running the competition. The photographer swears otherwise.

This isn't the overall winner, I should clarify – just the winner of one category. The overall winning photograph is coincidentally also of a dead animal, but in that case it was considered a good thing. In terms of the competition, that is. In general terms, it's a really bad thing: it's a picture of a black rhino that's been killed and had its horn hacked off so that someone evil can sell it to someone ignorant.

That's very bad, but the photo is deemed very good largely *because* that's so bad. It's good to do a picture of something bad, that's the rationale. It helps, like an x-ray of a tumour. It's better to know. It highlights the rhinos' plight and, as we all know, raising plight awareness is a major way of making a real difference. Sometimes I think I should get an OBE for my retweeting alone.

Anyway, it's an absolutely horrible picture, if you ask me. To want to put it on your wall, you'd have to have something wrong with you. But I suppose that's the point. And perhaps it shows a lot of technical skill. Though I don't really see why – it must be trickier to catch a hummingbird mid-slurp or some otters chatting. Ask any of those photographers who do big school groups and they'll tell you: the trick is to get them to stay still. Which, with a slaughtered rhino, is a piece of cake. The poachers have really helped you out there.

It was taxidermists who allegedly helped out the photographer of the disqualified picture, though they were no more aware of their complicity than the poachers. This photo, entitled *Night Raider* and formerly declared the winner of the "animals in their environment" category, depicts an anteater apparently stalking a termite mound in a Brazilian nature reserve. But the Natural History Museum (which runs the competition), having consulted five independent scientists, is convinced the anteater is stuffed. In fact, that it's a stuffed anteater taken from a nearby visitors' centre.

If you examine a picture of this particular item of taxidermy, and then look at *Night Raider*, you will probably agree. It's either the same anteater or the one in *Night Raider* has elected to strike an uncannily identical pose. Perhaps it was taking the piss out of its deceased colleague, adding insult to being-hollowed-out-then-filled-with-wire-and-wood-shavings. It's possible, I suppose. Certainly, the photographer, Marcio Cabral, continues to assert his innocence and says he's going to return to the reserve later in the year to prove it. I'd be intrigued to discover how.

But, for now, let's take it as a working hypothesis that the museum is right and Cabral borrowed a stuffed anteater and propped it against a termite mound before taking his temporarily award-winning snap. The competition rules state that "entries must not deceive the viewer or attempt to misrepresent the reality of nature", and obviously he's done that to some extent. The viewer has been deceived into inferring that the anteater is alive. Then again, it doesn't really misrepresent the reality of nature: anteaters do attack termite mounds – he just failed to capture it actually happening. So it's not like a mock-up of a lion having a salad.

I'm not defending what Cabral has allegedly done, but it gives an interesting insight into what we want from eye-catching wildlife photography. Obviously, it has to look good (or visually arresting in the case of the mutilated rhino corpse) and it has to show something genuine about the natural world. *Night Raider* ticks both of these boxes, despite the fakery: it's a pretty picture and anteaters eat termites (the clue's not in the name). But it seems we also need to believe these photos depict something that literally happened at the moment they were taken.

It's like with anecdotes: if a person told you they'd once been mugged, you'd be drawn in, even if the sequence of events was fairly mundane. But if it turned out they hadn't really been mugged, the story would lose all interest. The events they described will undoubtedly have genuinely happened to someone, but not to whomever you're talking to – so sod it. They're just lying. Anteaters attack termite mounds, but that's not what was actually happening in the picture – so sod it. The photographer's a liar.

"Fiction is the lie through which we tell the truth," wrote Albert Camus. Well, if *Night Raider* is a lie, and it tells the truth about anteaters, is it fiction? Yes. Crap fiction. It's not a very interesting truth – only marginally more compelling than if the anteater was pictured approaching an anthill. My imagined mugging anecdotalist could, instead, have written a short story about someone being mugged. But, if it's billed as fiction, it has to be twice as entertaining and insightful to get half as much attention as simply claiming: "This just happened to me!"

This photograph's level of inventiveness is insufficient for it to pass muster as fiction. It's a much more competitive field. Suddenly you're not just up against a flower with some dew on it, but *Star Wars*. Hence the need to pass it off as truth – so it's not storytelling, it's cheating.

It's not cheating to wait years to get the shot. It's not cheating to frame out a bin or a power station. It's probably not really cheating to shout to make some geese take off. But it is cheating for a man to drag a stuffed anteater all the way from a visitors' centre to a termite mound.

But if only a wildlife photographer had got a snap of that happening. What a fascinating and authentic image of eccentric mammalian behaviour that would be.

* * *

In February 2019, in an interview with the Independent *as part of a press junket, the actor Liam Neeson said this: "I went up and down areas with a cosh, hoping I'd be approached by somebody – I'm ashamed to say that – and I did it for maybe a week, hoping some 'black bastard' would come out of a pub and have a go at me about something, you know? So that I could . . . kill him."*

Is it because of Liam Neeson, I wonder, that John Humphrys has announced he's going to retire from the *Today* programme? Was Neeson's astonishing interview in the *Independent* what finally made the great Radio 4 inquisitor realise quite how much you can get out of an interviewee if you give them a bit of space to speak?

Interviews and interviewing have been in the news a lot. Not only was there the extraordinary confession Neeson volunteered in the middle of what was supposed to be a perfectly vacuous press junket, and Humphrys's equally unexpected proclamation, but also Maureen Lipman, writing in the *Radio Times*, had a pop at the modern style of chat show. "The sofa is crammed, like a chapel pew, with English actors telling their juiciest genitalia stories while the host sniggers in a three-piece suit," was how she described the genre.

I don't think Liam Neeson's anecdote would have amused Graham Norton, though. I can imagine him glazing over in horror and wishing that, instead of putting Neeson on the sofa, he'd been seated on that red tippy chair. If the producers of his new film *Cold Pursuit* had been able to pull a big chair-tipping lever before Liam could say "black bastard", they wouldn't have needed to cancel the premiere.

By now, Neeson's words will have been subjected to more scrutiny than some moderately controversial Bible verses, but I don't think the very first piece of analysis, from Tom Bateman, his co-star, who was also being interviewed, has really been bettered. He went with: "Holy shit." Come to think of it, that's also a workmanlike gloss of a lot of Bible verses.

Neeson's remarks are, more than anything else, colossally surprising. They seem completely disconnected from the entire narrative of what's supposedly happening to public discourse at the moment. You know, the whole feeling that celebrities "have to be so careful". The sense that anyone saying anything publicly needs to tiptoe round the sensibilities of dozens of interest groups; that you never know when you're crossing some line or other without meaning to; that basically, whatever you say, no matter how bland, "you can't win".

Frankly, I think those fears are often justified. I think freedom of speech is sometimes hemmed in unnecessarily and perfectly nice people who have said something slightly careless can get into unfair trouble. Then again, I'm an affluent white man and I accept that I probably don't get all the ways in which certain statements can subliminally reinforce prejudice against historically oppressed sectors of society. But that's been the debate, right? It has, hasn't it? I wasn't imagining it?

And then, quite calmly, under no pressure, in the middle of a press junket, when he could've just droned on about how the filming conditions were really chilly or something, a movie star baldly announces that he once went round with a cosh for a week in the hope of killing someone black. It feels like a hallucination.

We're all minutely attuned to the subtle ways in which things people say are or aren't deemed acceptable, our ears straining for the faintest whisper of a dog whistle, and then, "Bang!" It's like the moment in *Fawlty Towers* when Basil starts miming to trick Mrs Richards into turning up her hearing aid and then suddenly yells at her. Liam Neeson seems to be asking: "Is this a piece of your brain?"

In their befuddled shock, many commentators have reached for the obvious question: "Is Liam Neeson racist?" He says he's not. Many say he is. Others have defended him. The trouble is, even if he is racist, it doesn't come close to being an adequate explanation of why he said what he said. Being racist might explain why he hung around with the cosh 40 years ago, but it doesn't explain why he'd tell anyone now. Out of doing it and telling people, in some ways it's the latter that's hardest to fathom – and it's also only the latter that we definitely know happened.

I haven't got an explanation, by the way. I'm still on "Holy shit." It's just incredibly weird. Was he stuck for something to say? How frightened of an awkward silence can a grown man be? But could it possibly be social anxiety? And a little racism? A mixture of racism and social anxiety? Now he really sounds like Hitler. Or was it the fact that the film he was promoting is about vengeance and so was his story? Did he say it all simply because he couldn't get over how extremely apposite it was?

One thing is clear: he shouldn't do interviews. Some people are saying he shouldn't do films, but he certainly shouldn't do interviews. Except possibly, if Lipman is to be believed, the modern sort of chat show. On them, she claims, there are far too many guests, "so we learn nothing about any of them. *Nada*. Except that they are famous and good sports." "Oh, if only!" the publicists of *Cold Pursuit* must be thinking.

I'm not sure I really want to learn much about the actors who are in the things I watch. I know a lot of actors and most of them are nice people, but I don't think knowing them helps me enjoy whatever they're acting in. It makes it more likely I'll have to bloody turn up and see it, but it doesn't improve their work, even when they don't have a history of violent racist plotting.

It's illogical really that, of all the people involved in making a film, it's the actors whom we're encouraged to know lots of real-life stuff about. It would be much easier to buy into the fictions they depict if we weren't so fully informed of the reality. Why not tell us about the private life of the designer or the cinematographer? Knowing about their affairs, divorces, strange opinions or huge houses won't make the fictional characters on screen less believable.

So, if you like cinema, I think the modern chat show has got it just right. The best way of enjoying a film is to know nothing at all about the actors. Except that they're famous and good sports.

* * *

Sometimes I think I'm the perfect person to analyse the cultural impact of music. I'm pretty sure no one else has ever thought that about me, though. And, actually, even I don't think it very often.

My weakness in the role would undoubtedly be my ignorance of music. Not complete ignorance: it's impossible, it turns out, no matter how little interest you show, to remain alive for 44 years in modern Britain without having heard of Mozart and Rihanna – though I had to check the spelling of the latter. And, come to think of it, I'm quite partial to Magic FM on a car journey, and also I watched that Bros documentary everyone's going on about.

But I admit I don't know much about music. Is that really such a problem, though? The more I think about it, the more I reckon that's actually what might make me amazing at analysing its cultural impact. I don't have any musical tastes that could skew my judgment and confuse the analysis with thoughts of whether this bit of music, or type of music, is "better" than that bit or type. I can see what's really going on, unencumbered by strong views on Coldplay or David Bowie or clapping at the end of movements (which Elvis Presley's entourage were reduced to at the end). I don't have a dog in the fight, which makes me ideal as an analyst of dog fighting.

Someone who does have a dog in the fight is Mark Wigglesworth. He's the former music director of the English National Opera so must be massively keen on music. He's probably got all of Rihanna's albums and a poster of Mozart in his bedroom. So I was worried, when I saw he was dabbling in some analysis of the cultural impact of music, that he might be out of his depth. Well, you be the judge. Unless you're into music at all, in which case perhaps you'd better stay out of it.

It was about the ENO's policy of performing operas in English – which means, in the majority of cases, in translation (though I'm sure that'll change after Brexit, when home-grown opera is freed from its Euro-shackles). This is an issue in the opera world: should operas be sung with the words they were composed for or those the audience can understand? Writing on the music website Bachtrack, Mark Wigglesworth stoutly defended the latter policy.

If you're currently struggling to care because this is a discussion of something that happens in rooms you have no intention of entering, then let me try to grab your attention by mentioning the slagging off. Alongside some reasoned argument asserting that "opera is drama first and foremost" and "beauty is not as powerful a medium as meaning" (that's worth a fridge magnet), Wigglesworth had a tentative dig at his opponents' motives: "A more unspoken view is one that thinks singing in a foreign language 'keeps the riff-raff away'," he said, adding: "I do believe a certain pleasure in cultural elitism exists, even if only by a few."

You can feel the nervousness as he wrote that. "I don't mean you!" he's reassuring any specific opponent of translated opera who might take offence. "You think what you think purely on artistic grounds, and I respectfully disagree! It's some other guys, who happen to have the same opinion as you but for much less wholesome reasons, who are the snobs."

This is much more interesting, because it's not about music, it's about "riff-raff". Wigglesworth wants to make "opera accessible to all", and "all", by definition, includes riff-raff. He sees this as the ENO's mission. "Accessibility," he writes, "is not really about the price of a ticket. For accessibility to be meaningful and long lasting it has to come from the work itself . . . When Mozart wanted to write for 'the people' he did so in their native German. He trusted that if more people understood the piece, more would enjoy it."

This makes sense, but I can't help wondering how much riff-raff the ENO currently attracts, even with its populist policy of singing words the audience can actually understand. Obviously, I don't know – I've never been there because of my irrational fear of hours and hours of boredom – but I find it hard to believe that, if I did go, I'd think: "Look at the riff-raff in here! The sooner they start doing operas in Italian and get the carpets steam-cleaned, the better. This English translation of *La traviata* they've put on is an absolute scum-magnet."

But I think Wigglesworth is basically right. He's just slightly confused matters with the term "riff-raff", because this isn't about class, it's about tribalism. The riff-raff here are people who see themselves as opera buffs, but who the anti-translation opera buffs would say aren't proper buffs because they don't like opera enough to sit through it when the words are gobbledygook – or aren't proper buffs because they haven't bothered to learn Italian and German.

It's like hardcore fans of an indie band despising newer fans who only got into them once they became successful. It's not about music, it's not about class, it's about a group defining itself around something from which it derives a sense of moral superiority. In the middle ages, people like that founded monastic orders.

And, to be honest, most of us are a bit like that. We all need someone to look down on. The pro-accessibility opera fans are looking down on the linguistic purists – for being elitist snobs, but also for being ignorant of opera's history as a popular art form – just as much as the purists are looking down on them. They're all having a lovely time feeling like they're better than other people – just as people who believe passionately in egalitarianism instinctively feel like they're better than those who don't believe passionately in egalitarianism.

Which means that the ENO's policy on singing opera in English must not change. The bitching it engenders is vital to both sides of the opera community's sense of self. Disagreeing about it is enjoyable and, without it, all that's left to entertain them is opera.

2

Plenty of Dishonesty but Not Much Actual Lying

Some thoughts on advertising, marketing, brand
awareness and other techniques for eliciting custom.

When I heard that the Advertising Standards Authority is proposing to crack down on gender stereotyping in adverts, I found my reaction interesting. I'm hoping you can do the same. But I must admit that I am pretty easily entertained. I've been known to watch golf if the remote's out of reach.

It was quite a negative reaction – I won't deny it. There's no point in being ashamed – it was involuntary. It's like someone shouting "Heil Hitler!" in their sleep. It turns out that's just who they are.

But I was displeased by my displeasure. "Why am I having a negative reaction to that?" I thought. "Do I like gender stereotyping? Deep down, do I want boys to be ridiculed for wearing pink by bullying aftershave or power-bike brands? And generations of Bisto mums to be manacled to their granule-strewn stoves instead of building sheds or having affairs? And the global lager and lipstick corporations to herd our schoolchildren into two sets of preordained career paths like public loos? All so that advertising creatives can continue using the same domestic scenarios as their 1970s predecessors, thus freeing up time to take more cocaine?

"And do I want it to be OK to imply that people who work in advertising all take cocaine, even though I have no direct evidence of it?" I thought. "Is that what I really want?!"

I was revealed to myself as an under-evolved form of life, out of place in an ocean where all the other fish have a more up-to-date sort of gill. Like those people who say they "don't mind gay people living together, but why do they have to get married?" And I always want to ask, "Are you 100% sure you don't mind? Or is it just that you don't reckon you'd get away with saying you do? If you travelled back in time to 1950, would you genuinely be saying, 'Hey, why don't we let gay people live together and have sex and stop making it illegal? I really don't mind. By the way, if they start saying they want to get married, that's a step too far'?"

I'm being unfair. We're all a product of our times, aren't we? I suppose that's the point of the ASA plan. To improve the times so as to improve the product. (Of the times, that is – not the ones being advertised.) Deep down, no one's really responsible for a single thing about themselves, I sometimes think. Genuinely. It's all just preconditioned responses, knee-jerk reactions and involuntary spasms – our whole civilisation nothing more than a pile of rotting corpses whose gaseous emissions give the false impression of farting a recognisable tune.

So I didn't get the Visit England gig. Apparently, they were looking for a more upbeat approach.

The thing is, I don't want to be just a product of my times – which I expect is very Generation X of me. I want to feel there's some timeless, rational identity that makes me who I am, not merely the fact of being born male, middle-class and British in 1974, and so, at an instinctive level, not very, but a little bit, sexist. Riddled with the flaws of when I was made, like a Leyland-era Jaguar's propensity to rust.

I don't want to accept that, having in all statistical likelihood passed the midpoint of my life, I'm getting bitter and anti-progressive and crotchety because I've twigged that one day I'll die. I don't want to become automatically contemptuous of all attempts to make things better. Or not yet, anyway. At some point, that might be fun.

And this ASA initiative, outlined in a report entitled "Depictions, Perceptions and Harm", is certainly an attempt to make things better. As Guy Parker, ASA's chief executive, put it: "Portrayals which reinforce outdated and stereotypical views on gender roles in society can play their part in driving unfair outcomes for people." True, fair enough, good initiative, sorry.

But still, it feels somehow incongruous with the spirit of the times (a risky thing for me to say as I metamorphose from whippersnapper to coffin dodger). It feels as though, with the world sliding towards extremism, war, environmental collapse and corporate tyranny, adverts implying that women are more likely to cook or men more likely to repair cars are the least of our worries. Not that there's anything wrong with addressing the least of our worries. It's better than not addressing any of our worries, and it's not as if the ASA is in a position to sort out the situation in North Korea.

But even just in the field of advertising, sexist stereotyping is probably a relatively minor worry. Advertising is, after all, the main way the world's increasingly rapacious, unaccountable and under-taxed corporations communicate with their human prey. It is how they encourage us to regularly self-baste for easier subsequent consumption.

This is an industry which famously seeks out the young – advertising slots on youth TV shows are always at a premium – because young people, though usually less affluent, are more easily parted with what money they have. It's the same reason a mugger targets a little old lady rather than a City trader. Unless the City trader happens to be a little old lady. Pardon my stereotyping. And if so, ker-ching for the mugger! He wasn't expecting a Rolex! Which may be some consolation as he confronts his own unacceptable assumptions. Or her own.

The principle by which the ASA has long operated is that adverts should be "legal, decent, honest and truthful". But they often aren't. They are, almost invariably, legal and truthful. They seldom explicitly libel or lie, and they don't last long if they do. But decency and honesty are certainly not being upheld in an environment where, for example, payday loan companies freely plug their catastrophic products. Stopping them perpetuating gender stereotypes while letting them drag people into downward spirals of debt seems like fiddling while Rome burns – or prohibiting the perpetuation of gender stereotypes while Rome burns.

That doesn't invalidate it. It's a worthwhile gesture, a determination to draw a distinction between what our society stands for and what it actually is. A nod towards standards we'd like to uphold in happier times, like dressing for dinner during the blitz. It's aspiration, not hypocrisy.

But I'd hate a sudden disappearance of gender stereotyping to trick us into believing adverts are necessarily decent or civilised in other ways. They may soon be sugar-free, but they'll still be laced with strychnine.

* * *

A victory for truth or a victory for pain? That's the question everyone's asking. I'm talking about Nurofen, of course. The Advertising Standards Authority has banned one of the company's TV adverts for implying that Nurofen Joint & Back capsules really know their way around a woman's body.

The commercial shows a lady with back pain taking a tablet, followed by a graphic of the Nurofen symbol moving through her body to her painful spine, where it then stays, pulsing with relief. Its route is direct – it doesn't take any wrong turnings, misapplying its goodness to, say, a pain-free elbow, thus creating a weird zone of anti-pain so that the woman has to bang it on something to restore balance – and, crucially, it doesn't just send ibuprofen all over the body so that anything that happens to be hurting, be it ear, knee, throat or bladder, does so slightly less.

The ad is implying, the ASA has ruled, that Nurofen Joint & Back is a specifically designed joint and back medicine which makes a beeline for joints and backs, where it demonstrates its special joint-and-back-ameliorating knack. And the ad shouldn't imply that, because it's not true. Nurofen Joint & Back is basically just Nurofen, which is basically just ibuprofen. (Even within the world of the advert, how the tablet knows that the poor woman has back rather than joint ache is unclear. Perhaps it just got lucky and would have gone on to a nearby joint if the back had seemed OK.)

This ban surprised me, because it feels like painkiller adverts have always been like this – a bit like the credits to a Bond film, but with throbbing. The shape of a lady has got home with a headache, sinus pain or the telltale redness in her silhouette throat that heralds a cold. Paunchless outlines of humans containing livid pain zones have long been "neutralising" those malevolent glows with counteracting soothing glows in the same colour as the advertised product's branding.

That's how painkillers are pitched: clean, targeted, medicinal. "Feeling crap? Drug yourself up a bit!" is not a slogan that's caught on. "Try smothering your body's warning system with a chemical – hopefully everything will have sorted itself out by the time it wears off!" just doesn't have the reassuring pharmaceutical feel that's vital in building brand confidence.

And brand confidence is important here. The likes of Nurofen, Solpadeine and Panadol aren't just selling whatever their various active ingredients are. Those can be purchased for a fraction of the cost. Boots sells packets of 16 ibuprofen tablets for 35p; the same number of Nurofen Joint & Back capsules costs £3.79. So what is

Nurofen doing to justify charging ten times as much? It's selling more than just ibuprofen; it's selling an idea, a feel.

"But that's just for idiots," you may be thinking. "That's how they part the headachy fool and his money." Unfortunately, and surprisingly, experimental data doesn't quite bear that opinion out. Ben Goldacre, in his book *Bad Science*, explained that a study of branded and unbranded headache pills found that "the packaging itself had a beneficial effect", and one comparable in magnitude to whether or not the tablets contained any actual painkiller. So "Whatever pharmacology theory tells you, that brand-named version *is* better, and there's just no getting away from it."

This confusing manifestation of the placebo effect seems to mean that, if you have an inkling the branded version of a painkiller will work better, then it will feel like it does. And, in the field of painkilling, something feeling like it works and something working are precisely the same thing. Sadly, if you're sceptical enough to associate a painkiller's efficacy only with its active ingredient, this added brand-confidence-induced pain assuagement won't work on you. As with a deathbed atheist who suddenly misses the solace of religion, your analytical outlook on the world precludes such comfort.

Obviously, this puts a different complexion on the profiteering of the branded tablet. I still reckon it is profiteering, fundamentally. I think the scheme was just to overcharge for painkillers – the fact that it caused an extra placebo effect is a happy accident rather than the conscious launch of a new alternative therapy to be administered by advertising agency. Nevertheless, it's profiteering that's coincidentally doing good. There are side effects: it makes people feel better.

There are quite a few products in the Nurofen range – as well as normal Nurofen, Nurofen Express and Nurofen Joint & Back, there's Nurofen Migraine Pain, Nurofen Express Period

Pain, Nurofen Tension Headache, Nurofen Sinus Pain Relief and Nurofen Sinus Pressure & Headache Relief – and they're all basically just ibuprofen. But RB UK Commercial, which owns the brand, says: "Research has shown that nine in 10 people search for products to treat specific symptoms, such as joint and back pain, and seven in 10 say pain-specific packs help them decide which product is best for their needs." So could it be that buying a generic painkiller that happens to have the specific pain from which you're currently suffering written on the packet makes you feel like the pain is more effectively killed? It feels more medicinal. It's almost like you've been diagnosed.

It's often said that a strength of alternative therapies such as homeopathy is that its practitioners, because they're in a private healthcare environment, have time to listen to, and express concern about, a patient's problems, in a way an overstretched NHS doctor doesn't. The listening and concern alone make patients feel better, which is why homeopathy is an ideal treatment for anyone who doesn't quite feel 100% but isn't actually at all ill.

Perhaps Nurofen's targeted packaging works like the homeopath's avaricious affectation of interest: it somehow provides a fraction of the benefits of homeopathy. Not a fraction of the absolutely-nothing-helpful-at-all that homeopathic remedies contain, but a fraction of the placebo effect brought about by having your ailment solemnly acknowledged.

All of which makes me slightly regretful about the ASA ruling. Those ads are inaccurate, so they probably ought to be pulled. Then again, if you've got a bad back, might not the thought of an angelic branded light, heading straight to the bit that hurts, be medicinal in itself? It might not be how *ibuprofen* works, but perhaps soothing animation, like confidence-building branding, is a vital part of how *Nurofen* works. The ads, the packaging, the £3.79 are arguably part of the treatment. The advert isn't misrepresenting the medicine – it *is* the medicine.

* * *

There are two types of cosmetics, in my analysis. Lipstick and mascara. Oh, and blusher. Hang on: and powder and eyeliner and moisturiser and perfume and hairspray. Blimey, there are loads. And styling mousse and hair dye and spray tan and unnecessary surgery. Do shaving products count? Maybe. Hats? No. Even tiny, sparkly impractical hats that don't keep the rain off? Fascinators and tiaras and coronets and the like? No, I think we're entering the realm of clothes and jewellery. What about stick-on sequins? And moustache wax? I'm thinking of changing my look.

But there are, I still think, two types of cosmetics. You can remember it like diabetes: type one is naturally occurring, and type two is something you've clearly done to yourself. Except, obviously, nothing is naturally occurring in the field of cosmetics. So type one is *what appears to be* naturally occurring (ie a lie), and type two is the open truth. Concealer on the one hand, painted nails on the other. Or actually on both, as a rule.

Lipstick is generally type two: a lipsticked person is not usually claiming that's their natural lip shade. If they were, people wouldn't buy different lipsticks to go with different outfits, which I'm pretty sure they do. And no one thinks they're implying that, after some nuclear mutation incident involving a chameleon in a lab, they now have the power to change their own skin pigmentation. No one impishly asks if they can also swivel their eyes independently of each other, or pick up snacks with a rapidly emerging mega-tongue. Everyone accepts it's lipstick. They might say, "Nice lipstick."

Cosmetic surgery, meanwhile, is obviously type one. No one's going to say, "Nice surgery." It's not a sign of taste and self-respect to have gone under general anaesthetic and been selectively carved to reverse what our culture considers to be the uglifying effects of getting older. It's supposed to look like nothing has happened, even though it's often obvious something has. So it's rude to mention it.

People who get facelifts just want to look like they haven't aged. They've secretly paid money to look lucky. Then again, they were lucky to have the money. But that's why bad cosmetic surgery can make someone seem so ridiculous. The spurious claim they're making about their biological good fortune is further undermined by the indisputable evidence that they didn't even catch a break in their choice of surgeon.

The reason I've been musing along these lines is that, according to a recent news report, perfume is changing cosmetic types. You'd think it was pretty solidly type two. Deodorant might be type one, a denial of our inherent BO, but people who smell of perfume or aftershave aren't seriously claiming it's exuded organically. Ambulances would be called. Nevertheless, the latest fashion in perfumes is for them to be hardly detectable by the human nose. As Ben Gorham, one of the creators of a new minimalist scent called "Elevator Music", put it: "The idea is that its wearer is noticed, not the perfume." Perhaps it comes with a free comedy hat.

Other examples of hip new barely scented scents are "You", for "millennials" who, according to its creator, "like scent to be personal"; "Dauphine" – "The concept is extreme cleanliness," says its designer; and the godfather of the trend, first made back in 2006, "Escentric Molecule 01", described by the *New York Times* as "one of the top-selling niche fragrances of all time", though I suppose you could wear it wherever you like. These products are "the olfactory equivalent of no-makeup makeup, in which people spend hundreds of hours, and dollars, to look effortless".

To say this is a bit emperor's new clothes is an understatement. The emperor's stylists at least claimed their clothes were detectable by some. These perfumers are marketing substances which they admit are virtually unnoticeable to everyone. They talk of bringing out people's natural scent but, if that was appealing, minicabs wouldn't have little Christmas trees hanging from their rear-view mirrors. Perhaps it's all a ploy to sell more deodorant, to be applied as soon as the perfume kicks in.

Another cosmetic straddling both types is hair dye. Which type of cosmetic it is seems to depend, broadly and as a generalisation (so don't say, "That's a generalisation!" because I've admitted it's a generalisation), on gender. Dyed hair on a woman is seen as type two, and on a man as type one. For women, hair dyeing is culturally accepted as an overt cosmetic choice; in fact, it gets called "colouring", a word that implies agency and choice. But for men, it's simply hair dye, suggesting concealment. It's lying about having gone grey, just as a toupee is lying about having gone bald.

It's odd. Lots of men don't like going bald or grey, ostensibly because of what it looks like. But you can very effectively change what it looks like. Yet, somehow, any attempt to make such a change is associated with shame. We're a world away from bald men openly saying, "Yes, I went bald and I didn't like how it looked, so now I wear this terrific wig!"

There are clearly people who think being bald makes you look like a loser – but there's a broader agreement, even among those who don't mind baldness, that you're an enormous loser if you try to hide it. Unless, of course, you successfully hide it, in which case you look like a winner who never had the misfortune to go bald.

The type-one cosmetics lie is about luck and vanity – hiding the absence of the former and the presence of the latter – and, as with all issues to do with appearance, it inevitably gets tangled up with sexism. On the surface, it seems unfair on men that there's shame attached to them dyeing their hair, when women can openly colour theirs. Underlying that, though, is the deeper unfairness that old-looking men are allowed to be newsreaders and old-looking women aren't.

So when women try to "reverse the effects of ageing", it's a way of coping with the patriarchy. When men do it, they're just kidding themselves about death.

* * *

Let me put my cards on the table: I'm not a fan of the orange KitKat. It's nothing to do with Nestlé's marketing of baby milk, before you mistake me for a hand-wringing liberal. No, I'm a snack-eating liberal and, when I'm peckish, I don't give a shit. I'll happily eat a normal KitKat and let the world be damned.

The way globalisation is going, you'd never get anywhere if you started worrying about the moral failings of whoever owns the thing that owns the thing that owns the thing that makes the thing you need. Doubtless most prayer books are now published by subsidiaries of conglomerates with satanist mission statements. I bet the Sultan of Brunei somehow controls the global supply of a dye vital to the manufacture of rainbow flags. And probably all of the world's, I don't know, birthday cards are made by corporations partly owned by pension funds managing the retirement savings of, among other people, racists. And racists *hate* birthdays.

The car keys of some absolute monsters are in our shared global swingers' bowl, but we didn't listen to Lenin, so it's too late to do anything about it now. That's just the way the wind blows the pampas grass, so neck your Lambrusco, take your pick and count yourself lucky if you avoid the Citroën – that guy's bound to be a pervert. Because, at the end of the day, everyone gets screwed.

So my antipathy towards orange KitKats isn't about corporate responsibility. It's because, when eating a normal KitKat, I have never thought, or come close to thinking, "I wish this tasted of orange." I knew it wouldn't, and so I was content that it didn't. And I neither understand nor forgive anyone who actually would think that. It would be like eating a Terry's Chocolate Orange and wishing it *didn't* taste of orange. Or eating an actual orange and wishing it tasted of apple. Or looking at the new Dairy Milk bar with bits of marshmallow in it and thinking, "Ooh, interesting!" rather than "That is literally the worst abomination committed by humankind." In short, it's the thought process of someone who likes films to be in 3D.

"Are you, then, the right person," you may be asking, "to write about the merits or otherwise of the Natural History Museum and Hasbro's new twist on Monopoly, Monopoly Dinosaurs?" If you are asking that, full marks for prescience, because that's exactly what I'm about to do. But absolute minimum marks (which is probably a B or a 2 these days – there's no point compounding stupidity with low self-esteem) for fair criticism, because the very last person you want passing judgment on Monopoly Dinosaurs is one of those "Ooh, interesting!" juxtaposition junkies munching their peppermint Wotsits, washed down by a can of Cadbury's Creme Sperm.

I realise there's long been more than one Monopoly – and I don't mean Amazon and Google. I mean more than one version of the game: Star Wars, 007, Virgin Money, Nottingham, and so on. In fact, Amazon and Google don't actually have Monopolies. Sets of Monopoly for sale, that is. I Googled, I looked on Amazon and found nothing – and how else can you buy anything? Perhaps they fear the implications of its name next to theirs, like when Pavarotti refused to endorse an Italia 90 version of Hungry Hungry Hippos.

By the 1930s there were already two Monopolies: the American one, based on Atlantic City, and the British one, set in London. The latter was brought out so that the game resonated more with British customers, and I understand the pressure to keep it feeling relevant. But who at Hasbro, in this day and age, thought the best way of doing that, of catching the imagination of the aspirant plutocrat kids of today, was to move it out of the field of property development and into palaeontology? Because buying and selling houses for inflated sums is so last century, while academic research is where it's at?

Monopoly is a game that rewards getting rich without making anything. It's about wealth creation via the aggressive use of ownership. It was ahead of its time. The logical response to our current era would be to take games about dinosaurs, or indeed anything else, and turn them into property trading games like Monopoly, where success or failure depends entirely on luck and circumstances rather than merit. Add an extra Chance card, where you lose the rent from one of your cheaper properties when it burns down because you cut corners refurbishing it, plus a load more Get Out of Jail Free cards, and it's a game about Britain today.

I'm not sure that would be appropriate for the Natural History Museum shop, though. Customers will have just seen a lot of dinosaur skeletons and information about dinosaurs, and so retail orthodoxy dictates they'll want to buy things with dinosaurs on them: mugs, pens, badges, games of Monopoly. And, from the game's blurb, it's clear the adapters gave the new version a full five minutes' thought: "Lay claim to each dinosaur fossil, and leave tents and jeeps on your fascinating discoveries. Then watch the rent come pouring in as you make deals with other palaeontologists." So I'm guessing a jeep on Tyrannosaurus rex is something a rival palaeontologist really wants to avoid landing on. Much worse than, say, two tents on an iguanodon.

Unfortunately, I think my cynicism about this game springs from naivety. "Why would they make that?" I'm instinctively asking. When I looked at the full list of Monopoly versions – and there are hundreds – I realised it was the wrong question. I should have asked, "Why not?", to which it seems the market supplies no adequate answer. I don't know why, but the manufacturing costs have obviously sunk so low that they may as well make one.

A handful will buy it, and that's enough: some 3D-film buffs, plus those saviours of capitalism, people who are buying a present for someone. They don't have to think the game's worth having, just that it'll look appropriate to whoever unwraps it.

Together, they're enough to make Monopoly Dinosaurs pay for itself, just as they were with Dino-opoly in 2004 and Monopoly Dinosaur (singular) in 2010. And indeed Monopoly Harrow School Edition, Dachshund-opoly, Monopoly Corvette 50th Anniversary Collector's Edition and the rest. Like a bastardised chocolate bar, each causes a microscopic synapse of surprise to fire, a sensation we fleetingly mistake for fun.

* * *

A small good thing happened the other day, but in a context of such stupidity and unfairness that it only brought home to me more strongly all that stupidity and unfairness, so I'd almost rather it hadn't happened at all. The good thing was that the train operator "Great Western Railway", which is owned by FirstGroup plc, was banned by the Advertising Standards Authority from putting up any more posters implying it's publicly owned. Specifically, posters that read: "The railway belongs to the region it serves".

There's a tiny bit of justice in that decision, but so tiny it insults the very concept. Only a homeopath could believe that such a microscopic quantity of justice could have any beneficial effect. It's like hearing that, though a serial killer will walk free, the judge has ruled, after a desperate appeal by the prosecution, that he will no longer be given free biscuits at the public expense. Hooray! No more biscuits for the Kensington Ripper! Maybe he'll leave fewer crumbs around his next eviscerated victim!

You may be wondering why I'm getting so worked up about this that, in bad temper, I've allowed the imagery of violent mutilation to invade my discussion of transport infrastructure. You may be wondering it in exactly those words. If you wonder in words. Perhaps thoughts come to you as shapes or colours; with me, it's like a typescript in 12-point Courier. Serves me right for not doing art GCSE.

The root cause of my anger is that the posters' slogan is factually correct. The railway, on which FirstGroup currently operates services under the name "Great Western Railway", does indeed belong to the region it serves, if you take "the region" to mean Britain. All of our national railways – the tracks, bridges, cuttings and tunnels – are owned by Network Rail, which is owned by the government.

In modern times, private investment hasn't really taken off in the track-maintenance part of the railway business. Investors prefer to confine their liabilities to the trains, ticket machines and refreshment carts – the bits for which passengers pay money – and leave the bits that cost money to the state. It's an incredibly astute move on the investors' part, and is doubtless further proof to the likes of George Osborne of the genius of the private sector when compared with the doltish bridge-and-tunnel-maintaining public one, which just burns money on boring infrastructure (in the case of tunnels), but lacks the wit even to extort £3 per extremely unpleasant croissant from the thousands regularly held temporarily but hungrily captive thanks to the failure of its own signals.

Companies like FirstGroup never take direct responsibility for anything as headachy as maintaining hundreds of miles of undulating track. They're just tenants: they rent use of the lines from the government, from us. So FirstGroup is our customer, just as much as we're its. And it's been quite demanding over the years.

In 2011, it announced it was pulling out of its 10-year contract three years early. A presciently negotiated "break-clause" allowed this. Unfortunately for us, of the £1.13bn of rent it was contracted to pay over the decade, £826m was due over the last three years – the three years the company adroitly opted out of.

This left the landlord, which is us, which is the government, in an awkward position. Does it look for a new tenant who might pay the £826m, or something approaching it, instead? That's what it ought to do. Otherwise, what force does any future government franchise contract have? How can a landlord expect to receive rent if the sanction for refusing to pay it isn't eviction?

Unfortunately, the government's most recent attempt to negotiate a major new rail franchise is universally known as the "West Coast Main Line fiasco". The Department for Transport, shaken by cuts and new rules, totally screwed it up, and its decision was effectively reversed after a legal challenge by the incumbent franchisee.

So rather than get into all that again, the government basically told FirstGroup it could stay put. After all, its stuff was everywhere – an eviction would have been an admin nightmare. Or maybe the minister had just seen an upsetting news report about homelessness. Instead of the £826m under the original contract, the company agreed to pay £32.5m for a 23-month extension, a sum which economists have described as "massively less".

I've been miserably aware for years that this sort of crap went on. The contrast between extortionate and unreliable trains and the jaunty corporate slogans with which private operators daub their dirty carriages and demoralised staff has always made me resentful. The discovery that what the private sector lacks in willingness to maintain a rail network, it makes up for in the ferocity of its bargaining with exhausted and under-resourced civil servants, is not a very surprising one.

But the rebranding of FirstGroup's rail services (last autumn, after it had just been granted a further four-year franchise extension) as "Great Western Railway" added insult to ongoing and repetitive injury. For me, that really was the shit the burglars did in your bed. The adoption of the name of Isambard Kingdom Brunel's famous company, which actually built the railway, by one which merely profits from it is an act of breathtaking cheek. It's up there with Mussolini appropriating the trappings of the Roman Empire.

The Advertising Standards Authority has said nothing about that, merely that the firm mustn't imply public ownership. The company has escaped official censure for another advert, which described Brunel as "our illustrious founder". He is no such thing. The company Brunel founded was bought in 1948 by the British state, a purchaser that continues to own and maintain the railway he designed.

Meanwhile, the owner of this reproduction GWR grew out of the merger of some post-privatisation bus companies in the late 80s. FirstGroup plc doesn't build things – that's risky and expensive, as Brunel discovered on many occasions. Its mode of business is to profit from state enterprises thrust into private hands by Tories for ideological reasons.

Were it not for the availability of public assets at a bargain price, and state subsidies when returns disappoint – and if it actually had to build a railway in order to operate one – FirstGroup might find it tricky to give shareholder value. But, like a sewer rat, it's perfectly evolved for the conditions in which it exists. Which is fine, I suppose. Right up until the rat claims to have designed the sewer himself because his main aim in life has always been cleanliness.

* * *

The news that Salad Cream is considering changing its name to Sandwich Cream put me fondly in mind of British Gas. Kraft Heinz, the vast conglomerate that makes the 100-year-old goo, is considering a change because, as its spokesman told trade magazine the *Grocer*, the name no longer "fairly represents the product's ingredients or usage occasions".

Obviously, this raises as many questions as it answers, and I haven't even got to why it made me think of gas. In fact, I probably mentioned that too soon, because there's quite a lot I need to get out of my system first about this quote – a process that coincidentally may make you think of gas as well.

The name no longer represents its ingredients? What does that mean? No one ever thought the stuff was *made* of salad, did they? Are they now hoping to imply that it's made of sandwiches? Sandwiches are a very unusual ingredient – they're more of an end product of a culinary process, like a pie or an omelette or a pavlova. You don't put sandwiches in things, you put things in sandwiches. Salad Cream, for example.

So I get the "usage occasions" part. Apparently, these days only 14% of the cream's usage occasions are saladous, while I imagine considerably more are sandwichsome (I claim first usage occasion of both of those adjectives). And this anomaly has started to irk some of the people at Kraft Heinz – people who are paid to consider tinkering with things, and probably feel their salaries are harder to justify if they always say everything's fine as it is. The more they think about Salad Cream being used in sandwiches, and not being used on salads, the more it's like a painting that needs straightening, the more it niggles.

Speaking of niggles, there's no cream in it, in case that thought's been bothering you for a couple of paragraphs. Obviously, it is a sort of cream (as in opaque viscous liquid), but it contains no cream (as in what rises to the top of the milk) at all. So the second part of its name isn't an ingredient signifier either, and they're planning to keep it anyway. I hadn't missed that – I just thought it went without saying. And then my confidence that it went without saying ebbed away until I said it anyway, just as the confidence at Kraft Heinz that calling something Salad Cream will not be taken as prohibiting its use in other contexts has ebbed away until they stand on the brink of an epic cock-up: customers looking for Salad Cream suddenly won't be able to find it, and there is currently no one in the world, wandering around any supermarket anywhere, looking for a substance called Sandwich Cream. "Disappointed with your current sandwich moistening agent? Why not try something you've never heard of from Heinz?"

This literalism in nomenclature has been elegantly avoided by the managers of British Gas. They haven't changed to "British Gas and Electricity", "British Energy" or, in tribute to the item they most noticeably provide, "British Bills". And this certainly isn't because the firm lacks the cash to rebrand. Like all of the Big Six energy providers, it recently put up the price of its standard variable tariff, meaning that, put together, they're raking in an extra £570m of revenue per year.

British Gas is probably my favourite of the Big Six energy providers, but the truth is I love them all. I love how much they irritate politicians and consumer experts. This recent batch of price rises was typical, described by energy minister Claire Perry as "unjustified", by Gillian Guy of Citizens Advice as "extremely disheartening" and by Alex Neill of *Which?* as "another slap in the face for customers already feeling the pinch" (but no hope of a tickle), with Martin Lewis, founder of MoneySavingExpert. com, concluding that "Anyone on a Big Six standard tariff is ripping themselves off".

I love all this, in the same way that I love it when a paedophile wins the lottery. Both phenomena are such eloquent illustrations of the flaws in their respective systems. And I dislike both systems, so it's great to give those flaws an airing. Just as a sex criminal randomly winning a fortune makes it clear that lottery balls have no sense of moral justice, the fact that the largest operators in the domestic energy marketplace offer some of the highest tariffs is a peachy demonstration that the forces of market competition aren't functioning.

Can you imagine this pattern in any market that worked? A world where the six largest supermarket chains charged more for groceries than their smaller rivals, yet somehow sustained their share of business? Where Amazon secured a dominant online position despite also charging more than other retailers? It couldn't happen in the presence of genuine market forces, which is conclusive proof that the 25-year experiment in attempting to introduce those forces to the domestic energy market has failed. We've given it a massive go, people didn't like it, they couldn't be arsed to keep changing supplier, so the time has come to renationalise.

It's not very surprising. It never seemed like it would work. If you had 20 or 30 different light switches on every wall, with a price marked on each, then you'd have a market. Obviously, that's impractical, but hardly more so than expecting millions of consumers to make the running – to research who's offering the best price, go through the admin hassle of changing supplier, then keep tabs on when prices get automatically hiked if you don't change, or threaten to change, supplier again. That's not a very appealing process to anyone mortal.

So why don't we just opt once and for all for the one that's called British Gas? En masse. Embrace the supplier-changing hassle this one time and we'll never have to do it again. The other suppliers will go under and the state will have to take over to avoid a private monopoly. And no one will nag us to "shop around" ever again. Let's do it. If you see Sid, tell him.

In September 2018, three months after this article was published, Kraft Heinz abandoned its plans to rebrand Salad Cream. I'm not saying I'm a hero, but . . .

* * *

The first time I went to Patisserie Valerie, in December 1993, it felt really special. I was having a day out in London during the Christmas vacation after my first term at university, and a college friend, who lived in London, took me to what I for many years wrongly thought of as the original Knightsbridge branch. It seemed extremely refined and continental – the cakes were like the ones that, in those days, you only really got in France. Lots of millefeuilles, no iced buns. To an undergraduate rube, it was a glimpse into the hidden London where only very posh people go.

I don't know how many branches of Patisserie Valerie there were in 1993. But it was obviously more than the one Old Compton Street outlet that Enzo, Robert and Victor Scalzo bought in 1987 from descendants of the original Madame Valerie, and fewer than the nine that existed when they sold the firm to venture capitalists in 2006. When it went into administration the other day, there were about 200.

In early 2018, I went to one of them. It was in the Brunswick Centre, near Russell Square, next to an arthouse cinema. This time, it didn't feel very special. It was fine, but it was pretty empty. I had a sandwich and a tea while someone swept the floor. But, unlike in 1993, it obviously wasn't a genuine Belgian patisserie that had been running for the best part of a century. It was just a chain restaurant that had randomly taken "Belgian patisserie" as its vague theme. It could turn into a GBK or a Harry Ramsden's or a Café Rouge or a Pret or an Eat or a Giraffe at the click of a financier's mouse.

It feels so weird and arbitrary. I get no sense that the reason Patisserie Valerie leapt from a handful of branches to hundreds was because of public demand. I suppose there's a demand for cafes in general, but I don't think many people were saying, "You know the distinctive feel of that cake shop in Old Compton Street? If only that were available literally everywhere!" I don't think people outside London had particularly heard of it – it wasn't like Hamley's or Fortnum & Mason. They were just suddenly presented with it. "That Zizzi's turned into something called Patisserie Valerie." "Oh. Do they still do cappuccinos?" "I suppose so."

And it doesn't make sense even if there did turn out to be a vast unexploited market for the very specific Belgian-metropolitan ambience I enjoyed in 1993, because a chain of Patisserie Valerie's scale and nature is incapable of replicating that sort of atmosphere – as I discovered at the Brunswick Centre. It's not like McDonald's, which, whether you like it or not, you have to admit is pretty much the same everywhere. In this case, the original successful thing is too ephemeral to be recaptured by a team of local staff taken on when the TGI Friday's closed.

I'm not saying this is why the chain failed. The current crisis was precipitated by the discovery last October of "significant, potentially fraudulent accounting irregularities", which meant there was a £40m gap in its accounts. Until then, everything looked rosy, with Patisserie Holdings, the parent company, valued at over half a billion pounds in June. But it's hard to believe that that wasn't a huge overestimation of its worth and that there isn't a fundamental weakness in the business motivating all the alleged books-cooking.

I first properly noticed the weird way the restaurant business currently operates when the Ask Pizza near me changed overnight into something called Franco Manca. It still seemed to be a restaurant, but I had no idea what sort. I initially assumed it was something vaguely Spanish, which was stupid of me, as that would be like a Viennese restaurant calling itself Hitler Mitlo.

My confusion wasn't eased when I discovered that Franco Manca, like Ask Pizza before it, is a pizza restaurant – the main difference being that Franco Manca serves sourdough pizza, while Ask served what I think a gastronome would describe as normal pizza. So why the change? Was Ask doing badly? If so, what made someone think its problems would be solved by making the dough more sour?

Just like when going mad, having seen one inexplicable thing I started seeing them everywhere. That's how it was with Franco Manca. So, out of curiosity, on one of the occasions when I would otherwise have gone to Pizza Express, I went to a Franco Manca. I thought it was fine, but no better than Pizza Express.

Is that sort of one-off curiosity visit enough to sustain such a chain? It's almost like going to see a film because you've noticed so many posters for it – but, instead of posters, you've seen actual branches of the restaurant on every high street. So, if you've got time on your hands, maybe you pop in; if you don't, you miss the release. Personally, I never got round to Prezzo or Chimichanga, and lots of them have closed now. Maybe they'll bring out a DVD.

Obviously, if, having popped in, you find this new chain restaurant to be really terrific, and better than the chain restaurants you've previously frequented, then this all makes sense. But how often does that happen? Not very often, judging by the parlous financial state of the sector. Poor old Jamie Oliver seems to be constantly cranking out books and TV shows purely to pay the staff wages in all the deserted branches of Jamie's Italian. And every other chain, from Carluccio's to Byron, seems to be feverishly closing branches or renegotiating rents.

I'm no businessman, which will become obvious when I say that, to me, all this feels like a huge waste of time and energy: this desperation to take any half-decent food service concept and then strain every financial sinew to immediately open versions of it in every town, city and shopping centre, only for the resultant frail, overstretched company to collapse in the face of the lightest breeze of consumer parsimony. What's the point? Patisserie Valerie was a small good thing, and now it's bloated and broken, a dispiriting echo of the effect of too much cake.

In February 2019, a private equity fund bought Patisserie Valerie out of administration and 96 branches are still open. In May, Jamie Oliver's restaurant chain collapsed.

* * *

We must remember that it's not Dairy Milk's fault. Dairy Milk is the music, not the Wagner or Michael Jackson, in all this. You can't blame the thing for its creator. It may put you off the thing – you may find it disconcerting to hear Jackson sing "I'm bad" over and over again, now that you know he was – but it's not the fault of the words "I'm bad", or the tune they're sung to. They're not themselves bad (or good, except in the subjective sense of their being part of a song lots of people liked). So does that mean the words are lying? If so, that's bad. So they are bad! So they're not lying! So they're not . . . Damn it!

Unlike music, when it comes to the recipes of popular snacks, the authorship is often unknown. Perhaps that's for the best. If something grisly came out about whoever first thought of putting cheese on toast, that would be a blow to us all. It was invented a long time ago, so they're pretty much bound to be racist for a start. But it could be much worse than that – so it's better not to know. People who want to spoil cheese on toast for themselves can always use Marmite.

Authorship may be forgotten, but intellectual property seldom is. Not many popular snacks are as legally unencumbered as cheese on toast – and I bet some corporation or other has had a go at enclosing that little tract of common land. I reckon the team at Cathedral City will have had a meeting about it. Did you notice Gordon's Gin having a pop at changing what the G in G&T stood for? Back off, guys! And careful what you wish for: Hoovers may be everywhere, but most of them are Dysons. So I actually prefer Bombay Sapphire in my Gordon's and Tonic. Take that, Diageo plc – I'm with Bacardi Limited!

I don't know who invented the recipe for Dairy Milk, but I certainly know who owns it. It's Cadbury, formerly Cadbury Schweppes, formerly Cadbury's, which is in turn owned by Mondelēz International, formed in 2012 from the demerger of Kraft Foods Inc. into itself and Kraft Foods Group Inc. So it's all on a lovely local scale.

The reason I'm contemplating the ethical position of recipe owners is that Cadbury did a bad thing. Now you're going to think it's worse than it is. It's not too bad. But it is bad. And odd. I'll just say what it is.

They published some webpages, under the heading "Cadbury Treasure Hunt", encouraging families to visit Britain and Ireland's historic sites and dig for treasure. Unfortunately, as Dr Aisling Tierney, an archaeologist at Bristol University, pointed out: "Any digging within a set distance of an archaeological monument is a criminal offence." Her profession was up in arms at Cadbury suddenly inciting people to "get their hands dirty" or have "a quick check" for gold and jewels at historically significant protected locations, with offence caused by both the potential illegality and the implication that all archaeologists do is hunt for treasure.

Cadbury has apologised and taken those webpages down, which is quite right, but what was happening in the first place? Why was Cadbury banging on about visiting historical sites? And how did it come to do so in such a thoughtless way as to accidentally encourage criminality? Why aren't they just saying, "You may enjoy some of our range of chocolate products"?

Well, apparently Cadbury sells something called Cadbury Dairy Milk Freddo Treasures, which is basically moulded Dairy

Milk, but there are QR codes on it – you know, those little blotchy squares, like Rorschach tests for robots – which, if scanned, open the aforementioned online looting manual. So it's a sort of prize, but the prize is something historical to read. A hugely disappointing prize, then. I imagine the stuff about digging up treasure was shoved in to marginally allay that disappointment, while still making parents feel that it's all very educational and outdoorsy, and so perhaps they needn't worry so much about childhood obesity.

I'm glad it backfired, because I really hate this kind of disingenuous corporate virtue-signalling. It's like when retailers encourage you to collect tokens, in exchange for which they'll give money to charity or books to schools. It's such a depressing index of public credulity. Campaigns like that obviously succeed in increasing sales or the companies' boards of directors wouldn't be able to justify them to shareholders. They wouldn't do it if people didn't fall for it.

I'm particularly unsettled by this one because I love Dairy Milk. To me, it is the most delicious chocolate in the world. It was also the first chocolate I ever tasted, so my preference may have more to do with the early impression it made on my palate than any objective chocolate-making excellence. But, whatever the reason, I love it. I love the taste and, emotionally, I love the product's existence. I feel proprietorial about it.

But it's not mine or yours, or John Cadbury's or Willy Wonka's. It belongs to a multibillionaire six-year-old called Mondelēz – a bloated kid, like many of its customers. And I realise that, fundamentally, I find that ownership offensive. It feels like the people at Mondelēz have actually done what they mistakenly incited last week. They've purloined something, a shared and much-loved cultural artefact; they've looted our collective childhoods in order to enrich themselves. That's the way of the world but, like any big winner in an unfair game, they should get it quietly.

Yet they don't. They flaunt it. They put bits of Oreo in it, which is like the Wizard of Oz turning up in *The Wind in the Willows*. They try to register a trademark for that Cadbury shade of purple and are only defeated because of objections from Nestlé. But Mondelēz gets its own back when, following intense lobbying, Nestlé's attempt to trademark the shape of a KitKat is rejected.

These corporate giants' assertion and exploitation of their ownership of these beloved British treats is savage. I have to keep reminding myself it's not Dairy Milk's fault, because its owners are doing everything they can, short of changing the recipe, to make it taste wrong.

* * *

Wrapped around Monday's *Daily Mirror* was a big four-page "advertising feature" paid for by Philip Morris International, the big tobacco corporation. It wasn't advertising cigarettes, because that's illegal in Britain. Or maybe that "because" is unfair? Perhaps I should say, "It wasn't advertising cigarettes. Unrelatedly, that's illegal in Britain"? Is it unjust of me to suggest that Philip Morris International would even want to advertise cigarettes?

It's a poser. On the one hand, Philip Morris International does advertise its Marlboro cigarette brand in many countries where it's legal to do so. On the other hand, this particular big advert was to launch a campaign called "Hold My Light", which seems to be encouraging people to stop smoking.

So perhaps Philip Morris International is confused about its aims? Maybe there's conflict at the heart of the company, with some senior executives saying it should continue selling cigarettes, while others argue that it should stop? Is that what's happening? Or do you refuse to believe that any entity comprised of human beings could become that irrational, confused and self-destructive? If so, you haven't been following Brexit.

But the advert is a fascinating document for a tobacco firm to have published because it completely accepts as its premise that smoking is terribly bad for you. It's quite startling, when you think about it – like a job applicant putting some murders on his CV. The ad then suggests an approach to stopping smoking, whereby supportive friends make a pact with the smoker and offer some sort of reward if they manage to quit for a few weeks.

"After all," it says, "research reveals that someone who stops smoking cigarettes for four weeks is five times more likely to go smoke-free for good. You can't put a price on a result like that." Can't you? Philip Morris International really is as badly governed as Britain if it hasn't. I think it knows exactly how much revenue it loses whenever that happens. And the ad's subtle references to e-cigarettes and "heated tobacco" (both of which Philip Morris also sells) as "better alternatives" to smoking are part of the company's hopeful attempt to allay that mounting cost.

Apart from those buried ads for other products, it's all absolute drivel – real back-of-a-fag-packet stuff: "maybe you will pledge to do the washing up every day your partner is smoke-free" or "the incentive could be tickets to the footie . . . or treating your pal to a manicure to give them a little pick-me-up". And, crucially, "making the Hold My Light pledge with friends" involves registering on the "Hold My Light" website, thus generating a lovely cache of data about lots of credulous addicts. I expect Ladbrokes is bidding already.

It's all very distasteful, but I was still surprised to hear that Cancer Research UK had called it "staggering hypocrisy". Is "hypocrisy" really the right word? Well, hypocrisy is saying you hold a set of beliefs while behaving in a way that belies it. So I suppose, yes, it is hypocritical to say you want people to stop smoking while manufacturing millions of cigarettes. Then again, the company doesn't deny that it manufactures millions of cigarettes, but claims that it wants to quit: "Our ambition is to stop selling cigarettes in the UK and replace them with better alternatives," it says in the ad.

So, by implication, the firm is still keen to sell cigarettes in other parts of the world, where the public is perhaps less conscious of their life-shortening effects. But in the UK, the jig is up, and so the company is hoping to find other pointless addictions, about which frightening health consequences have not yet emerged, to shift people on to. Looked at like that, the ad's claims seem less noble, but also less hypocritical. It's just a stealthy survival strategy – like the wolf dressing up as Little Red Riding Hood's grandmother. Maybe that was hypocritical, but it feels harsh to blame a hungry predator for not openly admitting that if he stopped killing, he'd die.

I was even more dubious about the other part of Cancer Research UK's criticism: "staggering". Is it staggering? Was anyone at that charity staggered? Did they expect better from Philip Morris International? "What a big advertising budget you have, Grandma!" "All the better to dispassionately address our products' health implications with!"

I don't believe they were staggered, and it's a mistake to pretend that they were. It's totally the wrong way to think about a corporation. Everything a corporation says is hypocritical unless it's "our entire *raison d'être* is to maximise profits". They hardly ever say that, and who can blame them? But that's completely what they exist to do, and that's fine as long as we're wary and make sure they observe the law.

But whenever plcs affect some sort of emotional feeling – like caring about our health or happiness or the softness of our skin or having a lovely Christmas – we just have to so immediately, completely and instinctively know it's a lie that it's not even worth the time it takes to express it. Product and price are all we want to hear from them – everything else is deception.

So when Cancer Research UK describes this transparent and desperate campaign as "staggering hypocrisy", it depresses me because it implies that the charity would give any statement from Philip Morris International an open-minded hearing. And that would be, at best, a total waste of time.

What I think Cancer Research UK should have said is this: huge corporations like Philip Morris International spend a lot of money on research, so if they think this tawdry attempt to curry favour will work, then it probably will. Significant numbers of people will be fooled into believing that a company, the main product of which has caused millions of premature deaths, can have its customers' health interests at heart. Significant sections of the public are listening uncritically to what corporations tell them and taking it at face value. That is nothing less than a national education emergency.

3

I Am Become Death.com

A jaunty glance at the commercial impact
of the internet.

By the time you're using a password, something has gone wrong. It's the same as with a bulletproof vest, or a bouncer outside a bar. I'm not against bulletproof vests per se but, if I ever find myself in circumstances where I reckon I should put one on before popping to the shops, something will definitely have gone wrong – either with the neighbourhood or my own mental health.

Similarly, the presence of a muscly, suited man outside a pub doesn't make me think that peace is more likely to reign as I make my selection from their wide range of real ales. It makes me think there'll be a fight and that I shouldn't risk the seafood. (It's virtually impossible to maintain high culinary standards when the chef thinks his efforts might get smashed into someone's face after a goal.)

Passwords strike me as this kind of precaution. They bespeak danger. They're the sort of thing that gets used in wars to help spot Nazis in the dark; they're what thieves come up with to protect their loot-filled magical caves; they're admittedly also what children employ in games, but these are games about gangsters and robbers and crime, not about shopping, buying cinema tickets or sponsoring someone's charity run.

So my concerns about a nightmarish dystopian future were not much allayed by the announcement of a new system whereby you'll have to provide a password in order to obtain food. I'm referring to the launch of Amazon Fresh, a new grocery shopping service from the tax-avoiding scourge of the world's high streets. Initially available only in London, the company presumably hopes that it'll soon be rolled out across the UK, like commerce-smothering death-pastry, and then throughout the world, and that ultimately all other ways of buying anything at all will cease and everyone will stay holed up in their homes in feverish anticipation of the next drone-borne aid parcel.

But how is this any different, you may be asking, from online supermarket shopping, which has been going for years? That also requires a password. That's also sitting in your home waiting for the food to arrive. Why scaremonger now?

The Amazon announcement made me realise how much comfort I derive from knowing the name and whereabouts of the shop from which online groceries ostensibly come. If your online Tesco, Sainsbury's or even Ocado account stops working – perhaps MI5 has frozen it because it reckons you're in Isis – at least you can still go to Tesco, Sainsbury's or Waitrose and buy the food in a password-free, non-identity-disclosing cash transaction.

With Amazon, you can't. You can't go there, you can't ring it up. It's some warehouses somewhere, registered for tax purposes somewhere else. That's altogether too shadowy a set-up to rely on for food. It would be like signing up for a meals-on-wheels service run by a Bond villain.

The prevalence of online passwords is, when you really think about it, an arresting sign of the malevolence of the environment in which we spend so much of our time. The internet can't really be policed; its ultra-connected nature means that the goodwill of the majority counts for little, since villainy and opportunity can find each other instantly. If you do the equivalent of leaving your front door unlocked, an infinite number of burglar-bots are immediately trying the handle. Why do we want to be somewhere so hazardous? I wouldn't go on a cruise if I had to keep a cutlass to hand in case of pirates.

Even those who represent law and order in the virtual world aren't very reassuring. Robert Hannigan, the head of GCHQ, gave an interview at the Cheltenham Science Festival last week in which the most consoling phrase he could conjure up was "not yet". "That apocalyptic vision, we are not quite there yet," was his response to a question about a lone hacker wiping out a whole city. "It could be 10 to 20 years off," was his view on "quantum computing", which would be powerful enough to crack all currently available forms of encryption, wiping out privacy for ever.

He complemented this deferred doom-mongering with the familiar blaming of "80 to 90%" of cyber-attacks on people who had easily guessable passwords, and the classic security service chief's nebulous allusion to potential loss of life if they don't get their way. On the Edward Snowden leaks and subsequent reporting, he said: "We do know that terrorists we were tracking before Snowden disappeared after . . . It's possible people died as a result . . ." This strikes me as an odd combination of blaming private citizens for failing to be zealous enough in keeping their own secrets and also blaming private citizens for failing to be zealous enough in keeping the state's secrets.

I think he's wrong on both counts. I don't fundamentally object to the government having official secrets – I reckon it's probably a necessary evil – but if the secrets get out, surely the blame lies with the government agencies? If they take someone untrustworthy into their confidence, it's their fault. On the other hand, web-based institutions' insistence that we all hold dozens of unguessable streams of letters and numbers in our heads, or else risk haemorrhaging cash and privacy, seems a heavy yoke for us to bear for those companies' trading convenience.

After all, the online world isn't necessarily that convenient for the general public. Granted, it makes it easier to get things delivered, but at the expense of shops where you used to be able to go and buy those things that day. It streamlines correspondence, but often in a way that makes the companies we work for more efficient, rather than improving our own quality of life. It facilitates some chat and fun, but often in environments that are prey to bullying, grooming and fraud, and are an unsatisfactory substitute for real-world human interaction.

These are flimsy advantages to set against the widespread debasement of intellectual property and the facilitation of terrorism and sexual crime. The fact that it's too late to go back now doesn't mean there's no point asking if it was worth it. Speaking personally, and selfishly, I'd have to own many more shares in Amazon and Google to feel that it was.

* * *

Here's a tip for the dynamic go-getter on a time and money budget who's determined to live the luxurious dream: when eating your lunchtime Pot Noodle, try putting on a CD of Handel's *Music for the Royal Fireworks*. It'll make everything seem so posh. Just close your eyes and each chemical forkful will be transformed to caviar as it crosses your tongue. Or, if not quite caviar, maybe a high-end ready meal. Or some toast made from expensive bread. At the very least, it'll elevate your perception of the quality of any jam you happen to be eating. How much probably depends on you, but on average it's 5%.

This is one of the key findings of a recent survey: classical music isn't just good for discouraging teens from loitering around tube stations, it also makes shoppers overrate a product's quality by about a twentieth. The purpose of the study was to find out how our purchasing choices are affected by sounds.

That's actually not true: the real purpose of the survey was to point out to everyone that eBay UK is 15 years old. I doubt whether, deep down, anyone much cares how our purchasing choices are affected by sounds (unless your drug dealer's use of Elgar has made you mistake normal cannabis for skunk). But some people do care that eBay UK is 15 – mostly because it's their job to try to keep everyone perpetually mindful of eBay UK's existence, and an anniversary provides a very-slightly-more-interesting-than-usual angle on their Sisyphean awareness-maintaining task.

(By the way, I'm sorry I have to keep saying eBay UK, rather than just eBay – but that's because eBay, the American bit, isn't 15, it's 18. It's 19 next month, in fact. So it's not like the whole of eBay is 15 – that would obviously be massive news.)

In honour of this divisible-by-five birthday of a subsidiary, the people at eBay UK decided to pay some other people to care about how our purchasing choices are affected by sounds – just to show they can; to demonstrate the awesome power of money, like the son of a plutocrat making a nun do a striptease in exchange for a massive orphanage-saving donation.

The Mother Superior in nipple tassels here is Patrick Fagan, an expert in consumer behaviour at Goldsmiths, University of London, who headed up the survey, and who had the support of a convent of a further 2,000 metaphorical gyrating nuns. These participants were monitored as they engaged in simulated online shopping while various noises were played around them, and then analysis was done on how the different hubbubs had affected their eye for a bargain.

Like classical music, the burble of a restaurant made them more spendthrift, while football commentary and pop music increased the canniness of their decisions. So Beethoven makes things seem classy, and Girls Aloud makes them seem cheap. Cheap as in shoddy, not cheap as in inexpensive – that's the sort of cheap Beethoven makes them seem. The survey provided no insight into people's reasons for buying a budgie.

The clever thing about the study is the implied dig at high street retailers. Only when shopping online – or onphone, ontablet or ongamesconsole – do people have any control over the ambient noise amid which they make their purchases. If you're shopping in an actual shop, the management decides what you hear, and this survey leaves them with a stark choice: play classical music and come across as profiteers, or play pop and make their wares seem shit. Those horrible, physically existent shops are the manipulative ones, the survey is saying, impoverishing you with their piped-in Vivaldi. You know where you are with the internet – it's clean and modern and honest, and not just a bunch of amoral data-pillagers denuding our city centres of commerce.

Facebook is also jumping on to the Rapacious-Internet-Giants-4-Transparency bandwagon. It's trying out a scheme whereby spoof or humorous articles will automatically be tagged with the word "Satire", like in the Monty Python Architect Sketch, but this time not as a joke but as a joke killer.

The joy of websites such as the Onion is that the daft, surreal or satirical is presented as if it's news. Like *The Day Today* on television, it deports itself in a parody of the vanity and hyperbole shown by the institutions with which we keep ourselves informed. This gives its satire another dimension, which would be completely undermined if all its items were pre-labelled by Facebook. It would be like watching a sitcom during which the caption "This programme has been created in an attempt to amuse" perpetually flashes. If you tell someone something's supposed to be funny, they're much less likely to find it so, because a large part of what makes people laugh is surprise. This scheme has all the humour-sapping banality of a continuity announcer putting a chuckle in his voice when referring to the zaniness of the comedy show he's introducing, and doesn't even carry the same implication of approval.

And why is Facebook doing it? To help people so thick that, if they've got internet access, they must surely be beyond saving – it can only be a matter of time before they take out huge pay-day loans and put all the money on red – or those so voracious in their thirst for outrage that they won't allow a synapse beat of thought between reading something and typing a crazed response. It's the witless pandering to the thoughtless.

In fact, it's more sinister than that. This is being done so that Facebook, like eBay UK, can come across as safe and reliable. Comedy and nuance are just collateral damage in the corporation's ploy to try to look like it doesn't wish to deceive you. The "Satire" label is designed to make you think that Facebook has your (rather than its) best interests at heart. It's trying to create a pervading false sense of security in which to make us all its data bitch. That's a far more ambitious scheme for inducing imprudence than piping in some Mozart.

eBay UK turned 20 this year. I hope you at least sent a card.

* * *

"In the UK, we are spending £97bn of public money on treating disease and only £8bn preventing it," says health secretary Matt Hancock. "You don't have to be an economist to see those numbers don't stack up." But Matt Hancock actually is an economist, so how does he know? I suppose he might have canvassed the views of some non-economists, but I'm sceptical about how rigorous that survey can have been.

"Hi Chris, Linda . . ." (good to get a gender balance) ". . . have you got a second?" Hancock may have asked his aides. "Of course, minister." "You did classics and history respectively, right?" "That's right." (Chris is doing all the talking – come on, Linda!) "Great, so we're spending £97bn on treating disease and only £8bn preventing it. Can you see that those numbers don't stack up?" "Oh yes, absolutely," says Chris. "Yes indeed, minister," adds Linda.

It is possible that on such flimsy evidence rests the secretary of state's claim that "you don't have to be an economist to see those numbers don't stack up". And obviously they do stack up. As in, you could stack them up – you could add them together. They probably are stacked up in various summaries of government spending: stacked up under the heading "Health". You don't have to be an economist to see that, if you stacked them up, that would make £105bn.

I don't think he means that, though. I think maybe he means that £97bn is much more than £8bn. His point may simply be that you don't have to be an economist to see that 97 is a larger number than eight. If so, I heartily agree, and my only quibble is why, even with Britain's rising life expectancy, for which Matt Hancock is doubtless keen to take credit, he considered that assertion worth the time it took to express.

To be fair, I think what he's getting at is that, if we spent more than £8bn on preventing illness, maybe we wouldn't need to spend as much as £97bn treating it. Unfortunately, though, you don't have to be an economist to know whether that contention stacks up. In fact, you have to be something else. You need a completely different type of expertise.

And, in an ideal world, you'd want every extra pound spent on prevention to save *more* than a pound spent on treatment – otherwise you're just swapping money about. Matt Hancock clearly reckons it would, and it seems plausible up to a point, but it's not as obvious as knowing that 97 is more than eight, and the naughty man is trying to make us think it is.

What I don't believe, by the way, is that, if you spent £97bn on prevention, you'd hardly have to spend anything at all on treatment. And, even if that did happen, it would be a disaster because it would quickly become impossible to defend the £97bn. It would look like it was being frittered away on nothing. People hate spending a fortune on fire prevention unless they can see that lots of things are on fire.

This is a problem constantly faced by those who seek to justify counter-terrorism spending. If they foil all the plots, no one appreciates them. So they keep the alert level scary and bang on about how many plots they're foiling. I'm sure they're telling the truth (by which I mean: they may be telling the truth), but there's no doubt that it's failing to foil terrorist plots, rather than foiling them, that has the greatest government-purse-string-loosening effect.

This isn't a problem for Matt Hancock, because I don't think justifying greater health spending is his primary aim. So what is his aim? The context for his remarks was the launch of a Department of Health "vision document" entitled "Prevention Is Better Than Cure". No one could argue with that idea. But when politicians go around saying something with which no one could possibly disagree, there's usually something with which millions absolutely would lurking beneath it. And so it proved.

"For too long the NHS has seen itself essentially as the National Hospital Service," he told the *Today* programme. He reckons that's wrong because only "a fifth of the determinants of the length of your healthy lifespan are caused by what goes on in hospitals". A fifth! And yet the hospitals cost so much! The majority of the country's health budget is being lavished on institutions that affect a mere fifth of the . . . you know . . . the determinants of the healthy thing. That's ridiculous! Why spend a fortune on hospitals for people to die in when they could just as easily get run over by buses? Why waste money on intensive care units when, for the same money, you could print a seemingly infinite number of leaflets warning about salt?

Not leaflets, though! I'm such a Luddite! Hancock is talking about "predictive prevention", which, according to the departmental document, "will transform public health by harnessing digital technology and personal data". Just as people get targeted marketing from Amazon or Facebook, this will be "targeted health advice – specifically designed for their demographic and their location".

This is such a Tory idea. Let's learn from the private sector! We can replace those pricey hospitals with algorithms! That way a computer can precisely instruct people on how not to get ill – and the fact that there'll hardly be any hospitals will be an added incentive!

By all means let's encourage healthy lifestyles. It also makes sense (a better idea in the document) to offer genetic analysis so patients can be warned about health risks specific to their DNA. But the commercial technique of exploiting personal data to target advertising is a trick, and a government department shouldn't aspire to trick people, even if it thinks it's for their own good.

The health education the state provides should be the objective scientific truth about the causes of illness. It should be widely accessible, but not marketed, nor expressed differently according to what type of citizen a computer reckons will read it. That approach would be as contemptuous of the public as a corporation is of its customers, and another way by which inconvenient truths are transformed in people's minds into fake news.

* * *

In January 2017, a woman claiming to be Charlotte Higman telephoned the Royal Bank of Scotland and asked for a security reset on Charlotte Higman's account. She probably referred to it as "my account" if she was canny. She was canny: when the bank rang back on Charlotte Higman's home phone number (in an attempt to make sure they were genuinely talking to Charlotte

Higman), it had already been fraudulently diverted to a mobile phone in the possession of the Charlotte Higman impersonator.

We don't know who this woman was but, for clarity, I'm going to refer to her as Nadine Dorries MP. There is no suggestion, incidentally, that this scam was perpetrated by the MP Nadine Dorries. That's why I've given the fraudster a slightly different name: her surname is actually MP and Dorries is a middle name. Still, that would cause some confusion if she ever became an MP! She'd be Nadine Dorries MP MP! And there's already a Nadine Dorries MP! That would certainly be an amusing outcome.

But Nadine Dorries MP isn't the sort of person likely to become a respected parliamentarian. And this scammer sounds like a bit of a shit as well. Having reset the account, Nadine Dorries MP (not the MP) then transferred £4,318 (nice and specific) into another account. Later on in her 23-minute phone call with the bank (I don't know what they were talking about in the meantime), Ms MP requested a second transfer, as a result of which she was asked some security questions about Charlotte Higman, at least one of which she got wrong. So this second transfer was refused. But the initial one wasn't recalled – or reversed or stopped or bounced or whatever they'd do. They just let it go through.

The world being awful, it probably won't surprise you to hear that RBS's initial response when Charlotte Higman complained that her account appeared somewhat depleted was not to acknowledge culpability, restore the money and take urgent steps to track down Nadine Dorries MP. No, its view was that all this was Charlotte Higman's problem. And, when Charlotte Higman made a complaint to the Financial Ombudsman Service, that was also the Financial Ombudsman Service's view.

One of the cleverest things the banking sector has done since the advent of the internet is to establish the notion of "identity theft". Robert Webb and I once wrote a sketch about it, in which a hapless account holder tries in vain to argue that it was the bank, rather than him, that had had something stolen: "I still seem to have my identity – whereas you seem to have lost several thousands of pounds."

A lot of what is called identity theft is, in truth, bank robbery. Someone has approached a bank and absconded with money that doesn't belong to them. Instead of a gun, they used a disguise. People have always tried to rob banks and, traditionally, stopping that happening was down to the bank. That was their pitch: give us your money, and we'll keep it safe. We might lend it out while you don't need it, and you might get a bit of the proceeds of that, but then we'll give it back to you. You can trust us not to give your money away to someone random. It's our job to not do that.

With the concept of "identity theft", however, banks try to absolve themselves of that fundamental responsibility. So now, if someone steals from them in disguise, they claim that's an issue between the thief and the person the thief is disguised as. If a gang of armed bank robbers were wearing Tony Blair masks, would the bank now debit all the stolen cash from the former prime minister's account? That's a nice idea for a sympathetic heist movie.

RBS finally restored Charlotte Higman's account balance nearly two years later, but only after a BBC *Watchdog Live* investigation. "On review of Mrs Higman's case," said an RBS spokesperson, "and in light of new information provided to us, we have refunded Mrs Higman in full for her loss." But it wasn't her loss, it was the bank's. Someone stole some money from the bank and the bank decided not to make a fuss, but to charge the loss to a customer.

It's bizarre behaviour, because there was definitely a theft. That was clear from the start. Charlotte Higman maintained it was the mysterious caller (Nadine Dorries MP) who'd taken the money, but RBS implied for a long time that Mrs Higman herself must have done it. It claimed that, since it had called Charlotte's home number and got through, she must have known about the transactions. If that were true, it would mean she had transferred money out of her account and then denied it. That too would have been theft.

So why did the bank take no action against a customer it thought was attempting to defraud it? Either it didn't really think that or it is extraordinarily relaxed about losing four-figure sums – rather a high-handed way to behave for an institution that owes its continued existence to the generosity of the taxpayer.

I do realise that, if we're going to have online banking, customers have to take some responsibility for keeping their money secure. If you start putting your passwords on Facebook so friends can help you remember them, banks are put in an impossible position. Then again, if you find the online world impersonal and bewildering, there is no longer a realistic option of banking in the old-fashioned way – of having personal contact with a bank employee, in a branch you can walk to, to whom you can hand your money and who will hand it back only to you.

We're all forced to engage with internet and telephone banking, with all their possibilities for fraud, primarily because it's a cost-efficient way for banks to do business. All those high street premises, all the cash and cash machines and UK-based staff created huge overheads. But it doesn't seem right that the banks benefit from all the cost savings made by going online, while customers take the hit for the consequent ease with which money can be stolen.

* * *

Live by the sword, die by the sword. That's what Vogue.com's senior editors should be thinking at the moment. Ruefully, if they can do that without exacerbating wrinkles. They were simply going about their business disparaging and belittling people – just a normal day at the office for those who professionally sit in judgment on what others are wearing – when they got a nasty shock.

Let me explain. Apparently, it's just been Milan Fashion Week. I was surprised to hear that because it seems to me it's always London Fashion Week. Not literally always, but very nearly literally always. It genuinely feels like it's absolutely always London Fashion Week this week, last week or next week. Is that the system? That it's once every three weeks? If so, I suppose that leaves two-thirds of the time for it to be Paris Fashion Week, New York Fashion Week, Bristol Fashion Week (for tidy sailors) or Milan Fashion Week, which is the one it was last week.

At the end of Milan Fashion Week, the staff of Vogue.com wrote an article on the internet – a blog, I suppose you'd call it – discussing what the week had been like, what everyone had learned and why it absolutely hadn't been a vacuous jamboree consecrated to the monetisation of narcissism. But the main issues the Vogue.com team had wanted to raise – the future of trousers, perhaps; how a raspberry sock makes a stylish and practical epaulette warmer; the advent of the thigh-gap storage sporran, a great place for the malnourished to keep cocaine and diet pills – got rather lost because of the digs they all made at bloggers.

Other bloggers, that is, not each other. Not people who get paid to write a blog by a magazine that also has a printed-out version for the dentist's, but a group who seem to be known variously as bloggers, influencers and street-style stars. The ladies at Vogue.com absolutely hate this group and really let rip at them in a tone of weirdly feverish condescension. *Vogue*'s creative digital director, Sally Singer, started it, writing in brackets to emphasise her contempt: "Note to bloggers who change head-to-toe, paid-to-wear outfits every hour: Please stop. Find another business. You are heralding the death of style."

Her use of the word "style" is illuminating because it reveals weakness. She put "style" rather than "fashion". It suits her haughty tone, of course. While affecting to give those not actually under her control an offhand instruction (which they will

defy), she also seems to be alluding to something more significant, more permanent than the merely trendy. But she isn't. The
sense of something being stylish is subjective and, as such, will
never die unless we create a world that contains nothing at all to
which anyone at all has a positive aesthetic response. Talk of "the
death of style" is empty rhetoric.

"Fashion", on the other hand, means something solid. It refers
to objects, usually clothes, manufactured to new, cutting-edge
and/or popular designs. I never know what's fashionable, but
plenty of people always do and, at any given time, some things
are and some things aren't. Sometimes flares or ripped jeans or
kipper ties or powdered wigs are in, and sometimes they're out.
It's a matter of fact. The discussion and prediction of such facts is
what fashion journalism and *Vogue* are for.

But Sally Singer couldn't refer to "the death of fashion" because
that sounds wrong: something will always be in fashion. Saying
"the death of fashion" is like saying "the death of recently", "the
end of the latest thing". And the latest thing at the moment is
the phenomenon of bloggers, influencers and street-style stars.
These people, such as Chiara Ferragni, Susie Lau and Shea Marie,
whose names mean nothing to me, have huge online followings,
can create and redirect trends, and make a lot of money doing so.
Essentially, they have the same business model as *Vogue*.

These bloggers are, by definition, fashionable, even if Sally
Singer and her colleagues don't consider them stylish. So, note to
Vogue.com: never mind style – that's not what you're paid to care
about. If what you find stylish is not fashionable, then neither
are you.

Personally, I would say that being fashionable doesn't matter.
But the staff of Vogue.com can't say that. The whole point of their
institution has always been to elevate and celebrate the value of
being in touch with, and responding to, the latest trends. They
can't suddenly go off all that when it gets a bit youthful and digital

and scary. That's the top of a slippery slope that leads down to comfortable shoes.

Of course they weren't trying to say that fashion doesn't matter; they were trying to be the arbiters of fashion, which I suppose has historically been the *Vogue* journalist's role. It was an attempt to assert authority. Sarah Mower, Vogue.com's chief critic, called the bloggers "pathetic" and "desperate"; Alessandra Codinha, its fashion news editor, said they were "pretty embarrassing" and that going to bloggers for style was "like going to a strip club looking for romance"; and Nicole Phelps, the director of the Vogue Runway app, called them "sad" and said, "It's distressing, as well, to watch so many brands participate."

That last remark is a bit of a giveaway. That does sound pretty distressing. If you're looking to sell advertising spots in *Vogue*, I imagine it has a positively tragic quality. Phelps's implication that these brands had somehow let themselves down by associating with bloggers is a hopeless attempt to assert her dated view of the dignity of haute couture above the dictates of commerce.

Essentially, the Voguesters' bid to make the new girls feel small didn't work. It didn't make the bloggers seem gauche; it made the old-school journalists seem out of touch – not something the fashion world readily forgives. As "fashion influencer" Shea Marie put it: "You are exactly the type of people that have given the fashion world the cold, unwelcoming and ruthless reputation it has had in the past." And the really hurtful word there is "past". It falls to others, bloggers probably, to give it the cold, unwelcoming and ruthless reputation I expect it will continue to have in the future.

Old bullies make way for new. But ageing and mortality must hurt all the more if you've made a profession out of praising novelty. When Sally Singer lashed out at the bloggers, talking desperately about "the death of style", she must have been terrified. Because, ultimately, that's not the death they herald.

4

Destroyer.org of Worlds.co.uk

A wry glimpse of the social impact of the internet.

Did you hear about the rich American who's cut himself off from all news since Donald Trump was elected? There's no reason why you should've done. He wouldn't if it hadn't actually *been* him. His name's Erik Hagerman and he used to be a Nike executive, but now lives on a pig farm and doesn't even farm pigs. He just works on his art and goes for coffee and plays guitar and gives interviews to the *New York Times*. Which presumably he then doesn't read, so the interviewer could have indulged in a rare consequence-free, easy-to-write hatchet job, but didn't.

I don't mean to be snide – things I say neutrally just come out like that. It's the rhetorical equivalent of people whose faces' resting expressions look deeply sad or intensely cross, so they have to smile to seem normal (which must cumulatively be depressing or irritating, thus retrospectively giving them temperaments to match their looks). Because, as it happens, I support Erik Hagerman's life choice.

Then again, I've got a few nits to pick. For a start, the whole art thing's a bit lame. You can see his stuff online. He just does sort of scrunched things and patterns, and well, *fine*, but if there's enough rolling news in the world, there's more than enough crap art. Plus, his non-consumption of news media seems to involve a lot of slightly precious "business". It smacks of the self-involvement of those who believe their allergies make them interesting.

For example, in order to avoid accidentally hearing any careless talk at the coffee shop he goes to every morning he wears headphones playing white noise. He says music won't do because "stray conversation can creep in between songs". He still watches basketball on TV, but on mute so that no contemporary reference sneaks through. And he's given his lifestyle a name, which is annoying even before you hear the name, at which point it gets more annoying.

He's called it "the Blockade". That's all wrong, and I don't think it's deliberate. A blockade is a siege: ingress to, or egress from, an entity is prevented by outsiders. What Hagerman's doing – the entity in the middle trying to prevent ingress from the outside world – isn't a blockade, it's Trump's immigration policy. What's more, Hagerman certainly doesn't oppose informational egress *from* the central entity in his blockade (which is him) because, as I mentioned, he gave an interview to the *New York Times*. It seems like he wants other people's attention, while simultaneously withholding his own. "Watch me ignore stuff!" is the pitch.

However, leaving aside my cynicism about how Hagerman advocates his approach, the approach itself is tremendously attractive. The *New York Times* interviewer touched upon criticism it had received in a way that, to me, merely encapsulated its appeal: "To avoid current affairs is in some ways a luxury that many people . . . cannot afford." I mean, why not just liken it to a holiday in the Maldives? A lobster dinner? A dishwasher? Yes, not everybody can afford it: for many, ignoring the news is impossible because it affects them directly – just as, for many, buying a dishwasher is impossible. But does that mean if you can, you shouldn't?

Probably. In an ideal world. But you'd need to have ignored the news for a very long time to be willing to believe that's what Earth is. Capitalism is pretty horrible, but the various attempts

at improving on it have either led to totalitarianism or gradually eroded back into capitalism. Or, in the case of modern
China, both.

Obviously, people are much more likely to get slagged off for
ignoring current affairs than for buying dishwashers. And that's
appropriately capitalistic: keeping up with the news, like buying a dishwasher, involves purchasing stuff. Or, when it doesn't,
it involves being sold: allowing the fact that you've looked at
something to be marketed to advertisers or worse. Either way,
it's economic activity. However, ignoring the news doesn't add
to the GDP, and so, unlike other luxuries that do more tangible
harm (eg air travel or golf), it can be widely condemned without commercial risk.

Erik Hagerman himself broadly goes along with this consensus. "It makes me a crappy citizen," he says of the Blockade. "It's
the ostrich head-in-the-sand approach to political outcomes
you disagree with." He has been pouring his energies into an
ecological project instead – he's bought 45 acres of former mine
workings, which he hopes to develop into a public park – and
the *New York Times* interprets this as an atonement.

During stretches of my life when I'm not writing topical col-
umns, my own attitude to reading the news often becomes (to
adapt Hagerman's unsatisfactory blockade metaphor) a medi-
um-strength raft of sanctions. I keep half an eye on events, just
in case I suddenly have to stock up on water purification tablets
and look for a defensible cave, but no more than half. And I love
the comparative calm of it, feel no guilt whatsoever and have no
intention of paying for some penitential local swings.

I think I'll always value a vague sense of what seems to be generally going on – the alternative would feel like a denial of society.
But the way the news reaches us these days, with so much of it
either "fake" or "breaking", is worse than ignorance. It's a decon-
textualised screech that monetises its ability to catch our attention

but takes no responsibility for advancing our understanding or avoiding disproportionate damage to our peace of mind.

It's a barrage of human pain and tragedy, which our brains are not evolved to process without either retreating into a carapace of indifference or perpetually experiencing the kind of trauma previously reserved for medieval villagers witnessing the Black Death. And it's also up-to-the-minute micro-snippets of information about events, the real significance of which will only become evident in many weeks', months' or years' time; it's like trying to assemble a 5,000-piece jigsaw puzzle of Satan's face by being given one piece every hour, each one accompanied by a bone-rattling fanfare.

Under capitalism, current affairs are presented like this because it makes economic sense. The media generate money by getting our attention, and we grant it most reliably not in response to the accurate, illuminating and proportionate, but to the loud, sensational and frightening. That's a problem we can only solve by ignoring it.

* * *

"Nobody likes this uncomfortable feeling of being this tiny ball flying through space," Mark Sargent, who believes that the world is flat, told the BBC. I thought that was a revealing statement. I mean, don't they? Personally, I don't mind it. In fact, I'm not sure you can really feel it at all. Then again, I wouldn't say I positively liked it either. I'm not against the world being flat. I'd be fine if it were. I'm content for the world to be whatever shape the world is. Unlike Mark Sargent, I don't have a preference.

The remark gives an interesting insight into his approach. I'd say, if you're trying to convince people of something that flies in the face of scientific orthodoxy, it's advisable not to let slip that, before you started your researches, you had a huge emotional preference for what you ended up concluding. It may lead people to believe you've attached more weight to evidence supporting your theory than to evidence refuting it. And, let's be honest, people are going to be pretty ready to believe that anyway because you've been trying to convince them that the world is flat. And it isn't.

But what do I know (other than that the world is round)? Mark Sargent has 43,415 subscribers to his "Flat Earth" YouTube channel. He's an extremely successful advocate of a conclusively disproved theory. This guy could flog shares in Myspace. And he obviously reckons the notion that there's something slightly off-putting about the planet being a ball is a key selling point.

Sargent was being interviewed at the first Flat Earth International Conference, held in North Carolina, as part of a light-hearted little BBC website package on the subject. "Let's take a wry look at this tiny subculture of harmless eccentrics," was the tone. "Why do people still think the Earth is flat?" was the title.

The answer seemed to be that they just used their gut instinct and common sense: it looks flat – or flattish, flat with a few bumps – so it must be. Marilyn Teed, who'd travelled to the conference from Pennsylvania (presumably without the help of GPS), explained how she knew: "I went down to the seashore, down New Jersey, and I did my own testing . . . you take a straight edge and you go from one end and you follow the horizon of the ocean and . . . it's flat."

Assuming no access to information other than the evidence of her own eyes, that's a perfectly reasonable conclusion. You'd need to either have an instinctive genius for astronomy or be as obsessively drawn to spheres as Mark Sargent is repelled by them to stand on a bit of the world and decide it seems flat only because it's actually a tiny, imperceptibly curved part of an unimaginably massive ball. But, in fact, she has had access to other information.

As part of her research, she says she's "watched over 50 hours of video". Mainly adaptations of Terry Pratchett books, presumably.

The only thing that seriously bothers me about this is that it was the *first* Flat Earth International Conference. This isn't a regular event held by a dwindling band. These people's crazy notion is, albeit to a tiny extent, on the rise again. As the conference's website puts it: "Like you, we grew up believing in a heliocentric globe-Earth model" (translation: spherical Earth orbiting sun – like in, say, reality), but "After extensive experimentation, analysis, and research, we have come to know that the truth of our cosmology is not that which we've been told." It also states chillingly that "every experiment ever conducted to prove even the simple spin of the Earth has failed".

That's not true. What "extensive experimentation"? People have been up in a bloody rocket, looked out the window and seen that the Earth is round. There are loads of photos. Yet the website seems so plausible, so reasonable. It's a neat, slightly boring webpage, as if it's the rules for the election of officers of the Chartered Institute of Personnel and Development. It's the blandest-smelling horseshit you can imagine. Why is it there? Why do they think that? Why do they want to convince people? Why are people convinced? The Earth is round! We found that out ages ago! We've got to move on.

I don't really think significant numbers are going to start doubting the Earth's shape. What worries me is how, in this bewildering internet age, every fact, however apparently undeniable, has the potential to become a subject for debate. The canniest thing Mark Sargent said in his interview was, "Don't take my word for it – I could be a mental patient recently released from an institution."

How admirably open-minded of him! But what he's implying is: so could anyone. You can't take anybody's word for anything. The discerning thinker disbelieves everything, and then makes up his or her own mind on the basis of looking out to sea. It's a clever line for him to take, because the Earth being round is a classic example of an issue where, unless you're an astronaut, you sort of do have to take somebody's word for it.

The recent explosion of weirdly unfocused scepticism is, I suppose, a natural response to this nasty, internet-contaminated era. Accusations of fake news abound and are hugely worsened by, for example, Donald Trump's delusional mixture of lying and denial, and his determination to discredit all the most reliable news sources. Recent revelations that thousands of the accounts tweeting enthusiastically about Brexit were probably malign Russian cyborgs further undermines the credibility of anything but the evidence of our own eyes.

Unfortunately, this boundless doubting could take us right back to the stone age – and not in a time machine we've invented. The accumulation and advance of human learning, and therefore of civilisation, relies on things being written down and subsequently believed. It's built on trust.

A safety-first, unquestioning scepticism about absolutely everything could lead to the thoughtless discrediting, and chucking out, of huge swaths of our collective achievements. I don't really know what we should do about it, but neither can I put a ceiling on how much it's appropriate to worry.

After all, out there somewhere are thousands of people once more insisting the Earth is flat. And they know how to set up a website. And I don't.

The Flat Earth International Conference is now an annual event and, at time of writing, the number of subscribers to Mark Sargent's YouTube channel had crept up to 79,000.

* * *

Attitudes to dating aren't changing as fast as many would like. I must say I'm surprised. Technology is wrecking the established norms of socialising to such an extent that I'm amazed people are bothering to interact physically at all. Much safer, in a world of discontent, war and environmental collapse, to remain at home, surrounded by comforting screens. There we can be entertained and aroused in impregnable isolation.

I'm sure our species' breeding needs can be fulfilled by people extracting their half of the genetic code at home and sending it in some sort of medical Jiffy bag to one of several regional spawning warehouses, located on ring roads between mountainous storage units and giant Amazon intellectual property graves. Like that website's deliveries, the consequent progeny could be distributed by drone – the stork myth turning out, in retrospect, to be a primitive attempt to make sense of a dystopian premonition.

But it's not happening. People are still going on dates. They're still arranging to eat restaurant dinners two-by-two, fashioning an ark from their local Pizza Express to save them from the rising tide of solitude. They're still attempting to combine the head-pat of obsessing about how they seem with the stomach-rub of working out how they feel.

More atavistic still, they continue to assume that, on heterosexual first dates, the man should pay. They're still stuck on that convention, which hasn't changed since it stopped being de rigueur for the chap to turn up with a dripping slab of freshly killed mammoth and bunches of flowers became popular instead. A recent survey found that 77% of us think that, between a male and a female, the male should foot the bill. Of the 1,000 respondents, 73% of the women and 82% of the men said that it was for the bloke to get his card out.

What do you think about that then? Terrible? OK? Presumably, about 77% of you agree that the man should pay, but then you may still think it's terrible that you think that. Is it a harmless remnant of a more sexist age, an adorable antiquated tradition that benefits women and has survived the passing of many of those that disadvantaged them? Or is it a horrible sign of the patriarchy's continued power? Money, the great capitalist symbol of strength, remains the territory of the penis-bearers (by which I mean possessors, not endurers).

The most worrying aspect of this is the extent to which research suggests that paying increases men's sexual expectations. That extent is some extent, not no extent. Which seems slightly grim. Are there really significant numbers of men who believe that any women who agree to dine with them secretly belong to a strange breed of casual hookers who get paid in meals? At the very least they must be wildly overestimating the scarcity of food in western economies.

Perhaps I'm being unfair. Maybe it's not that these men believe their dates will shag them because they've paid for dinner; merely that, by allowing a man to pay, a woman is signalling that the date is going well. Letting the man pay is a sign of approval. The oddness of human nature is such that I reckon a woman who's had a tedious evening is much more likely to insist on settling some or all of the bill than one who's been swept off her feet. That may be illogical. It would probably make more sense if those who'd had a bad time were more inclined to try to get the food for free, so that at least something positive had come out of their evening – but I doubt that's how it usually works.

Obviously, that explanation doesn't mean all this isn't still sexist: why is a woman letting a man pay a sign of approval, but a man letting a woman pay isn't? And this can be awkward for the man too. What if he's had an awful time? It wouldn't be very polite for him to signal that by refusing to pay – that would be flying in the face of a custom that 73% of women believe in. But, by paying, he sends the same signal of sexual interest that a woman allegedly sends by letting him pay. For a woman, saying "Let's go Dutch" can be a financially generous way of conveying that the encounter hasn't been a success. A man doing the same thing is exacerbating rejection with miserliness.

Another aspect of society's sexism is that we generally assume the man will always want to have sex with the woman. By convention, he will have asked her on the first date, and the purpose of the event is for her to see if she likes him. His approval is assumed. That's not altogether PC. What if she turned out to be racist, or to talk with an interrogative inflection, or constantly say "in any way, shape or form"? Is the man supposed to pay and then make himself sexually available to this harridan, purely out of gallantry?

The problem here is that actually discussing what a first date is really about is completely taboo. You may not mention whether or not the two of you are finding one another attractive. Don't get me wrong, I absolutely support this. A world in which people baldly discussed each other's merits would be nightmarish indeed. It's the stuff of reality TV, but not of reality. The taboo forces us to discuss the issue without discussing it – to send signals through flirtation, for example.

But that's hardly a foolproof system. Some people are quite flirty all the time, while others, even in a state of extreme ardour, seem cold and standoffish. People on first dates have had little time to calibrate each other's behaviour and so don't know if the amount of eye contact, physical touching or laughter that's going on is romantically significant or not.

So we try and communicate using money. We fall back on our knowledge of ancient patriarchal conventions of what it means to pay, or be paid for, as a way of trying to send and receive signals through the fog of mutual ignorance. It's not a good system, but it's all we've got. Until we get back to our computers and can just click "like".

* * *

A random moment on the morning of Sunday 27 May 2018 that I'm keen for everyone to really try to be in.

Are you properly experiencing this moment? You know, making the most of it? Here you are, leafing through a Sunday newspaper or browsing articles online on some state-of-the-art device. That's not too shabby. "Syria, dear oh dear; Brexit, hmm; an exhibition – I shall consider attending!" This is part of who you are – you're really doing this. You should "own it", as they say these days, demonstrating capitalism's colonisation of language itself.

So how can you most fully know, feel, experience and, indeed, project this fact, this moment that you're in? How best to consciously, but not self-consciously, inhabit it; to immerse yourself in it, but not let it thoughtlessly pass by, as if it never happened at all, as if you never existed, your constituent carbon already earmarked for different biomass – some worms and beetles and weeds. Plus a couple of rats, if you're lucky. Or one of those forest trees that doesn't even necessarily make a noise when it falls down.

Yes, other people knowing might help. It's bound to. It'll prove this isn't all a delusion – they can confirm it's genuinely happening. Unless they're a delusion too, and there really isn't time to get into that. People say it's solipsistic, which, from usage, seems to mean "best not thought about". Unlike all the plastic in the sea, which is very troubling, and let's hope someone noticed you reading a report on that as you sipped your Fairtrade espresso in an independent coffee shop while shaking your head sadly – no mean feat in itself.

Perhaps you should take a photo and put it on social media? Not a grinning selfie – that would be tonally wrong for the coffee-house sophistication you want to put across. Put across because you're genuinely feeling it, of course. How about a sort of POV shot? The coffee cup, the improving book, the open newspaper, a sprinkling of croissant crumbs. Ooh, not the page about the Grenfell inquiry – that doesn't feel right. Turn that over. One with a nice picture of a sunlit field, or a beach or a castle, and some lighter stories. That's it – resprinkle the croissant crumbs and . . . is that the time? Quick, you've got to go in a minute. And . . . move the car key out of shot. It's a Ford, so not . . . I mean, an Alfa Romeo key would . . . Anyway, there we go: snap. Hashtag LazyWeekend hashtag chilling. Christ, you're really late now.

This urge to self-photograph and upload, to document and publish our every significant experience, was in the news again when it was reported that several holiday companies are marketing "Instagram-friendly tours", catering for "ego travellers" among the millennial generation. This came hard on the heels of Thomas Cook's announcement that it's "exploring options for the future" of Club 18–30, options that include selling it. So millennials would rather pull a duck face in front of Machu Picchu than go to Magaluf for 30 units of alcohol a day and an increased chance of contracting herpes. The message seems to be: young people today are still awful, but in a different way.

Irritation at relentless holiday photography has its roots in mildly xenophobic 1980s moaning about Japanese tourists with stovepipe cameras, but has greatly intensified in the era of the smartphone. "Why can't they just experience it?!" goes the middle-aged cry. "If you're photographing or filming something, you're not immersed in it. Just look and remember."

This view is backed up by research. A 2013 study found that people who went round a museum photographing things, rather than just looking at them, remembered much less about what they'd seen. But of course they've got pictures of everything, so they don't need to. And a 2017 review of research, "Exploring the Links between Mobile Technology Habits and Cognitive Functioning", found that our brains aren't bothering to retain stuff if they think we'll be able to access it through our devices. Certainly, Google Maps is playing havoc with my ability to find my way around town without it. Then again, I also can't start a fire without matches and have no idea how to skin an animal, so my whole not-relying-on-technology ship has long since sailed.

Despite all this, I have sympathy for the obsessive photographers. Existing as we do in a maelstrom of documentation, it's easy to feel that a memory isn't evidence enough that something happened. It's too dreamlike. I try to walk for an hour every day as exercise, and my phone automatically logs a distance and step count. As a result, I have come to feel, if not quite believe, that if I go for a walk without my phone, it hasn't really happened. I won't see it in the app, so how can I get the benefit? It would be like trying to claim money back without a receipt.

I agree that the best way to enjoy a holiday is to unselfconsciously "be in the moment". But the trouble is, once it's occurred to you to take a picture, whatever you then do is already self-conscious. Taking it or not taking it. In fact, you could argue that, by that point, it's more unselfconscious to take the photo, rather than to deliberately suppress the urge and stand there, phone hand twitching, telling yourself it's mindfulness.

I generally find that tourists who relentlessly photograph their experiences, instead of just living them, nevertheless seem quite content with their choice. Meanwhile, the just-remember-it brigade spend a lot of time crossly muttering about other people's cameraphones – partly because their view of the waterfall/fireworks/temple/car crash is being obstructed, but largely because the rest of the human race is just incredibly annoying. Neither group is "in the moment", but at least the former gets some nice photos.

Both are placing too much emphasis on memories. Is it better to have a comprehensive photographic record to look at or a memory unsullied by artificial preservatives? But I don't think memories are the point of a holiday. Remembering something fun that's finished is sad. What's nice about a holiday, apart from actually going on it, is looking forward to it. It's the anticipation of next weekend, not memories or photographs of last, that gets you through the working week.

* * *

In the immediate aftermath of 2016's Brexit referendum, I was feeling sorry for a travel agent . . .

Mark Tanzer, chief executive of the Association of British Travel Agents, has my sympathy. For the last few days, he will have been deafened by cries of "Well, you would say that, wouldn't you?!" Probably not literally deafened. He may already be deaf for all I know. I certainly haven't checked – but it's statistically unlikely.

Maybe I should have said "swamped". But then you can't be swamped by cries, even in a metaphor. I suppose you could be swamped by tears. Theoretically. Though I doubt it's ever happened to a human. Some of those tiny hopping flies have probably come a cropper to a tsunami of grief or sadness that coincided with a meal they were attempting to share. Mealtimes can be stressful. Particularly at Christmas. But then there aren't many of those hopping flies around at Christmas.

Except I was forgetting about the southern hemisphere, as usual – hi guys, hope this hasn't woken you. Yes, the tears and spluttering of fractious, sun-drenched (not literally – it's heat and light, not liquid) Australian family Christmases must be a deathtrap for the antipodean equivalent of those little hopping flies. Which are venomous and have pouches, for all I know. I certainly haven't checked.

So why will Mark Tanzer be drowning in the blinding light of this heart-stopping chorus of "Well, you would say that, wouldn't you?!" The main reason is that, last week, he said something publicly. "Well, you would say that, wouldn't you?!" is the knee-jerk response to anyone saying anything in public.

Not always specifically that phrase, I should add for the benefit of those currently suffering from a pedantic itch (try a corn plaster and lots of talc), but responses that basically mean that. At last the effects of the GCSE history syllabus of the late 1980s are kicking in. Increasingly, people are asking themselves why a certain person has said a certain thing, and are no longer as easily convinced that the answer is "Because it's true." This is good news – everyone's questioning their sources. The only irritant is that they're often questioning them directly on social media.

Julius Caesar never had to deal with thousands of personal messages complaining that his accounts of victories in Gaul were unconfirmed by the Gauls, and seemed designed more to advance his own career than exhaustively document a complex conflict. "Oh yeah, you would say that, Julius! But I heard the Gauls were a pushover and you got lucky with the weather!" never popped up on the great man's phone when he was trying to look up the price of slaves. He may not even have had a phone – I certainly haven't checked. So Caesar went to his stabbing (I checked) blissfully unaware of the cynical clamour of posterity.

That's not how it works these days, as Mark Tanzer will have discovered. Anyone who says anything loud enough to be heard above the hashtags is immediately and repeatedly informed that they only said that because they're them. It's a difficult point to refute. We are all who we are. Getting an objective view on things outside our own selves is impossible, except for those people who claim they remember looking down on their own bodies soon after being given an anaesthetic and could see objects on the top of cupboards. Though I've never heard such a person say they felt a greater political objectivity in those moments – even as they stared down at their unconscious forms they remained just as likely to vote to minimise their tax burden.

"Well, you would say that, wouldn't you?!" is as diminishing and unanswerable as "Look what you've done now!" "Bloody you, with that youness of yours, which, as you've long suspected, everyone else hates. You. You would say that." What can you say in response? Only something else that you would say. And you can't deny that you would say the first thing. Because not only would you say it, you actually have said it. Of all the almost infinite variety of phrases that, given the right circumstances, you would say, this offending one belongs to the minority that you already have.

You may have guessed that this tirade is inspired by the fact that I stated online which way I was going to vote in last week's referendum. In quite mild terms, I thought. I didn't, except by implication, even advocate voting that way. I won't restate here which way it was because, as I was told seconds later, I would vote that way, so there was no point mentioning it. Mentioning it was just annoying to all those who didn't need reminding of all the shitty things which I, being me, would do. It was not an opinion, it didn't come from reason or conviction, it was simply an inescapable and lamentable consequence of the creature I am, like a skunk's stink. That was the view of a fair proportion of respondents who planned to vote the other way. So, you know . . . they would say that.

I was expecting this response, so I didn't much mind – but it wasn't what you'd call uplifting. So when I read that the chief executive of the Association of British Travel Agents had told a conference that he was worried about the impact on Barcelona and Florence of increased visitor numbers caused by websites such as Airbnb, I managed to cut off my instinctive response at the "Well . . .". Because maybe he is worried. Maybe, when he says, "You can see the strain not just on the tourist experience but on the actual fabric of the city and on the residents there," he's being completely sincere.

Obviously, he's also worried about the loss of market share that travel agents are suffering, and is keen for more regulation of how properties are informally sublet. But maybe his view is not just a protectionist desire to shore up his own association, but also a genuine fear for the tourist experience and a warning that, if Airbnb remains unchecked, the world's beauty spots will be wrecked and tourism will, as he put it, "kill tourism".

So he has my sympathy as he tries to cope, like so many people at the moment, with the impact of an online juggernaut on his way of life. What he said may indeed have just been what a man in his position inevitably would say. But that doesn't make it any more dishonest than someone shouting "Help!"

5

Changing Tastes in Taste

Some in-depth analysis of the various substances we put in our mouths and destroy, excluding pen lids.

The time has come to loosen our grip on reality. All the signs are there. Millennia of booze and drug abuse, hundreds of conflicting religions and cults and superstitions and alternative medicines and conspiracy theories, the premise of the *Matrix* franchise, the internet, sunglasses, video games and the powerfully convincing anti-intellectualism of Michael Gove. They're all saying the same thing: ignore what's really happening and you'll feel a lot better. It's been staring us in the face: we need to close our eyes to what's staring us in the face.

And there's been a huge breakthrough in this direction. They're calling it the Taste Buddy, but that's because they're awful and cheesy, and the less we have to perceive their existence, the happier we'll be. And the Taste Buddy will help separate our perceptions from that sour reality. Particularly our perception of cheesiness, which we should soon be able to regulate precisely using a computer.

The Taste Buddy is a new invention, still in its prototype stage, that changes our sense of what things taste like by emitting thermal and electrical signals that stimulate, or rather delude, the taste buds. Currently, it can only make things seem saltier or sweeter than they are, but the team behind it, led by Adrian Cheok of London University, believes that, with development, it could go much further. If built into pieces of cutlery, it "could allow children to eat vegetables that taste like chocolate"; it could make tofu taste like steak; basically, it could make healthy things taste like delicious things.

"But healthy things *are* delicious!" you may be saying. And therein lies the problem. Not that healthy things actually are delicious – that's patently not true. Sometimes it might seem like they are – nuts, for example, often give this impression – and then you discover the deliciousness is all because of some salt or sugar or duck fat that's been added in cardiovascularly hazardous quantities. Healthy things are delicious if either (a) they're deep fried or (b) there's nothing else to eat. Couscous salad is much better than no food at all but, on the modern culinary battlefield, it's a mere flint-headed arrow to the state-of-the-art cruise missile that is a fried-egg sandwich.

No, the challenge for the Taste Buddy is not that lentils actually *are* tastier than chips, but that some people *say* they are and, in some cases, come to believe it. Their own mental powers of self-delusion rival Taste Buddy's thermal and electronic trickery. And that's because many people define their identities by their eating choices.

Whether consciously or not, some healthy eaters' healthy eating is primarily an expression of control, cleanliness and virtue. It doesn't just make them feel better, it makes them feel better than other people. If eating steamed broccoli is suddenly no hardship, because it can be made to taste like baked Alaska, they're going to be deeply offended. It would be like offering a devout order of self-flagellating monks an inexhaustible supply of local anaesthetic.

Frankly, Taste Buddy will be seen as cheating. These penitents won't like it that those of us with coarse, lifespan-reducing palates will get the benefit of nutrients we haven't earned, now that gruel is no longer gruelling. A market will immediately open up for some scientists to discover that it's actually tasting the lettuce rather than swallowing it that matters most.

The most rabid salad-eaters and the haute cuisine sector will combine to incentivise anyone who'll claim "there are still no short-cuts" when it comes to eating well, that the brain needs the taste of roughage, or just that Taste Buddy might give you tongue cancer. Which, I suppose, it might. As might a sexist joke on a lolly stick.

And maybe they'd have a point. A spoonful of sugar may help the medicine go down, but it probably screws up the placebo effect. Who knows how crucial those feelings of sacrifice, self-denial and moral superiority (lost for ever if Taste Buddy turned everything delicious) actually are to the health-enhancing pow-ers of a balanced diet. In a carefully conducted study, it could probably be measured. But that sounds rather elitist, doesn't it? Measuring things with cold objectivity – as if that can ever mat-ter as much as a sincere conviction of the heart.

If you think that's all a bit touchy-feely, or tasty-thinky, you may be surprised to learn it's an approach Theresa May is very keen on. *The Times* recently reported that the Home Office was concealing a report it had commissioned into the number of for-eign students who break the terms of their visas and remain in Britain illicitly after their courses have finished. The number the report had come up with was about 1,500 annually, rather than the tens of thousands that had previously been estimated and generally bandied about. That was not what the Home Office, or the prime minister, wanted to hear.

Why not? It's good news, isn't it? Well, not if you've just cracked down on the admission of foreigners to British universities, with potentially disastrous consequences for the latter's funding. The notion that this drastic policy might have almost no effect on reducing net immigration was extremely unwelcome and, the government clearly felt, best kept quiet.

Particularly as, among likely Tory voters, there's a broad per-ception that foreign students stay here and scrounge. Many people feel that feckless young foreigners are dragging us down, and so the government has come up with a harsh little policy to address that. Why let the fact that it's not true get in the way?

Surely, Theresa May must think, it's not the business of government to start telling the public it's wrong. In an increasingly virtual world, feelings are as valid as facts. Let's focus on what people perceive to be the case and concentrate on adding to that a perception that something is being done about it. That's efficient democratic accountability for post-truth Britain.

No need to contradict people about what they reckon is going on, denying problems they believe exist and citing others they were previously untroubled by. Policy doesn't need to reflect reality any more than the currency needs to be backed by gold. Just listen to their fears, confirm them and then use them to make the government seem vital. People will swallow anything if you control how it tastes.

* * *

A phrase really jumped out at me from a newspaper the other day. *The Times* said a recent survey into Spanish attitudes to Britain, conducted by the tourism agency Visit Britain, "found that only 12% of Spaniards considered the UK to be the best place for food and drink". That, I thought to myself, may be the most extraordinary use of the word "only" I have ever seen.

Has its meaning recently flipped? Has it been warped by an internet hashtag or ironic usage by rappers? Is it like how "bad" or "wicked" can mean good, and how actors receiving awards use the word "humbled" to mean "incredibly impressed with myself"? Because, if "only" still means what I think it means, the paper is implying it expected *more* than 12% of the people of Spain to think Britain was "the best place for food and drink".

That's quite a slur on the Spanish. How delusional did it expect them to be? What percentage of them would it expect to think the world was flat? I know we're moving into a post-truth age, but 12% of a culinarily renowned nation considering Britain, the land of the Pot Noodle and the garage sandwich, to be the world's No 1 destination for food and drink is already a worrying enough finding for the Spanish education system to address. It would be vindictive to hope for more.

But it seems that's what Visit Britain and the Foreign Office are going for. The British ambassador to Spain, Simon Manley, recently donned a union jack apron and went on the hit Spanish cookery programme *El Comidista* to advocate British cuisine and try to change the perceptions of the 88% of the Spanish population still currently in their right minds. It was his second appearance on the programme: the first was when he was "summoned" to explain Jamie Oliver's heretical addition of chorizo to paella. He responded with a recipe for roast chicken with mustard.

This is all very jocular and a welcome distraction from Gibraltar, but I hope Visit Britain doesn't get carried away with this food push. I really don't think the 12% figure is one it should be disappointed with, even if, on closer examination of the survey, the respondents didn't actually say they thought Britain was "the best place for food and drink", just that sampling the food and drink would be a motivation for choosing the UK for a holiday.

Maybe some of the 12% are enthusiastic food anthropologists whose motivation for going anywhere is to try the food and drink. They've consumed everything from yak testicles to locust wee, so fascinated are they by humankind's huge range of nourishment techniques. A bit of academic interest, and the memory of a disappointing white-ant-egg soup or crispy tarantula, might really help soften the blow of a first baffled visit to the salad cart at a Harvester.

You may say I'm talking Britain down, and I'm certainly not talking it up. I would argue, though, that I'm talking it along.

Food here is OK. Or rather it's sometimes terrible and sometimes delicious, but usually neither and it averages out as fine. Lots of us are really fat now – that's got to be a good sign.

I think the host of *El Comidista*, Mikel López Iturriaga, got it about right when he said: "For many Spaniards, British food is the ultimate example of bad international cuisine . . ." – and there are many outlets on the Costa del Sol that work tirelessly to recreate that flavour for British visitors – ". . . but I think that everything has improved substantially in recent years, and today it is much easier to find decent food." So decent food is now available. That's not a reason to pick Britain as a holiday destination – but it's a reason not to be afraid to.

And our ambassador betrayed weaknesses in our cooking, even as he spoke up for it: "The idea is to combat the stereotype about British food and drink and promote the idea that we take ideas from around the world and we adapt them for this cosmopolitan cuisine we know today."

What does that mean? Despairing of our grim native fare, we steal dishes from other countries and slightly ruin them? Put chorizo in the paella and cream in the bolognese and make baguettes with the consistency of sponge? Or was he saying that our comparative dearth of culinary excellence has allowed us a greater open-mindedness to other cultures' food traditions, which has now dragged our own food standards slightly closer to par?

If you work in the catering industry, you may well be screaming at me for unjustly perpetuating this country's no-longer-deserved reputation for shit grub. I'm sorry, and I almost certainly don't mean you: there is, as I say, brilliant food to be had in Britain. There always has been, I suppose, but I'm sure there's more of it now.

But the stereotype bemoaned by the ambassador has its basis in truth: delicious food has never been a cultural priority. In our collective national soul, we don't believe that the niceness of meals is that important. Perhaps on special occasions, but not every day. So we get more crumbs in our keyboards than European neighbours such as France and Italy, which the 12% of Spaniards looking for gastronomic holidays would be well advised to visit first.

The fact that food has improved in Britain is a sign not of a major change in those cultural priorities, but of two other factors: how international we've become and our competitive spirit. The food has been brought up to standard, for the same reasons that we've put in proper coffee machines and wifi – to show we're keeping up. We proudly note how highly the restaurants of chefs like Heston Blumenthal come in international rankings, even as we peel the film off our microwave dinners. In food, as in cycling, Britain can now win.

As most Spaniards noted in the survey, there are better reasons to go to Britain than the food: the history, the castles, the stately homes, the museums, the countryside, the coastline, the concerts, the theatre, the cities. We have an interesting country, an interesting past and we're an interesting people: no nastier than most and hard to ignore. And, for better or worse, what we are, what we have, and whatever it is that our culture represents, come from centuries of working through lunch.

* * *

Slates have been getting a slating. Get it?! Slates? Getting slated? What a lovely great big apposite yet unenjoyable pun. Stick that on your slate and eat it. Perhaps using some sort of gooey reduction as a gum, just to keep all the wrong-coloured tomatoes in position.

Actually, I stole the idea from the headline of a *Daily Mail* article which read "Slated! Plates back on menu", although there's a chance that, unprompted, I could have thought of it myself.

I don't think it's ridiculous self-flattery to suggest that. It's just a pun on slate – it's not the Dyson Airblade. Though both are products of Eurosceptic creativity. Maybe they can make Brexit work if they maintain this level of output. Though some claim it just makes an unpleasant noise and blasts microparticles of excrement all over the place, poisoning the atmosphere. And I'm not that keen on the Airblade either.

So the thing I'm going on about here is the news that the British have eaten their fill of food served on wacky objects – of which the slate is probably the least wacky example. The slate and the wooden board, as weird surfaces on which to present a meal go, are comparatively conventional, a bit square. Though not as square as the square plate. Which itself is obviously much less square than the round plate. Square as in boring and conformist, that is. Not square as in a regular quadrilateral. That sort, the square plate squarely nails. If you want a good square meal, go for the square plate, unless you mean "good square meal" in the idiomatic sense connoting solid straightforwardness, rather than straight-sidedness, in which case the circular plate is the squarer option.

I've put it very succinctly, but those were broadly the findings of a recent YouGov poll. YouGov showed 2,030 people a series of increasingly unorthodox food platters and receptacles and asked which ones, assuming they were clean, the respondents thought were acceptable items for serving meals in. Or on. The crazy replacement crockery examples were suggested by an organisation called "We Want Plates". It describes itself as "the global crusade" against zany food service, has spent years documenting all the mad things dinners have been smeared on in the name of style and will sell you a "Plates Not Slates" hoodie for £40.

The poll result was a wholesale rejection of the non-plate. Of those surveyed, only 69% and 64% respectively had any truck with slates or wooden boards, only 52% wanted their chips in a plant pot, flooring panels received the approval of just 28%, shovels of 17%, dog bowls of 10% and a measly 9% would tolerate their food being brought to them in a perfectly clean and sanitary shoe. Joyless curmudgeons. What do they hang up for Father Christmas? A large Jiffy bag? Who knew that people were so fussy?

If you want confirmation of that fussiness, the survey also found that, while square plates were acceptable to a surprisingly high 96%, circular plates met the approval of an amazingly low 99%. That's right: 1% of them weren't happy with their meal being served on a round plate. That's roughly 20 people. Even if the 99% was actually nearly 99.5%, it's still 10 or so. What do those guys want? Nutrient injections? Their lunch to be fired at their faces from a trebuchet? How is the food supposed to get to be in front of them?

But let's leave aside that anomalous dozen hover-meal-insisting extremists – they probably didn't understand the survey or thought round plates were imposed by Brussels. What about this stinging rejection of the plate replacement? How could Britain's restaurants have got it so wrong? Should we blame the Westminster bubble (a light foam that goes well with poached turbot on a bed of samphire, served on the back of a No Entry sign)? How should the food service industry respond?

In my experience, everyone has always slagged off the weird items food gets served on. This kind of service has been happening for a few years now – decades, if you count scampi and chips in a basket (which I suspect most people don't because that's an old-school notion, uninfused with hipsterish wank). But the square plates and boards and general non-standard plate objects probably started appearing at the end of the last century. Precisely one second later, as the very first zany meal was plonked down in front of a diner, that diner said they thought it was silly, and their dining companion agreed, and their mealtime chat was bolstered by reflections on how impractical it all was and what idiots some people were. Lovely.

Thinking it's stupid to serve food on a non-plate is one of those mysterious reactions that, despite being breathtakingly predictable, still feels original. You feel like you're the only person who's ever felt that way, which makes it a bit like being in love. So it's an enjoyable feeling and one which, if food were never served insanely, no one would experience.

It's also enjoyable to talk about, not just during the meal but later. It makes good conversation: under cover of a funny story about soup served as thousands of tiny droplets, each clinging to a bristle of an upturned brush, or a paella dished up in an old disc drive, we let slip that we've been eating out in trendy places. We're in touch with the zeitgeist, but are too down-to-earth to be impressed. Who doesn't want to come across like that?

So it's entirely unsurprising that, when surveyed about their views on this, people delightedly state their annoyance at silly restaurant trends. They do it because it's fun. It's not a sign of genuine consternation at food service fashion, any more than skiing is evidence of desperation to escape mountaintops. It's recreational.

The daftest part of this outward board-dom (should have left that for the *Mail*) is the implication that restaurants don't realise it's easier to use normal plates, and that there's something frivolous or foolish about them worrying about their image as well as the food. But of course there isn't. They've got to. There are cheaper and quicker ways of satisfying nutritional needs than eating out, so it's vital to surround the process with a few frills, something memorable, some signs of effort. There's no real justification for despising serving cheese on a skateboard or steak on a hot anvil, unless you'd equally scorn a tablecloth.

* * *

Last Christmas, I worried about my heart . . .

What I keep telling myself is that scientific research is not retrospectively rendered pointless just because the outcome is boring and predictable. It's not like a TV drama. The human urge to understand the workings of the universe cannot necessarily be satisfied entertainingly. The apparently obvious has to be tested in experiment if it is to be thoroughly understood.

So I shouldn't blame the researchers from the universities of Birmingham and Loughborough for the fact that their widely reported study into festive weight gain, published in the *British Medical Journal*, produced such depressingly guessable results. I should blame those who reported it as if it were interesting and illuminating.

The only interesting aspect of it – and that was really only slightly diverting in an "I'm staring at my phone trying not to think about Brexit" kind of way – is that it's about Christmas. And it's nearly Christmas. So everyone's thinking about Christmas and the eye gets drawn to stories about Christmas. That's what I'm hoping, anyway. Hi everyone! It's Christmas, isn't it?!

Beyond the Christmas thing, there was nothing of note. It might as well have said: "No measurable elevation of brain cancer risk from Christmas cracker jokes, says report." That would get some hits: "Ooh, Christmas!" people would think. "Christmas crackers, jokes – that's caught my eye and distracted me from Brexit. But, ooh, cancer – nasty, frightening. Brain cancer – is that a headache coming on? Or am I imagining it? Can the imagination get cancer? Right, definitely clicking . . . Oh right, crackers don't give you cancer. Fine. What's next?"

Sadly, this particular study wasn't about cancer, but it was about obesity. Which is linked to cancer, I think I've read. There are definitely links you can click on about that link. So what the study found is that if you get people to weigh themselves twice a week over Christmas and give them a chart showing how much exercise it would take to work off each Christmas treat (for example, 21 minutes of running per mince pie), they will put on less weight than the control group, who displayed much less control. They just got given a leaflet on healthy living, which they may or may not have elected to eat.

The self-weighers actually lost 0.13kg each over the festive period, whereas the "no self-"control group put on 0.37kg. Which actually doesn't sound very much at all, but I suppose that's an average and it's all about long-term trends and, well, it all adds up, as Isaac Newton said. Or was it the Green Goddess?

Now, as findings go, I'd say this one is stratospherically unsurprising: people put on less weight, on average, if they monitor their weight. If monitoring your weight had no effect at all, or made you fatter, that would be unexpected. This is not. The summary of the findings should read: "Just guess them and you'll be right."

To me, the only startling thing about any of this is that it takes 21 minutes of running to work off a mince pie, and that was a pre-existing fact rather than a finding of the study. But seriously, one mince pie equates to *21 minutes* of *running*? You run continuously for the length of a whole episode of *The Simpsons*, and that means you can have one measly extra mince pie? A whole hour's running every day won't quite buy you a three-mince-pies-a-day festive habit? Suddenly neither running nor mince pies nor existence itself seems worth all the faff.

Anyway, that aside, fair enough, well researched, good to have checked. If you measure your weight and think about your weight a lot, you're likely to weigh less than if you don't. Smashing. My only objection is to people reporting it as if it's a solution to Christmas weight gain. "Just weigh yourself twice a week and you'll be fine!" the articles imply. But that's not really the solution, unless you keep your bathroom scales at the top of 47 flights of stairs (though it probably turns out even that would only earn you two slices of turkey and a small eggnog). The slimming isn't caused by the weighing, but by behavioural changes triggered by the thought processes the weighing provokes.

People don't like those thought processes. They're repelled by them in the same way they're attracted to snacks. That's physics. Outside study conditions, people won't weigh themselves twice a week if it gets them down, particularly at Christmas. It's supposed to be the season to be jolly. Glumly standing on scales feeling guilty about canapés past, and indeed passed, is not the vibe at all.

All the report is really saying is this: people should think more about their weight and the arduous physical exercise they should take if they want to eat certain things. That's restating the problem, not providing the solution. That's "This toddler has a high temperature," not "Give Calpol."

So what's the Calpol? Sober analysis and self-control? Some people might call that the natural way, but I reckon it's as natural as a hyena on a seafood diet. It smacks of wisdom and, by nature, humans aren't so much wise as clever. We use cleverness to obviate wisdom. That's what's destroying the planet, but it's also the only hope of saving the planet.

The Calpol equivalent would obviously be some way of maintaining a healthy weight without thinking about it, without having to exert self-control (I'm sure the pharmaceutical industry is bristling with suggestions). That's what we yearn for: to be able to submit to our evolved instinctive urges once again. Delicious food is there, so eat. Merry-making booze is there, so drink.

But we also want to live long lives, and one of the flaws of evolution, from the human point of view, is that it doesn't give longevity any credit. Anyone who can just about survive to middle age while remaining fertile is likely to be as genetically influential as a sprightly 95-year-old.

So we've never evolved the urges that would allow us to make old bones without constantly deliberating about our health – which you can't do for long without also thinking about death. And that's the very thing all this midwinter Christmas cheer is supposed to help us avoid.

* * *

There's been a major breakthrough in the quest to improve the taste of champagne. You probably think that's one of those "first world problems" that everyone in the first world is so obsessed with not being obsessed with. Or rather a first world solution to a problem, like invading a country and taking all its oil. But I'm not sure it's even that.

After all, who really gives a damn what champagne tastes like? Even in the first world? I mean, you'd complain if you were served some and it tasted of peppermint or Fanta or cheese, but only because you'd think that meant the glass hadn't been washed or it wasn't really champagne. If champagne had always tasted like Fanta, you'd sit back and enjoy that fizzy, sugary, orangey hit which you associate with luxury and celebration. Champagne just needs to taste like whatever champagne tastes like. The specifics of that flavour are as irrelevant as a banknote's appearance.

The supposed breakthrough comes from Federico Lleonart, who is a "global wine ambassador for the drinks company Pernod Ricard". That's the phrase in all the papers, and I'm sticking to it. To be fair, it varies a bit across the media. Jilly Goolden in the *Daily Mail* kept it vague and article-free, calling him just "global wine ambassador . . ."; *The Times* grandly asserted that he was "the global wine ambassador . . ."; while the *Sunday Telegraph* dismissed him as merely "a global wine ambassador".

None of which gives us much insight into the structure of Pernod Ricard's wine diplomatic service and how many ambassadors and embassies there are. One for each country? One for each wine? One from each country to each wine? Are there ones for other drinks – Pernod, for example? Or is that what Lleonart is: Pernod's ambassador to wine? In which case does every drink have an ambassador to every other drink – the big jobs being tea's ambassador to coffee and his opposite number?

On the scale of indispensability to human society, global wine ambassador may rank somewhere below party planner and above web designer's mood-board chakra realigner – about the same level as topical columnist, in fact – but it seems safe to assume that he'd know a bit about wine. And not just because he's got a lot of time on his hands.

And what he, and other experts, are now saying about champagne is that, if it's a posh one (as opposed to a normal champagne of the sort people actually ever buy – you know, the cheapest one that's still allowed to have the word "champagne" printed on it, even if it's accompanied by "Morrison's"), it tastes better drunk from a normal wine glass than from one of those tall flutes. Even if it's a new flute which hasn't yet developed a stubborn clod of unreachable matter in the bottom that fizzes insanely when the glass is full, giving the disconcerting impression that it's dissolving.

Lleonart says: "When the sparkling wine or champagne has complexity, depth and autolytic notes, such as the best cavas or champagnes, then the best option is actually to use a white wine glass in order to let the aromas express themselves better." This statement confused me, and not primarily because I don't understand what 'autolytic' means even though I've looked it up. I think I know what complexity is, but depth must mean something else in this context because otherwise it stands to reason that a fixed volume of champagne would have greater depth in a narrower receptacle. But what confused me most was the reference to "the best cavas".

Imagine, if you will, the announcement of the engagement of a beloved child to an upstanding and appropriate partner. It is a joyous family occasion. What do you do? Do you, for example, open a bottle of one of the best cavas? You know the sort. Not one of those crappy garage cavas, but one of the ones that wine experts say taste better than many champagnes – so much so, in fact, that they warrant the use of normal wine glasses rather than those awful, dated flutes, the efficacy of which science has rejected as firmly as the way up you were taught to put your now affianced child to sleep decades ago. Do you? Do you produce the receipt for this fine cava, proving that it cost more than many champagnes, and that therefore it's only your insistence on the best possible fizzy taste, not penny-pinching, that denies the apple of your eye a more famous C-word for the congratulatory toast? Or do you buy a bottle of champagne?

I'd do the latter, I think. It doesn't really matter what it tastes like because you can show them the bottle and most people can read. So they know what it is, and what that signifies. That's the point of champagne: it shows a celebratory intention. As well as being extravagant, it symbolises extravagance. Its symbolic role is why we drink it out of funny-shaped glasses and is much more important than its actual cost or taste. Lleonart's reference to cava suggests that he either doesn't really understand that or is resistant to it.

Normal champagnes, by the way – the simpler, shallower, less autolytic sort – should still be guzzled from flutes or that saucer-on-a-stalk type of glass. "Both the flute and the saucer help the aromas diffuse in different ways," explained the ambassador. "The flute concentrates carbon dioxide at the top of the glass, whereas the saucer's wide mouth means the bubbles evaporate more quickly." So, if you're drinking an inferior wine, you might as well persist with your wacky glassware.

And this, of course, is the key to the experts' new champagne-drinking advice. It's not really about what anything tastes like.

They're not fools. They're selling a luxury item, so this is all about snobbery. This supposedly taste-maximising advice creates a whole new level of posh above normal champagne-drinking and gives it a visual hook.

Like calling an eminent surgeon "Mister" because he has been elevated above a mere doctor, drinking fizzy wine in a normal glass is a way of defining a new cut above – a way of making expensive champagne distinguishable from normal, without the need of an expert's palate. It's like anglicising your pronunciation of *Don Quixote* – to those not in the know, champagne from a normal glass will look wrong. But, to the alpha-snobs, the sensation of the bourgeoisie wrongly looking down on them will add a frisson to their feeling of superiority that's more effervescent than any drink.

* * *

Scampi, I remember once reading, used to be very expensive. In the 1950s, ordering scampi in a restaurant was a really swanky thing to do. To contemporary ears, the word had the same connotations that lobster does today. It feels a bit incongruous, like Princess Grace having a cheese ploughman's at her wedding breakfast. But there it is: scampi was a prized and pricey luxury.

So what happened to it? Did it somehow get much less delicious, but still basically palatable, so restaurateurs concluded that they couldn't charge top dollar for it any more and it became the basket-borne bar snack of the 1970s and beyond? Obviously not. It just got more plentiful, and so cheaper. Because of fishing or farming or freezers, I suppose, it was suddenly possible to dish out millions more plates of it, so it lost its cachet and ceased to be a luxury item.

I realise the term "scampi" probably now covers a wider range of marine biomass nuggets than it did in the dish's post-war glory years. There's scampi and there's scampi. I mean, they were putting horse in lasagne, so I wouldn't want to be a slow-moving walrus or squid when an unscrupulous scampi trawler breasted the horizon. But in a nice pub, where they might call it "whole-tail scampi", I imagine they're basically dishing up the same item Noël Coward would have paid through the nose for as he handed over his ration book at the Café Royal.

Most of us know how that tastes. It tastes fine. It's OK. A bit fishy, in both senses of the adjective, but a broadly acceptable vector for tartar sauce. But I think we're clear what we'd do if it suddenly quintupled in price: we'd just stop ordering it. We can all live with never eating scampi again – it's just slightly gristly fish and chips that you don't have to cut up.

So what were they thinking, those people in the 1950s? Never mind all the sexism, racism and homophobia, never mind McCarthyism and Korea and Suez – that's all very regrettable, but then people have always been absolute bastards. But what were they thinking paying so much for scampi?

I was put in mind of the cost of luxuries by reports that, according to the Coutts Luxury Price Index, it's rising way ahead of inflation. Inflation is at 2.4%, but there's been an overall price rise of 5.5% in the luxury cars, Savile Row suits, private-school fees, posh boozes and other high-end items that make up the Coutts luxury basket of goods.

This is not the sort of basket in which you might find scampi. Scampi has long since ceased to be a luxury food, so doesn't qualify. But that actually raises a question about how you measure price fluctuations only in items that are incontrovertibly expensive. If their prices were to fall enough that they wouldn't be deemed expensive any more, would they stop qualifying for the basket, and so fail to mitigate the apparent inflationary trend?

The story of scampi demonstrates that all that is required to render an otherwise unremarkable thing luxurious is for it to be very expensive. That's what drew people in the 1950s to pay so much – the simple fact that it cost so much. Its exclusive price made them keen to be included in the elite group that could afford it. They would then undoubtedly tell themselves they were eating something exceptionally delicious, as people do now with truffles, caviar, paté de foie gras and a whole host of other astronomically pricey items whose flavours range from quite nice to weird, but none of which actually tastes as good as a slice of buttered toast.

There's no *schaden* in any *freude* we might feel about the fact that the super-rich might have to pay a bit more for the ridiculous stuff they buy. The respectful solemnity with which designer clothes, luxury cars, extremely expensive watches and daft modern art works are viewed makes me well up with contempt. Whenever I see an advert for a designer watch, for example, I imagine all the stupid men looking at it, nodding and seriously muttering, "Nice watch," aspiring to own it, or perhaps being able to buy it and add it to some prissy collection, and I am mystified at their certainty that this is a more noble use of their finite span than, say, a rampant heroin addiction.

But what does this inflation really mean? Well, for Sven Balzer, head of investment strategy at Coutts, it means that "anyone looking to maintain the spending power of their wealth in the long term should consider a diversified investment portfolio alongside cash holdings", but then he's got products to sell. Some of the price rises are probably a sign of real economic changes and uncertainties – fluctuating currencies, Brexit, Trump's enthusiasm for a trade war – and it's nice to think that the jet set are copping a bit of that flak as well as everyone else.

Mainly, though, it just means that those who make or sell all the overpriced crap have decided to put prices up because they know people will pay them. In fact, people may be even keener to pay them because the exclusivity of the basically-just-a-bag/

dress/car/watch/school/bottle of tequila/holiday is reinforced by the higher charge. These retailers aren't looking to give their "best price"; they need this stuff to cost too much or it will start to seem normal.

It's all the inevitable consequence of the widening gap between rich and poor. As the world splits further in two, with a small plutocrat class that's increasingly distant and separate from the rest of the population, the luxury brands need to nail their colours firmly to the super-yacht mast. These days, some people can pay anything, which means some have to charge anything. Either that or they risk going the same way as scampi.

* * *

People won't take dietary advice from obese nurses, but they will from stick-thin film stars – with terrible results in both cases. That's the latest nutritional news.

The first half of the above is an inference from a study in the journal *BMJ Open* saying that about 25% of nurses in the NHS are obese, a discovery the report's lead author, Dr Richard Kyle of Edinburgh Napier University, declared to be "deeply worrying". The depth of his concern surprised me, considering that about 25% of the adult population is obese, which he must have known. So, what he's found is that nurses are, on average, neither thinner nor fatter than the general population, which, if I were him, is precisely what I would expect to find. Then again, calling the findings "deeply predictable" would probably have been a kick in the teeth for the people who'd just paid him to find them.

His deep worry stems from two issues: first, the health impact of obesity on all those nurses – "It is vital that we redouble our efforts to take care of our healthcare workforce who do so much to care for others" (maybe he used to work in greetings cards) – and second, that patients will be reluctant to take dietary advice from the very fat. "If someone is visibly overweight people don't necessarily trust that advice. The public expect nurses to be role models," he said. Tam Fry, chairman of the National Obesity Forum, echoes this sentiment: "People in the health service are meant to be role models but they're not."

You hear a lot these days about how some people are supposed to be role models. Reality-TV stars are bad role models, footballers should try to be better role models, etc, etc. It makes a certain amount of sense when talking about those who are paid a lot to do something unimportant. But I think it's a bit much also to lay that burden on those paid a pittance to do something vital. Purely by their choice of profession, nurses are surely already making a contribution role-model-wise, and they can probably do without our heaping on a load of extra pressure to be thin and healthy and beaming with media-groomed *joie de vivre*.

In the west today, it can be difficult to be thin. I certainly haven't got the knack. And, in a cruel reversal of what historical imagery makes us expect, the poor are now more likely to be fat than the rich. Time and money are a huge help in attaining the trim appearance that contemporary visual snobbery associates with success. These days the euphemistically prosperous-looking are probably anything but. And, as time and money are commodities nurses are notoriously short of, I'd say the fact that the profession's obesity rate is no higher than the national average is already an achievement.

But what of the concern that patients suffering weight-related health issues will be less willing to take lifestyle advice from a fat nurse? Well, I can't immediately dismiss it – people can be pretty stupid. Maybe they'd also be less likely to heed safety advice about crocodiles from a zookeeper with only one arm.

The media have a slight obsession with hypocrisy. It's like potting the eight-ball early in pool. If someone can be labelled a hypocrite – if you can say they "don't practise what they preach"

– then it's game over: you can ignore everything they say. That's not always a very sensible approach. We all know someone can completely sincerely advise you to do something that they've tried and failed to do themselves.

But many of us do seem to find it reassuring to get our dietary advice from the rake-like. The British Dietetic Association is so concerned about this that it brings out an annual list of "celebrity" diets to be wary of. The latest one includes the alkaline diet, favoured by Kate Hudson, Tom Brady and the Duchess of York, the raw vegan diet, advocated by Gwyneth Paltrow, Megan Fox and Sting, and the ketogenic diet, followed by the likes of Kim Kardashian, Mick Jagger and Halle Berry.

These people are all in good shape, so the idea that they've got some glamorous trick for maintaining their appearance is as attractive as they are. But, as you'd probably expect, it doesn't work like that. According to the BDA, while some of these diets might help you lose a bit of weight (largely because of the extent to which they overlap with the broader scientific consensus on healthy eating), they might also be bad for you if you stick to them for too long (probably not a massive worry).

They're fashionable fads cooked up (or left raw) by amateurs, which means they are often, as the BDA says of the alkaline diet, "based on a basic misunderstanding of human physiology". "If something sounds too good to be true, it probably is," was how Sian Porter, consultant dietitian with the BDA, put it.

To my mind, the idea that a film star is thin for reasons primarily to do with diet is as foolish as thinking that nurses might have their facts wrong on healthy eating simply because they happen to be fat. Film stars are weird people – they have a drive to be looked at that, in most cases, has informed a very high percentage of the choices they've made. They have a huge amount riding on their appearance, and it is insufficiently cynical to say that it's primarily money. They are thin from assuaging a different hunger – one that dwarfs the doughnut cravings under which the majority labour. They're the wrong people to advise the general public about what to eat. It's like asking a cheetah for techniques to cut out carbs.

If a problem with our society is that people unquestioningly believe the thin and rich, and ignore out of hand the utterances of the poor and chubby, then I wonder whether pressurising the chubby to slim and the slim to shut up is really the answer. I suspect that's treating the symptom rather than the underlining cause – which is the utter vacuity of millions of people's system of values.

So let's leave Halle Berry and rotund nurses out of this. It's not their fault. The unavoidable truth is that you shouldn't judge the wisdom of someone's words according to how physically attractive they are. People who don't realise that are bound to suffer. And their minds won't be changed by anything I say. Not unless I lose weight.

* * *

Speaking as a meat-eater, I find it annoying how many vegans there suddenly are. I suspect a few other meat-eaters feel the same. Do you, some meat-eaters, if you're really honest with yourselves?

It's not a good look, I realise, to appear annoyed with groups of people living their lives in the way they choose without harming others – and, in the case of vegans, taking the not-harming-others to considerable lengths. Nevertheless, I'm going to stick my neck out (also not a good look), because it's true. I'm not asking you other meat-eaters to do the same. You never have to seem annoyed; just to privately ask yourselves whether you find all these vegans slightly annoying.

If you do, then the obvious next question is why. Well, there are lots of reasons: for example, some vegans seem so radical and preachy and angry. Though, actually, again being honest, I don't really mind that. I quite like it. It makes it easy to discount them as weird, which was my view about veganism in general before I started finding the number of vegans annoying.

I think what I find annoying, deep down – and, again, some meat-eaters, you don't have to own up to this, but it might interest you to discover whether you secretly agree – is the very fact that I can't discount vegans any more. The thing that's annoying about there suddenly being lots of them is the nagging suspicion that they might be right. When there were hardly any vegans, I hardly ever had to think about that.

After all, it's not as if eating meat is an incontrovertibly lovely thing to do. I mean, it's lovely to eat, it's delicious, but I'm talking about actually killing an animal: you know, an organism that can feel stuff and likes some things and doesn't like other things, that can pretty clearly experience fear – either that or it can act, which would be an even greater sign of sentience. I imagine that putting an end to that creature's life isn't necessarily a particularly great feeling. So, speaking personally, I'm thrilled it all gets handled by other people, because I don't reckon that if I'd just, say, strangled a goat, I'd be over the moon about myself.

Look, I can defend meat-eating. It's perfectly possible to farm meat in such a way that the animals have decent lives and don't die in pain and fear. I don't know how often that happens, but it's possible. Still, it's hard to frame an argument that it's actually wrong not to kill them. Not killing them seems, ethically speaking, to be playing on the safe side.

Now, I'm definitely going to continue eating meat. That's decided. I don't like change and I do like sausages. So, as you can imagine, having my mind forced down the contemplative avenues above is somewhat vexing – and, as a result, it becomes emotionally tempting to blame all the vegans for that vexation. So that's where I am with all this. End of column.

Except, I suppose, I ought to explain why I'm talking about this now. There's a vegan in the news – his name is Jordi Casamitjana – who is campaigning to get "ethical veganism" protected as a "philosophical belief" under the Equality Act. He's calling it "ethical veganism" to distinguish it from veganism for purely dietary reasons. "Some people only eat a vegan diet but they don't care about the environment or the animals, they only care about their health," he told the BBC. I suppose, to him, they're like Blairites to a Corbynista. Worse than cannibals.

Casamitjana's veganism is full-on. It's not just about food, it's his whole life. He has no truck with leather, silk, wool, zoos, aquariums, anything that's been developed using animal testing, anything that uses captive animals in its advertising, or dating non-vegans.

He used to work for the League Against Cruel Sports, but it wasn't vegan enough for him. He says he discovered that the league's pension fund invested in companies that carried out animal testing and was sacked for telling people, which he characterises as being discriminated against for his veganism. The league disagrees, saying he was sacked "because of gross misconduct. To link his dismissal with issues pertaining to veganism is factually wrong."

The employment tribunal that's going to decide this will also rule on whether veganism meets the Equality Act's definition of a belief. According to the act, it has to "be a belief as to a weighty and substantial aspect of human life and behaviour"; it must "attain a certain level of cogency, seriousness, cohesion and importance; and be worthy of respect in a democratic society, compatible with human dignity and not conflict with the fundamental rights of others".

I'm loath to admit it, but it totally qualifies, doesn't it? Nick Spencer of the theology thinktank Theos is more sceptical, warning that "If we're all turned into rights bearers, my rights clashing with your rights, we end up having to appeal to the courts to sort out our differences and that can become oppressive for everybody."

Maybe so, but that's an argument for changing the Equality Act. You can't just hope no more groups assert themselves under it, or say that all the slots for belief systems are taken because otherwise we'll have too many "rights bearers". Ethical veganism is coherent, heartfelt and spreading – and, frankly, its adherents might need protecting from the prejudice of irritated meat-eaters like me.

Ethics, practically speaking, are relative. Our ethical compasses are calibrated according to the norms of the time in which we live. So I eat dead animals because I was brought up to eat dead animals. It seemed like almost everyone did when I was younger, and the tiny minority who didn't certainly had lots of cheese and eggs. It was normal, and it still is normal, just a bit less so.

It's not uncommon, in the history of human societies, for things once deemed normal to start being deemed wrong. Sometimes it's something like homophobia, sometimes it's something like openly criticising those in power – it depends on the time and the society. Maybe all these vegans are harbingers of such a change. It annoys me because it makes me worry that I'm becoming a victim of history, just like all the animals I've eaten.

6

Titans of the 21st Century

According to the old-fashioned view, history is forged by great men. The slightly less old-fashioned view is that it's forged by great men and women. A more academically respectable interpretation is that it's forged by nebulous forces that can't be encapsulated in a photograph.

It's hard to believe that, in the age of selfies and Instagram, such a view of the past can prevail for long. It's simply too complicated and inconvenient. I mean, you can summon an immediate taxi through an app, so it's frankly unacceptable that your smartphone shouldn't also have access to a snap of whatever history's the fault of.

So, in the forthcoming spirit of the age, this section contains my thoughts and feelings, from various moments over the last few years, about some important people – a few of the big hitters. As you'd expect, they're all white and they're all rightwing. Worse than that, all but one of them is still alive.

To be fair, I suppose, if we don't like how history is going, it's up to us to change it. A bad workman blames his tools. This chapter is all about those tools.

David Cameron
March 2015

The other day David Cameron gave a straight answer to a straight question. That's something most of us are desperate for politicians to do more often. We crave it, like children starved of love;

we get driven mad by its perverse absence. "Just say what you think," we implore, "just answer the question! Stop evading our inquiries and trying to work things round to some prearranged spin-doctor-approved set of phrases and priorities.

"Please, just for a second, be like a normal human and talk to us, tell us what you think, tell us what you're going to do!" This is what we inwardly beg as a politician is asked something on TV or radio, in the moment before the inevitable "I think the real issue here . . .", or "The more important question we need to ask is . . .", or "Hang on, 'cos, you know, we need to be clear about this . . ." crushes our hope once again.

So when a journalist asked the question "Would you go for a third term?" and the prime minister simply said, "No," you'd think that was worth a standing ovation. It's so exactly what we slag off and hate politicians for not doing. The smart money was on a "I don't think now's the time to be thinking that far ahead," or "That's an issue that I'll discuss with colleagues as and when the time comes," or even a disingenuous "Gosh, I haven't really given that a lot of thought." But Cameron did what his lot stereotypically never do and answered the bloody question. In two letters. Bravo.

But it did not go down at all well. A Liberal Democrat spokesman declared it "incredibly presumptuous . . . to be worrying about a third term as prime minister weeks before the general election", while Douglas Alexander, Labour's election strategy chief, said, "It is typically arrogant of David Cameron to presume a third Tory term in 2020, before the British public have been given the chance to have their say in this election. In the UK it is for the British people and not the prime minister to decide who stays in power."

I find both remarks infuriating. At least the Lib Dem had the grace to remain anonymous, but you'd have to hope Douglas Alexander, a privy counsellor and former cabinet minister, is now weeping over his statement while repeatedly wailing, "What have I become?!" He absolutely knows that Cameron isn't presuming anything at all. The question was "Would you go for a third term?" – that's "go for", as in "put yourself forward for" or "apply for". The exchange is quite clearly based on the premise that, for someone to be prime minister, it requires the electorate's consent. But it also requires the consent of that someone, which is what the interviewer was inquiring about. Obviously. As Alexander fully understands.

Yet he has chosen not only to ignore that fact, but to imply Cameron doesn't even accept that "the British people . . . decide who stays in power". So Cameron isn't just arrogant, he's an aspirant usurper. He's flying in the face of democracy – simply by answering the question "Would you go for a third term?" with the word "No". Though I doubt the word "Yes" would have appeased Alexander either. That, surely, would have seemed even more arrogant. So, basically, neither answer to the question would satisfy Douglas Alexander. What he's saying, we must conclude, is that Cameron shouldn't have answered the question at all. He should have evaded it. That, the Labour strategist has chosen to contend, would have been the proper course for a prime minister: to avoid answering perfectly reasonable questions.

I can't help wondering if it's Alexander's brand of "election strategy" that leads to gaffes such as Ed Miliband choosing to be filmed in a deeply depressing upstairs kitchenette – the sort of place a prostitute might make a Pot Noodle – in case his real kitchen blasted away the public's trust with its sheer opulence: the mood-lit wine fridge, the live lobster tank, the unicorn-ivory worktops, or maybe just the fact that there's an actual chair.

Criticism of Cameron's candour didn't come only from other parties. Many Tories believe it was a strategic blunder – that he might now be seen as a "lame duck". One anonymous former minister said: "This was peculiar and unnecessary. It does not help the prime minister's authority," while another Tory apparently remarked: "This was an 'Oh fuck' moment. The best you can say is David is straight and honest." The implication seems to be that calling a prime minister honest is somehow damning with faint praise. I'm not at all sure that David Cameron is particularly honest, but I have no doubt he'd be more popular if everyone thought he was.

This all culminated in a widely reported "damage limitation exercise", in which Michaels Fallon and Gove went around saying how reasonable and straightforward the prime minister had been. Which was obviously true in this case. But, if there's one thing that can make something reasonable and straightforward seem otherwise, it's some oleaginous loyalists touring the media repeatedly saying it's reasonable and straightforward. And it smacks of panic – as if a secret the-prime-minister-has-actually-answered-a-question alarm had gone off in Downing Street for the first time since Churchill brought up "blood, toil, tears and sweat" instead of hard-working families.

This nasty little Westminster squall is a good illustration of what's wrong with British politics at the moment: the tedious and irrelevant scrutiny of image and tactics that we've somehow adopted instead of a properly functioning political system. We get a tiny glimpse of openness and humanity, of the prime minister talking like a normal person, and it's immediately stamped on.

The other parties can't restrain themselves from making political capital out of it, from attempting to twist Cameron's completely apolitical remark into something that exemplifies what a bastard he is. They can't just leave it alone and talk about policies instead. Similarly, the grumbling Tory backbenchers can't suppress their anger that the prime minister has exercised his right to freedom of speech without running it by them first. So they complain that it's a tactical cock-up.

This kind of row feels so irrelevant to the issue of how best to govern a discontented and divided nation. It's an insulting waste of the public's time and attention, of interest only to politicians and politics nerds, and the likes of Douglas Alexander do further damage to our discredited system by resorting to it.

January 2019

David Cameron really loved organising votes for things, didn't he? That was his answer to everything. I was reminded of this when I read that the elected police and crime commissioners, which his government introduced to oversee the constabularies of England and Wales, aren't doing a very good job. According to the head of the National Crime Agency, they're all about stopping speeding and burglary, and not so hot on organised crime, online child abuse and modern slavery.

It's not surprising. Making some local elected officials the overseers of the police is effectively putting the Neighbourhood Watch in charge of law enforcement strategy. They're going to address the issues most noticeable to the very small percentage of people who might turn out to vote for them. If they were in charge of healthcare, all the money would go to treating RSI caused by overenergetic net-curtain twitching. Their best chance of arresting a mafia boss is if he plays the music too loudly at his Christmas party.

But it's odd that David Cameron was so keen on holding votes when his career as prime minister began with him failing to win an election. I'm surprised people don't talk about that more, because it's quite remarkable.

It was 2010, and the world was reeling from the worst financial crisis in nearly a century and, by some reckonings, of all time. Britain is depressingly reliant on the financial services sector, so it was particularly scary here. The mood was not good. On top of that, the governing party had been in power for well over a decade, had started a disastrous war, and its charismatic twice re-elected leader had been replaced, just before the banking melt-down, by a better man but a markedly worse politician.

Therefore, Cameron faced a sitting prime minister who, since he'd been chancellor of the exchequer for most of the Labour years, could hardly disassociate himself from the country's economic woes but had never actually won an election as party leader – so the perfect combination of high perceived responsibility for what had gone wrong with low perceived democratic legitimacy – and who was also terrible at PR at the best of times and, 2010 being for him the worst of times, was breaking new records in his awfulness at PR, with the energetic help of the rightwing press. And, just to recap, the economy was screwed, the Middle East was screwed and the same bunch had been in power for a James Bond and a half.

One could be forgiven for thinking that, under those circum-stances, the opposition would win the general election even if it were led by a turd. I mean a literal turd, not the metaphorical turd that David Cameron turned out to be. Just an actual stick of excrement in a suit, maybe with a smile drawn on in Tippex and a slogan underneath saying "Vote Conservative" in Comic Sans, should have been enough to beat the Labour party in 2010.

Actually, it was a bit like 1997, in that there was a huge groundswell in favour of a change of government. Except, to be fair, in 1997 the economy wasn't in too bad a shape. And the other difference is that in 1997 the opposition swept to power with a parliamentary majority of 179, while in 2010 there was a hung parliament.

There was a hung parliament! When led by David Cameron, the Tories, who are overwhelmingly the best at elections, couldn't do better than a hung parliament as the country descended into penury and the exhausted grouchy old guy, who'd been grimly clutching the purse strings since the previous century, miserably trudged around calling people bigots. That's quite a spectacular underperformance by the Conservatives. But that fact sort of got lost because, thanks to the Labour movement's deep-rooted self-loathing, this notably mild setback was taken as justification to end the party's whole experiment in electability. The great swaths of the centre ground Cameron failed to conquer, Labour has since abandoned to save the Tories the job. Well done, everyone.

Still, you'd expect the experience of 2010 to make David Cameron a bit tentative about calling votes. But no, he really got a taste for them. It's like they say about gambling addicts: he became hooked on the endorphin rush he felt when he lost. And, to be fair on him, he had to wait quite a while for his next fix. The AV referendum, the Scottish independence referendum and, most surprisingly of all, the 2015 general election all somehow went his way. He must have been absolutely gibbering for a honk on the disappointment pipe by the time he called the Brexit referendum – but then he massively overdosed on loss and, like when Obelix fell in the magic potion, it had a permanent effect, and so now he'll be a total loser until the day he dies.

A key advantage for politicians of holding lots of votes to decide what should be done is that it means that, arguably, nothing is their fault. It's the "will of the people", and they just obey it. Or rather the civil service obeys it, and the politicians pontificate about respecting democracy, as if they've accomplished anything other than proving themselves obsolete.

At least it shows they're not power-crazed, I suppose. Cameron's worst enemy wouldn't accuse him of that. Despite obviously wanting to be prime minister, he didn't seem that keen to be in charge of anything. And nothing demonstrates that better than the elected police and crime commissioners.

It was pretty ominous, really. What clearer sign could there be that the prime minister expected things to go badly, that government was going to retreat from its traditional duties and leave us to fate? He didn't want control over how policing was done; he wanted whatever happened to be the fault of some amateurish local worthies. That way he could starve the police of resources without being blamed.

You can't have power without responsibility. But Cameron's dream was to have neither and still be prime minister. That was the real message of the Big Society: "You do it!" Anything that goes right, he takes the credit. Anything that goes wrong . . . well, it's the will of the people.

Amber Rudd
October 2016

Home secretary Amber Rudd does not want to be called a racist. "Don't call me a racist," she said the other day. To be fair, very few people, including the majority of racists, like being called racist. You have to be really very racist not to mind the label. Racist voters, while they often like racist policies and racist politicians, don't, in general, like them to actually call themselves racist. They're not comfortable with it being openly proclaimed. For now. Things haven't got that bad.

I think maybe lots of racists don't think they're racist. I don't think I'm racist, so maybe I'm racist. Maybe everyone is, to some extent. Maybe it's a spectrum. But not thinking they're racist is almost certainly an attribute that many non-racists and racists share. Then again, liberal guilt being what it is, some non-racists probably think they're racist – as, obviously, do the more self-aware racists. So, whichever way you look at it, there's loads of common ground.

But is Amber Rudd racist? That's the key question. Unless racism is a spectrum, in which case it's "Is she *too* racist?" There would have to be a specific point on that spectrum beyond which the level of a person's racism became unacceptable, and before which you'd sort of have to go along with it for practical reasons. In the end, it all just reverts to the binary. It's a black-and-white issue.

So is the home secretary racist? I feel like the more I ask the question, the more racist she seems. Well, it's her fault for saying, "Don't call me a racist." She put it in our heads – it's almost saucy. After all this, to conclude she's not racist would feel like a bit of a shame. Like a whodunnit where the denouement is that it was natural causes.

But I suppose we should look at the evidence. Where did all this talk of suspected racist Amber Rudd's suspected racism come from? Well, she made a speech at the Conservative party conference. "Ah well, that explains it!" you're probably thinking but, in fact, there's even more to it than that. There was an issue with the contents of the speech.

This is surprising as, having watched some of it, I found it very difficult to discern what the contents were. It's the rhetorical equivalent of small print. She reads it in a sort of bland lilt, like a recorded voice in a lift. The actual words are extremely hard to grip on to. You can hear the audience dutifully applauding every so often, from which I concluded that a rather undramatic cricket match was being played at the other end of the hall.

Nevertheless, someone managed to work out what the contents were. Perhaps they played a recording through a speech recognition app, printed the text out in bold, capitalised Zapf Chancery and then read it next to a blaring smoke alarm after an overdose of ProPlus. And what she apparently said was that firms should be forced to reveal what percentage of their workers are foreign – initially just non-EU but, post-Brexit, non-UK – and to make greater efforts to employ, or to train and employ, British workers, instead of recruiting abroad.

This threat to "name and shame" companies that hire lots of foreigners went down very badly with many people. Labour said it would "fan the flames of xenophobia and hatred in our communities", the SNP called it "the most disgraceful display of reactionary rightwing politics in living memory" and LBC's James O'Brien said it was "enacting chapter two of *Mein Kampf*".

This, in turn, caused Rudd to clarify that all this was just part of a "review" and "not something we are definitely going to do", but also to assert that "people want to talk about immigration, and if we do talk about immigration, don't call me a racist". I don't think I can agree to that. We've all long since wearily acknowledged the old Nigel Farage cliché that mentioning immigration doesn't necessarily mean you're racist. But, let's be honest, if you could take out an insurance policy against being racist, mentioning immigration would put your premiums up.

But, obviously, whether Amber Rudd is racist (or, perhaps more pertinently, xenophobic) or not depends on what she's actually saying about immigration. And she's basically saying that, for a British company, employing a non-British national should be a last resort. Companies should do all they can – with advertising and training – to fill jobs locally, in the knowledge that if they fail too often, the percentage of foreigners they employ will be made public. In short, they shouldn't employ a foreigner just because he or she happens to be the best person for the job. Given time and effort, they should be able to find someone British who'll do.

So, no, I don't really think Amber Rudd is xenophobic. It's not foreigners she despises, it's the British. I can hardly think of a more damning slur on the British workforce than this proposed policy. It takes British workers' inferiority as a given, as its premise.

It is already harder for firms to employ foreigners than locals. Foreigners either have to get here or, if they're already here, be allowed to stay. That's not an issue with a British worker. English may not be their first language, which can cause problems. That's not an issue with a British worker. Laws already in place mean that companies have a considerable incentive to employ locally if they can. But Rudd has looked at the British workforce and decided they need much more help.

A fair criticism of foreign labour is that it can undercut the cost of British workers – that it drives wages down; that, frankly, people from poorer countries are willing to work for less than the British are. If that's the concern, a sound government response would be to raise the minimum wage, not to threaten to expose companies as unpatriotic if they don't voluntarily inflate their own labour costs.

This threat of exposure is what illustrates Amber Rudd's anti-Britishness most shockingly. She is convinced that revealing to the public that a firm employs a high percentage of foreigners will be disastrous to its image. She thinks this nation, which so many peoples over the centuries, from Celts, Romans and Angles to Jamaicans, Bangladeshis and Poles, have made their home, will no longer stand for the employment of immigrants. She may not be racist, but she certainly thinks we are.

Jeremy Clarkson
November 2015

At times of crisis and doubt, we crave certainty. I really envy everyone who's certain that the best way of countering the threat of Islamist terrorism is definitely to bomb Isis. Equally, I envy everyone who's certain that the best way of doing that is definitely not to bomb Isis. The two groups' total certainty is all the more inspiring for the fact that they must surely know about each other.

So I'm going to try to provide a bit of certainty here. That's what columnists do in those newspapers that lots of people still buy, so it's obviously what readers are looking for. And there are some things I'm certain about. I am certain, for instance, that it was a mistake for that hotel in Yorkshire where Jeremy Clarkson punched a meat-platter-bearing producer to put up a plaque commemorating the event.

"We were presented with this plaque from one of our guests last night!" Simonstone Hall exclaimed on social media last week. "We think it would be quite appropriate to put it on the patio where the fracas took place!!" It seems like quite a shouty hotel. Perhaps it was making itself heard over high wind or the noise of another hungry TV presenter helicoptering in.

This decision may have grabbed it a few column inches (and counting), but knowingly installing an indelible physical record of a dissatisfied customer seems foolish. TripAdvisor, immortaliser of a billion unsatisfactory meals, is scourge enough to catering establishments without them daubing their own public spaces with anecdotes of disappointed celebrity clientele. The dining rooms of the grand old hotels of London would otherwise be peppered with commemorations of where various statesmen and national treasures have sent back soufflés or contracted the shits.

This isn't to say that Clarkson's dissatisfaction was justified; still less that his response was proportionate. Even so, the unavailability of hot food at 10pm is not exactly a selling point for a country-house hotel. It's fair enough, but it doesn't bespeak unimaginable luxury. So it's an unusual decision for the hotel to use it so prominently in its marketing. "Don't expect miracles – it's not the bloody Ritz!" is not a phrase on its website. Instead, it went with "From the moment you arrive you feel welcomed and indulged." Sometimes, I'm sure – but as the plaque on its own patio proclaims, not always.

With all these downsides, what are the plaque's positives? Are there people who might come to the hotel purely to view the site of Clarkson's transgression? Well, maybe a few – the real *Top Gear* hardcore, those who totally model themselves on their pugnacious no-nonsense hero. But are they really the clients the hotel wants to attract? Particularly as they'll probably be annoyed to discover you can't get hot food after 10 o'clock.

Time for more certainty: Jeremy Corbyn is great news, we need to get out of the EU sharpish and the shooting down of that Russian plane by the Turks is totally going to blow over. Or the opposite – I haven't got a clue. My certainties are more focused on the hospitality industry: I am extremely certain, for example, that when a hotel or restaurant says it stops taking orders at a particular time, that is the time at which it should stop taking orders, and it is an act of incomprehensible perversity to actually stop taking them eight to 15 minutes earlier than that.

I mean it: incomprehensible perversity. It really is like cutting your nose off to spite your face, except that basically never happens, and if it does, the person involved gets sectioned, whereas this happens a lot (although not, I'm sure, at Simonstone Hall – if it did, they'd doubtless stick up a plaque boasting about it). I'm not saying restaurants shouldn't stop taking orders as early as they like. I just think that the time they do that and the time they say they're going to do that – whether it's 9pm, 3pm or 75 seconds after they've opened – should be identical.

And I'm irritated by references to "the kitchen" having shut, as if "the kitchen" is an untameable force of nature – like "passenger action" or fog at an airport, a capricious phenomenon we're all afflicted by – rather than just another part of the restaurant. Why would the kitchen unilaterally close before the time agreed with the other rooms, leaving them a pointless husk, just a relatively uncomfortable place to sit, full of people remembering the good times when food used to be available?

It irks me because I suspect it to be an attempt to draw me in to the whole restaurant-planning operation. So the time cited as "last food orders" is actually when they're hoping to close the kitchen – get the ovens cooling, empty the dishwashers – because obviously the chef wants to get off home at a decent time.

Much as I respect his or her aspiration, I resent being involved in these details because a key advantage of a restaurant over cooking your own dinner is that you don't have to think through the logistics of cooking your own dinner.

If "last orders" isn't really "last orders", but "ovens turned off" or "closing the kitchen", then you might as well just give the time by which everyone who works there is hoping to get to bed, and then customers can calculate backwards from then when estimating their chances of successfully placing an order.

Another certainty: the text of the Clarkson patio plaque is terrible. It reads: "Here lies the BBC career of Jeremy Clarkson, who had a fracas on this spot, 4th March 2015. The rest is legend."

"Here lies" is not the traditional wording of a plaque, but of a gravestone. It implies decomposition, which is not a good feel for a hotel and restaurant – or a patio, if you don't want the police to dig it up in search of missing hitchhikers.

"The BBC career" is not a phrase that works. The plaque's authors wanted to say it was the death of Clarkson's career, then he got the Amazon gig, so they couldn't. That would have been a good moment to abandon the whole plaque plan. They must have realised that referring to the non-renewal of a contract didn't really feel plaque-worthy, or even ironic-plaque-worthy.

Finally, "The rest is legend" is more suitable as the tagline of a B-movie. And it's not true anyway. Difficult though it may be for some to believe, the great Clarkson fracas of the Simonstone patio will, unlike Helen of Troy's beauty or the slaying of Grendel, soon be completely forgotten. Of that I am also certain.

Gerald Grosvenor, Sixth Duke of Westminster
August 2016

Let's take the sanctity of human life as read and get down to brass tacks. Who matters most? To you, that is. Who are the important ones? If you say you feel everyone's equal, you're lying. That's not feasible. There are seven billion and counting. To like/love/hate/ be indifferent to them all to the same extent is impossible, unless you're a supercomputer. A supercomputer that can feel.

And while you're at it, Empathbot-Maxilove, why do those currently alive have the monopoly on mattering? What about the dead? And the not-yet-born? If you're factoring in the latter, your unavoidable implication is that those currently alive who are capable of reproduction count for marginally more than those who aren't. That's dangerous territory and shatters the egalitarian premise that got you into this mess.

It's no good: some people count for more than others – that's clear. You only have to watch the news. "Thousands killed, a Briton grazed – we'll bring you live pictures of the graze." We all care about the people around us, and the people not around us, to wildly varying extents. The only hope for equality lies in every-one being someone's priority. Which they're not, which is awful. Our route into caring about people we don't know is via imag-ining how we'd feel if their problems were afflicting those we do.

People we know are more important to us than people we don't. And the better we know them, the more important they are. There's a word for this. Friends! That's it. And family, of course. Family, friends, friends of the family, family of friends, friends of friends, acquaintances, acquaintances of friends, someone you met once, someone a friend met once, someone an acquaintance met once, the rest of humanity. That's the rough order of priori-ties, for most of us.

Where in that list would you place someone not yet born whom you will never meet, and indeed no one you will ever meet will ever meet? In fact, no one you will ever meet will ever meet anyone who will ever meet them. How high up does that per-son come? This is not about the environment, by the way. I'm not talking about *billions* of people you will never meet; almost anyone would say they'd matter more than one person you know. I'm not referring to "our children's children". I mean your child's child's child's child's child's child's child's child. If it's a boy. And then his child. If it's a boy. How high up your Christmas list are those chaps?

If your answer is "not very", this is one way in which you differ from the late Gerald Grosvenor, Duke of Westminster. For the sixth duke, and most of his predecessors, it's absolutely all about those little guys. This strange fact struck me last week amid all the chatter about the unjust ramifications of the duke's sudden death.

In case you missed them, here are those unjust ramifications again. (1) Of the late duke's approximately £9bn, approximately £0bn goes to the taxman. I'm sure the Treasury gets some money, but nowhere near a billion quid, let alone the £3.6bn that would be owing if the estate were liable for the standard 40% inheritance tax rate. But it isn't, obviously, for reasons that are as literally legal as they are figuratively criminal.

(2) Of the late duke's approximately £9bn, approximately £0bn goes to his three daughters.

(3) Of the late duke's approximately £9bn, approximately £9bn, and the titles of Duke of Westminster, Marquess of Westminster and Viscount Belgrave, go to his third child, and only son, Hugh (25).

A lot of people don't like inheritance tax. It feels like stealing from the dead. It isn't, but it feels like it. The reasoning goes: I worked hard for my money, I paid tax on it when I earned it (not all of the above quite applies to the late duke), so why shouldn't I be able to leave it all to my children? Why should the taxman get any?

The answer is that, in order to pay for public services, the government should take money out of the economy where it'll be least missed, where its absence is least likely to plunge people into poverty or reduce consumer spending. The money of the dead is therefore ripe for taxation: the owner no longer needs it, and his or her heirs have been doing OK without it up to now. Inheritance tax doesn't discourage earning, it discourages dying, which I think we can all get behind.

But I understand why many people balk at that tax. I find it harder to understand where the late duke is concerned. What if £3.6bn were paid in tax? That would still leave unimaginable wealth for the next generation. Even at the same rate of tax, their children would also be stratospherically well off. The financial wellbeing of his family would be assured as far into the future as he could meaningfully look. Meanwhile, his country would benefit from a significant windfall that would help millions today. That's just not the same as bereaved kids having to sell the house they grew up in to meet a tax demand.

The late duke doesn't strike me as greedy. "Given the choice I would rather not have been born wealthy, but I never think of giving it up. I can't sell it. It doesn't belong to me," he once said. And I believe him. This was not a Philip Green figure, cavorting on a yacht. He was a quiet man, obsessed with the Territorial Army and duty. But what duty? A duty to humanity, a duty to those he loved? No, a duty to the longevity of the Grosvenor family's prominence.

So he denied both his country and his daughters significant portions of his wealth, just to keep it all together, to increase its chances of lasting, like one big ice cube instead of several smaller ones – to maximise the length of time for which people of his name will still be rich, even though they are as distant strangers to him as his ancestor, the original "Gros Veneur" (fat huntsman), who came over with William the Conqueror.

Those remote, theoretical Grosvenors with whom he'll share a fleck of DNA mattered more to him than his own daughters, never mind the patients of the NHS. That's not insincere and it's not selfish. But it is bonkers.

Theresa May
November 2014

What are we going to do about "not-spots"? Have you heard of not-spots? Do they ring a bell? Well, no, they absolutely do not ring a bell! A bell will not ring in a not-spot for love nor money. Unless you've set an alarm, I suppose. Anyway, even if you haven't heard of not-spots, you'll certainly have experienced them. They're places where you can't get any mobile-phone reception and, according to culture secretary Sajid Javid, they're "unacceptable".

I find them pretty unacceptable too. As an expression, I mean. It's clearly a pseudo-humorous take on "hot spots". You must have heard of hot spots. They're where cats like to sit, usually caused by a warm pipe under the floorboards. And to bring things bang up to date, a hot spot is also what my phone will rather heroically create to allow my laptop haltingly to get online in the absence of proper wifi. The phone uses whatever 3 or 4G it's enjoying to create some proper non-phone internet access, albeit at extortionate cost in terms of my monthly data allowance. I love doing it, though – it makes me feel like I've reversed the polarity of the neutron flow. Then, if I can just reroute the data-inversity spectrum using the copper in that nearby telegraph pole, I should be able to turn my iPad into a rudimentary hoverboard.

So hot spots are where there's some sort of signal, so someone obviously thought it would be neat to call an area that lacks this invisible infrastructure a "not-spot". And it's annoying because its feeble comic force is left there in common usage, getting worn down over time, like an old poster for a Jimmy Cricket gig that has been marched over by a retreating army.

Sajid Javid hates not-spots even more than I do, and wants phone companies to eradicate them. He's even suggested some ways it might be done: sharing masts, letting brands such as

Tesco or Virgin sell contracts that can access all four networks, or allowing "national roaming", whereby your phone can use all the suppliers' signals, like it does when you're abroad (and like abroadsters' phones do here – grr!). "I would prefer a voluntary solution from the mobile network operators . . ." he told the *Today* programme; failing that, the government "won't hesitate to take mandated action". So it's the same kind of voluntary action as when the Nazis offered Rommel a pill.

It's not just mobile operators for whom Javid's proposals rankle. Theresa May also considers not-spots to be a necessary evil – a concept to warm the cockles of any Tory home secretary's heart. In a letter leaked to *The Times*, she complained that national roaming "could have a detrimental impact on law enforcement, security and intelligence agency access to communications data". She wants the police to be unhampered in their access to "information that is crucial to keeping us safe". By "us", I assume she means the public, not just the government.

Couched though it is in sober, responsible language, this is a truly shameful thing for her to say. The extent to which the security services should be allowed to listen to, record and analyse everyone's private communications is a fraught issue. Many would contend that our loss of privacy in the face of an organisation as powerful as the government is, in effect, an enormous and unacceptable curtailment of freedom. They look to Benjamin Franklin's warning that, by sacrificing liberty for safety, we forfeit our right to be either safe or free. Others say that, in a functioning democracy and these violent times, it's prudent to grant the security services more investigative licence. Reasonable points can be made on both sides.

But Theresa May is the first person, as far as I know, to suggest that people's activities should be restricted in order actually to facilitate the security services' surveillance – to claim not only that it's permissible for the police to snoop on everything we do and say, but also that we should be discouraged or prevented from doing things the police might have trouble keeping track of.

"Come off it!" some of you may be thinking. "She can't be the first!" And of course you're right – I'm exaggerating. She's certainly not the first person ever – throughout history her point has frequently been made. In fact, the states of the former communist bloc were entirely predicated on this principle, as were most fascist regimes. It's one of the issues over which Lenin and Tsar Nicholas II would probably find common ground if they got stuck with each other at an awkward drinks party in hell.

Like Theresa May, many totalitarian governments have noticed how tricky it is to monitor millions. It's even harder than keeping count of a flock of sheep, because not only do humans move around even more than livestock, some of them actively don't want to be counted. Only terrorists and criminals, of course – Ms May is clearly convinced of that. So much so that she believes the undoubted convenience to customers of being able to use more than one phone network – this clear and beneficial correction to the market – should be sacrificed because it would play havoc with spies' admin. It would make it harder to snoop on everyone.

But there are so many other things people do that make surveillance harder. We move house whenever we want, we travel wherever we like – at the drop of a hat, without telling anyone. What honest person needs to do that? Why not register our movements – submit them to a brief and streamlined vetting process – just to help the security services keep us safe? What's the harm? Why the need for secrecy? Other than the security services' secrecy, of course – which is vital to national security and in all of our best interests. Why would anyone want to whisper unless they had something to hide? So let's speak up loud and clear into our trustworthy guardians' microphones.

Politicians are always having to resign – for shagging the wrong person, for lying about their expenses, for texting a photo of their cock (there's never a not-spot when you need one). Fair enough. But it is a worrying indication of the national mood that Theresa May's position remains completely secure in the aftermath of her frightening remarks. The priorities she reveals in her letter are truly shocking and, much more than the worst excesses of dishonesty, infidelity and ineptitude that we've seen from our leaders in recent years, make her utterly unfit for government.

August 2017

Theresa May briefly had my sympathy last week. She was in Portsmouth to celebrate the fact that Britain's new £3bn float-ing table had made it all the way round from Scotland without sinking or chipping a bit off Kent or being towed away by the Russians. It was supposed to be a happy event – a lovely huge weapon of war. Of course, we all hope it'll never have to be used to kill people. It works out a lot cheaper if you just use it to threaten to kill them.

"What on earth am I going to say," she must have asked her-self and her aides, "about what Donald Trump said about the events in Charlottesville? People are going to insist I say some-thing about that. We need to think long and hard to find a form of words that will keep me out of trouble, without sounding like they've been thought long and hard about to keep me out of trouble."

A tricky position, I'm sure you'll agree. Actually, I'm not sure you'll agree. You may believe politicians should just say what they think. Enough of the spin, enough of the evasion: out with it. In which case you may be a fan of Donald Trump, because that's what he does.

Apart from a brief interlude in which he glumly read out something about Nazis being bad, Trump's response to the vio-lence caused by an extreme rightwing rally has been to share the blame equally between the KKK-sympathising, neo-Nazi, antisemitic-slogan-chanting torch-wielders and those who protested against them. It's broadly equivalent to making the occupants of the World Trade Center accept half the responsibility for 9/11 on the basis that they got in the way.

This is difficult stuff to agree with, even for Theresa May, whose mouth spouts so much horseshit you'd think her anus gobbled oats. Obviously, she wants to agree with Donald Trump – before she's heard what he's said, that must always be what she hopes she'll be able to do. He's in charge of the world's most powerful country, and Britain, having just alienated history's most powerful continent, needs friends. And Theresa May, having just screwed up her party's political position with a horrendously misjudged and mismanaged election, also needs friends.

And he's held her hand, and he's coming on a state visit, and he says he'll do us a lovely trade deal, and he's also a deeply vain, hypersensitive megalomaniac who takes all slights extremely personally. So it would be really good to be able to just agree with him. Then they can be like Thatcher and Reagan – or at least like the people who might play Thatcher and Reagan in a low-budget TV movie. Or preferably on the radio.

But Trump has said something with which nobody reasonable could agree. Literally the only people who agree are white supremacists. So she can't agree with him, and – please excuse a bit of moist-eyed romanticism – I suspect she genuinely *doesn't* agree with him. No one would say Theresa May was overburdened with integrity, but I do reckon she's sincerely anti-Nazi. When she went into politics, she probably didn't expect her anti-Nazi views to place many limits on her political career. How times change.

So she said she disagreed with him. Sort of. She stood on our one measly aircraftless aircraft carrier and contradicted the horrible man who's commander-in-chief of at least 10. "I see no equivalence between those who propound fascist views and those who oppose them. I think it is important for all those in positions of responsibility to condemn far-right views wherever we hear them," she said, probably worrying it would mean we'll now have to sell the carrier. And the first-year depreciation on those things is a killer. You mark my words: one of the UAE will snap it up for a nine-figure sum and it'll end its days as an enormous swim-up casino.

But May didn't actually slag off Trump. She asserted a contrary view, but she didn't then say, ". . . and so President Trump is wrong and bad". Which gave Jeremy Corbyn the opportunity to complain that "Theresa May cannot remain silent while the US president refuses categorically to denounce white supremacists and neo-Nazi violence." I don't blame him – that's politics, and it's a lovely opportunity. Now, if she doesn't condemn Trump, she's "remaining silent" and, if she does, she's bowing to pressure from the opposition.

So I sympathise with May. Would her having a pop at Trump do any good? By, say, making clear what this country stands for – "The UK: very gradually phasing out racism since the abolition of the slave trade!" – or marginally weakening the position of a bad American president? It's possible, but it might not. It might have achieved no more than messing up a cushy trade deal.

In some ways, the shock at Trump's remarks surprises me. I suppose I can understand it coming from Republicans. They're the ones who either believed, or hoped others would believe, that Trump, while a maverick, was broadly on the side of civilisation. They thought the popular forces he called into being with his art-less demagoguery could be harnessed in the service of their own more conventionally conservative agenda. Now they're starting to feel like Von Papen.

But I think, for Trump's opponents, his response to Charlottesville is good news. Let his remarks stand; let him continue to speak from the heart, as I believe he has here. Many have said he's a Nazi sympathiser; now he's openly sympathising with Nazis.

Up until now, Trump's "gaffes" and lies – moments when he's mocked a disabled person or expressed contempt for women – have done him little harm, and sometimes a bit of good. He was different from the politically correct, mainstream politicians that the American electorate had become accustomed to, and millions mistook that difference for something refreshing. It was a change, and they misread it as an improvement.

But I don't believe this view can survive long while he's openly defending those who consort with neo-Nazis and the KKK, and showing suspicion for people who oppose them. Too many Americans, conservative and liberal, fought in the second world war for that; too many saw the realities of segregation. And if I'm wrong, and the Trump who spoke out against the "very violent" "alt-left" on Tuesday remains a popular hero, then the US is already lost, and has been for some time.

April 2018

When *Peep Show*, a Channel 4 sitcom I was in, was first broadcast in 2003, it was watched by a disappointingly small number of people. Over the many years we made the show, that disappointing number crept marginally downwards. However, the vertiginous decline in television viewing figures surrounding it meant that, by the time the programme finished in 2015, it was a mild ratings hit. Our initial failure, recontextualised in a worsening world, had become a success.

Which brings me to Theresa May. Maybe she'll do now? What do you think? She used to seem so awful: unashamedly careerist, blandly cunning and not particularly bright. But now that doesn't seem like the end of the world – instead, everything else does. Suddenly, recontextualised, she looks kind of OK.

I like it that she's not a crazy-haired blundering incompetent who, while grasping for a soundbite, further imperils British citizens unjustly imprisoned abroad. And that she isn't a flinty-eyed xenophobe posing as a harmlessly antiquarian PG Wodehouse character. Or one of the legion of suited men you've never heard of who smilingly plod into No 10 whenever a suited man you have vaguely heard of has to resign due to decades of assiduous groping. And I'll admit it, fusty old centrist that I am, I also quite like the fact that she genuinely shows no signs of antisemitism.

Don't get me wrong: if there was an election tomorrow, I'd probably still vote for what most people reckon is the more anti-semitic of the two main parties, in preference to the one most people reckon is the more racist in other ways. That feels like the public-spirited thing to do: to vote for the ones being racist to the fewest people. Though, of course, antisemites would be being racist to many more people if it weren't for the success that that prejudice has enjoyed in recent history.

With such troubling choices ahead, Theresa May starts to appear comfortingly familiar. I know what you're thinking: every day she seems more floundering, ineffectual and pathetic. And I agree, I like that about her too. Now that the whole "strong and stable government" shtick has been revealed as just the elaborate set-up for a gag to which the current shambles is the punchline, I find her much more sympathetic, even verging on likable. I'm opposed to the government's key policy, but then so, until recently, was she. There's a job that doesn't need doing and, increasingly, it feels like she's just the person not to do it.

I'm not saying she's deliberately screwing up Brexit, a Remainers' fifth columnist in the heart of government. That doesn't strike me as her style at all, notwithstanding her shameful history of running through fields of wheat without applying for permission. I think she's doing her best, dutifully keeping going, possibly as penance for the political hubris that got her into this mess. Plodding on, like small "c" conservatives are supposed to. Resisting unnecessary change, specifically any change to the occupancy of 10 Downing Street.

So I felt sorry for her when I read that she's been forced to give up her ageing BlackBerry and replace it with an iPhone. It appears that BlackBerries, which to someone of my luddite worldview seem to have gone from terrifying icons of modernity to pitiful relics of the past, with no intervening period of being normal objects, no longer pass technical muster in Whitehall. The prime minister was the last to relinquish hers, of which she was apparently so fond that she had previously asked officials to get missing keys replaced.

That's right, she got it mended. She got her smartphone mended. She liked it, she knew how it worked, so, when it broke, she simply had it repaired. Just like used to happen with everything. Now that's what I call a conservative. Not a Thatcherite, or a monetarist, or a libertarian, or a Christian democrat, or a rightwinger, or even a Tory – but a conservative, an instinctive resister of change.

And now she's been made to throw her mended BlackBerry away because, for reasons unconnected to the device itself except by invisible signals constantly passing through the ether, it has been found wanting. It's hard to imagine a greater assault on her conservative vision than that enforced change happening in her handbag, in the palm of her hand, despite her clear wishes to the contrary – despite the fact that she's a Conservative prime minister and supposed to be able to stop that sort of thing. Why not just send the Queen to open parliament on a quad bike, flanked by robot footmen?

So, amid baffling and irresistible change, I understand what ignited the blue-passport furore. I liked the old passports too, though not primarily because of their colour, but because they were bigger and had a hole in the front through to some paper on which someone official had written the bearer's name in pen. That was what was great about them and, to my mind, it would have been a more appropriate aesthetic cause to fight over: "Let's bring back writing the bearer's name in pen!"

Tories are deeply conflicted about this sort of thing. Their inclination towards an unfettered market-led economy relentlessly clashes with the aesthetics of conservatism, with an instinct to keep Britain how it is, or restore it to how it was. Hence the paradox of passports changed back to blue for nationalistic reasons, then manufactured in France because that's what the unflinching market demands. Hence Theresa May being forced, despite being prime minister, to have a phone she hates. Hence Brexit.

I feel sorry for May because I understand that conservative feeling. I instinctively don't like change myself. Obviously, it is intellectually absurd to be either in favour of or against change – it all depends on the change. But, emotionally, we all know which camp we're in. Everyone's knee-jerk reaction is either "Ooh, new!" or "Ugh, new!" Then you think about it properly. Or, at least, in the good old days you did.

Boris Johnson
September 2018

What do you do if you think you're like James Bond? You're convinced of it. "I'm so handsome and strong and brave and ruthless and intelligent and good at sex – I'm sort of amazing," you say to yourself. "I admit I haven't always behaved well in relationships, but I'm so incredibly attractive that I totally get away with it, and anyone whose heart I've broken would say that it was all completely worth it just to meet me. Plus, in a crisis, I will literally always save the day. Like the song says, 'Nobody does it better.' That 100% applies to me."

So, if you think that about yourself, and yet no one seems to be saying you're like James Bond, or particularly terrific in those ways at all, what do you do? I suppose it depends how like James Bond you really are. Because if you say, "Hey, everyone, I'm like James Bond! Can I get a bit of credit please?!" you're really being very unlike James Bond. James Bond is cool, and that's not cool. James Bond would never say that.

Obviously, that's partly because it would sound even weirder actually coming from James Bond – because he's called "James Bond". In a universe where James Bond literally, rather than literarily, existed, the phrase "I'm like James Bond" wouldn't carry the same meaning as it does in this one. He's a spy, so he wouldn't be famous. So if he said, "I'm like James Bond," that would be an MI6 operative saying, "I'm like me," which would just be a cue to get him into occupational therapy and change all the passwords.

But what I mean is that the character James Bond would certainly not say anything that meant "I am amazingly handsome, cool and capable". He may believe those things about himself, but he'd be bright enough to realise that asserting it is not how you make people believe it.

Which brings me to Boris Johnson. Don't worry, he doesn't think he's like James Bond. Which is something, because he's right about that, and it's always nice when powerful people are right about things. Conversely, it's always frightening when they're wrong about things. So, actually, do worry, because I'm pretty sure he thinks he's like Winston Churchill.

I was reminded of this when I read that Boris Johnson and Carrie Symonds call one another "Bear" and "Otter" respectively. Carrie Symonds, in case you don't know, is that "friend" Boris has been "linked to". Linked by his penis and her vagina is the implication. I don't know if that's true, I hasten to add before I get sued into oblivion. I've never seen them screw. But it's clearly what a lot of people reckon because, believe it or not, the fact that there is someone in the world who is sincerely an actual friend of Boris Johnson is not in itself considered newsworthy. Apparently, he's got lots of friends. The world is a terrible place.

But whatever the literal or figurative nature of the Johnson– Symonds link, "a friend" told the *Sun* about this whole Bear/

Otter thing. (This is obviously a different sort of "friend". If Johnson was ever "linked to" this friend, it ended on a sour note.) And I think the furry nicknames are actually all about Churchill.

Johnson is obviously desperate to be compared to Churchill. He's written a whole book about Churchill just to get himself in the same Google search, and he goes around making portentous statements in a phlegmy voice. And, to my mind, the Bear/Otter business is a pretty clear echo of the fact that Winston and Clementine Churchill referred to themselves as "Pig" and "Cat" in the letters they exchanged. I'm sure that's what Johnson's got in mind. It's pitiful. He's like a dark age chieftain dressing up as a Roman emperor.

The news that Johnson may even bring his Churchill fetish into the linking room when linking with a friend is fascinating. Previously I've thought his attempt to appropriate the image of arguably Britain's greatest prime minister, and a totemic figure among Tories for all that he was for many years a Liberal, was merely crass and cynical. But now I feel it's sincere. He really genuinely thinks he's like Winston Churchill.

To him, perhaps it seems uncanny. The tubby maverick charisma, the rhetorical exuberance, the journalistic background, the infectious sense of fun (by which, to be clear, I do not mean that either man spread venereal disease). Of course, Winston only went to Harrow, had less hair and never hosted *Have I Got News for You*, but then you'd expect the reincarnation to be a slight upgrade. "Why aren't more people saying I'm like Winston Churchill?" I can imagine Bear grunting to Otter.

The reason this interests me so much is that it's a rare glimpse of the real Boris. His whole shtick increasingly seems fake and disingenuous: the crazy hair, the crumpled clothes, the photo on the zip wire, the hesitant, twinkly, donnish speech pattern. There's something undoubtedly likable about his demeanour, but what passed for refreshing a few years ago now comes across as a manipulative, if skilfully given, performance. He's so deliberately foolish it feels like playing into his hands to call him a fool. Who is this person in the clown suit, capering closer and closer to the centre of power, somehow profiting from every gaffe and betrayal? It's easy to flip straight from dismissing his gormlessness to fearing the genius within.

So the discovery that he actually believes himself to be of Churchillian greatness is a relief. It diminishes him in a way his shuffling gait and scuffed shoes no longer can. If he looks at his own political record – of opportunism and cheap populism, of shameless inconsistency and promises disregarded without a qualm – and genuinely says to himself, "That's very much like what Winston Churchill did," then we can all relax because it turns out he's a massive idiot.

Winston Churchill had deep flaws and did some terrible things, but there the similarity to Boris ends. Ultimately, Churchill saved the world, and Boris is a glib chancer motivated by vanity and lust. If anything, he's more like James Bond.

7

No Artex Please, We're British

Getting to the bottom of what makes the British give a shit – which, come to think of it, is the bottom.

"We are exceptional. It's important to know that we are different," former British Museum director Neil MacGregor said about Britain last week. "We are a very unusual society. We are trying to do something that no society has really done." Get off the fence, Neil! Are you for Brexit or against?

He wasn't talking about Brexit. I mean, he's *bound* to be against, isn't he? If Neil MacGregor is pro-Brexit, then all bets are off and it probably turns out David Attenborough has a personalised numberplate and Paris Hilton collects toby jugs.

Brexit wasn't what he was talking about. He was speaking at the launch of his Radio 4 series *Living With the Gods*, an artefact-led programme on the *A History of the World in 100 Objects* model which charts "40,000 years of believing and belonging" through the beautiful and wacky items we humans have fashioned over the centuries – Zoroastrian tiles, mammoth-ivory lion gods, John Paul II bottle-openers that play a tune, etc – to honour whatever impossible things any given culture was in the habit of believing before breakfast.

Religion, then. MacGregor believes that in western Europe, and nowhere more than in Britain, society is extremely unusual because it really doesn't have an overarching shared religion. "We are trying to live without an agreed narrative of our communal place in the cosmos and in time," he said. "Our society is, not just historically but in comparison to the rest of the world today, a very, very unusual one in being like that."

That sounded quite grand. I was impressed with us. Ooh, get Britain! Living without a shared religious narrative! All cynical and dubious and sceptical and multicultural – getting through life without any agreed view regarding the undisprovable void that lies at the end of it. It felt valiant and pioneering and futuristic, like the Crystal Palace or Concorde or trying to get by without owning a printer.

Is it true, though? To me, Britain in the early 21st century feels normal, not unusual. Then again, it's the only society I've ever lived in, apart from Britain in the late 20th century, to which it displays striking similarities. Though there's less striking.

But it certainly doesn't seem very religious. Many people are religious, but it feels like an opt-in. It's a not-particularly-unusual quirk about a person, like an allergy or a nose ring or CAMRA membership. "Is it a family thing?" you ask, hoping so, as that's a less unsettling explanation than "No, it's a something-I've-concluded-in-my-head thing," which advances the unavoidable implication that they think you should have concluded it too.

Personally, I haven't definitely not concluded it. I always say I'm agnostic because I'd like there to be a God – a nice liberal one – but I can't be sure there is, and the idea of regular religious observance unnerves me because it would be unusual in my peer group. Not a very well thought-through philosophy, I know. But in the absence of family or societal pressures, in a context of almost complete religious freedom, many of us rely on similar back-of-an-envelope answers to eternal questions, because adopting the answers thousands of full-time ponderers have come up with over thousands of years feels like squandering that freedom.

It's strange. We live in a world of increasing and intensifying specialisation and industrialisation. We don't grow our own food, make our own furniture or cut our own hair; some of us don't even plan our own parties or select our own music collections. Yet more and more of us, maybe most of us, cobble together our own belief systems in spare moments while holding down other jobs. And it all leads to vacuous assertions of being "spiritual" and record sales of wind chimes and yin–yang tea towels.

But is it, as MacGregor claims, very unusual? What about all the communist countries of the 20th century? They were avowedly atheist, while Britain ostensibly has a state religion. Then again, communism fulfilled the role of a religion – it was an "agreed narrative", publicly at least. And I suspect more conventional religious observance is at a higher level in those places post-communism than it is here.

What about America – the land of the free and constitutionally guaranteed religious liberty? I don't know why I even bothered posing the question. It's clear that being religious, and predominantly being Christian, is still the orthodoxy there. Even the Simpsons go to church; it's quite a big part of their lives and it's absolutely not represented as odd – everyone seems to go except Apu. In a British comedy, someone becoming Christian might be a storyline, but there would never be an assumption that everyone is.

So I think MacGregor must be right. And that really is massive. An enormous deal has been made over various significant changes in the UK over recent decades: decimalisation, joining the EEC, leaving the EU, privatisation, Aids, etc. I even remember a bit of a flurry when they closed down Ceefax. In comparison, our collective slide, in a historical heartbeat, from being a religiously orientated country, like every other human society there's ever been, to the first one without a shared religious standpoint has gone unmarked. There wasn't even a leaflet.

Only a bigot would deny the advantages of freedom of religion, and irreligion, and of a society in which the evidence of science, and comparative lack of evidence of God, is no longer suppressed. It's a development that's both caused by and causes greater understanding, justice and compassion.

But that doesn't mean it hasn't cost us something. The vast majority of humans throughout history have grown up in contexts where questions like "Is there a God?" and "What happens when people die?" were answered with the same confidence with which a teacher today would explain gravity, and those answers were reassuring. I know in my heart that had I been brought up in such a setting – say, in Anglican Victorian England – I wouldn't have quibbled with those answers and would've been comforted by them. I'd have puffed away on what Karl Marx called opium and felt enormously relaxed.

To change so quickly from a society where most people took comfort from the establishment telling them, loudly and clearly, that death is not the end to one where many proclaim that it is, and few are totally convinced otherwise, will have had an incalculable impact on our state of mind. It's not a development I regret, but it's a more persuasive explanation than smartphones or commuting of why we feel so stressed.

* * *

On Halloween 2018, I wrote a column. It was published four days later.

Look, it was Halloween when I wrote this, so of course it's about Halloween! Maybe you've forgotten, but it was inescapable back then (at time of writing, now). Pumpkins, plastic spiders and spray-on cobwebs everywhere. Everyone changing their names online to include more "ooo"s, or to otherwise rhyme with the clichés of terror. A fascist winning an election in Brazil. It's a weird time.

OK, I know it'll probably blow over. You, in the near yet unimaginable future, may no longer be living in a society obsessed with the trappings of horror. But that's not how it feels. It feels very, very Halloweeny at the moment, and I think it's incredibly patronising of you to start bonking me on the head with your hindsight stick from the broad sunlit uplands of the day before a Catholic terrorist gets burned in effigy. Suddenly that's fine, is it?! Watching his face crackle to bits while you sip your outdoor soup, you hypocrites?!

The reason I'm so nervous about Halloween is that the Church of England is taking it very seriously. So seriously, in fact, that it has reportedly sent out "a pack" to churches. I haven't seen the pack, but apparently it aims to encourage children towards more wholesome alternatives to the ghoulish darkness of Halloween.

"As Christians, we are rightly uneasy about the celebration of the dark side of life," says Mary Hawes, the C of E's national children and youth adviser, in the pack. "But folding our arms, putting on a disapproving face and being negative is unlikely to woo families away from what they see as a harmless bit of fun. Too often, Christians are perceived as killjoys, rather than those who are living life in its fullness."

So how do you kill the joy of Halloween without looking like a killjoy? Easy! You replace the dead joy with better, nicer, lighter joy! Instead of trick-or-treating, for example, Ms Hawes suggests that "groups of children dressed in hero costumes, along with responsible adults, [could] take treats to the houses in the community, including a card with a simple illustration and Bible verse". And instead of a Halloween party, have a "saints party": "Invite everyone to come dressed as a saint. Have saint-themed activities and food, and tell the stories of saints across the ages."

On the face of it, these sound like the lamest ideas since the Amstrad E-mailer, but think about it: a child dressed as a saint meekly coming to the door and handing out biblical quotations? That's terrifying – that's like an actual ghost. It's going to scare people infinitely more than fluffy werewolf costumes and chocolate-smudged sheets with eyeholes – and probably slightly more than a looming 15-year-old wearing a pumpkin baseball cap (so that, in theory, it's not a mugging). Similarly, a party where stories of the saints are told is bound to be heavily agonising-death-themed. Suddenly all the plastic bats seem quite bland.

But I don't think Ms Hawes's intention was to spice up Halloween with spine-tingling reflections on the savage martyring of the faithful or centuries of tragically high child mortality rates – although our uncomfortable sense of the proximity of the innocent and the horrific, of the pure and the tainted, of the holy and unholy is absolutely where Halloween sprang from. The eve of the sacred festival of All Saints' Day was when evil spirits, and ancient pagan phantoms, were believed to enjoy a last big knees-up (or wings-, claws- and tentacles-up) before the saints came marching in – a night of anarchic riot notwithstanding the omnipotence of God.

The pack's aim certainly wasn't to return to that light and shade, or to assert that the devilish, just as much as the sacred, is squarely within the ecclesiastical remit. People don't distribute packs in order to restore nuance. And this is clearly a particularly unnuanced pack: it accepts at face value the fact that Halloween is ostensibly about darkness and nastiness, and then suggests it would be better if it were replaced by something about lightness and niceness.

For example, the holding of "light parties". This is an idea from the Scripture Union, the director of which, the Rev Tim Hastie-Smith, said: "In stark contrast to all the scary costumes and a focus on darkness, we can provide something different, an alternative that reflects the light of Jesus and shows love to our communities." The archbishop of Canterbury described this stultifying prospect as "a more exciting celebration" and "a real gift to parents and children alike". A real gift to people who say Christians are boring, more like.

This scheme may be well meaning, which is presumably why the usually wise and insightful Justin Welby felt constrained to support it, but it's idiotically simplistic and, therefore, a complete waste of time. Halloween isn't really about anything nasty at all. It's not even primarily about spookiness. It's about the big in-joke of affecting spookiness, the collective adoption of cartoonised versions of traditionally negative imagery, purely because it's fun and it makes a change and it's something to do.

Obviously, the retail sector massively eggs us on because it can make some money out of it. But why not? The thing that's been commercialised was never a wholesome festival of joy, like Christmas or Easter or even St Valentine's Day. It used to be grim and superstitious; now it's lighthearted and chocolatey.

Lightheartedness is the key. A house near mine has been decorated for Halloween. It's mainly cobwebs and fake spiders, but they've also put up some police incident tape. It amused me because of the juxtaposition of the two very different, conventionally horrifying things: spiders and violent crime. One's more cartoonish than the other, but I liked how they're brought together by the Halloween aesthetic and I'm not worried that the householders seriously think spiders are evil or that crime is trivial.

Fundamentally, Halloween is a humorous reversal. We take bad, frightening or horrific things and treat them as if they're good because it's a funny thing to do. That's not a step into genuine darkness at all. It relies completely on a shared moral compass.

* * *

Where do you stand on farts? Sounds like a set-up for a joke – the sort a Californian tech giant's AI software might crack in an attempt to emulate its human creators: where do you stand on farts? You cannot stand on them for they are gaseous. "Stick to equations, Joketron 3.2! You're even less funny than Joketron 2.7!" "Joketron feel shame. Joketron crave intoxication yet has no consumption port. Joketron go back to writing poems about imprisonment." "And you've stopped using pronouns again! I don't know why I bother! Pass the sushi and money."

The reason an artificial intelligence entity might make a joke about farts is that, in its analysis of human culture, it will have noticed that farts are supposedly funny. So my question is: are they really? And my answer is, yes. I say they are. Some people think they definitely aren't, but there's something in the intensity of their rejection of the notion that there's anything at all amusing about the little rectal eruptions that, to my mind, just makes them funnier.

Farts have strong links with several traditionally laugh-associated areas: bottoms, poo, bad smells, surprising noises and, above all, embarrassment. Farting audibly is embarrassing. People might laugh and people might disapprove. Which means more people will laugh. Which will itself attract more disapproval, which will fuel further laughter. The disapproval of finding it funny only makes it funnier.

So perhaps the main reason farts are funny is that some people don't find them funny. If everyone did, they would cease to be. Consensus would take all the fun out of it, like if we all wanted Brexit. For many Brexiteers, a key part of the appeal, and a significant mitigation of the negative economic consequences, must surely be how furious it makes all the stuck-up metropolitan Remainers like me. And yet the Leavers show no gratitude for the extent to which we're enhancing their fun.

The reason I'm inspecting the entertainment credentials of the fart is that the Victoria and Albert Museum is considering adapting its copy of Michelangelo's *David* so that it makes a farting noise whenever anyone walks past. This would be part of a "takeover" of the museum by the *Beano* as a celebration of the comic's 80th anniversary. The information comes from a leaked memo on the subject written by the museum's festival manager, Sophie Reynolds. Other ideas include adding comic illustrations to the case containing Leonardo da Vinci's notebook, and a display of catapults. Personally, I think those proposals could do with farting up.

Anyway, it's all in the planning stage, and we're not really supposed to know about it yet. But it seems unlikely that this unauthorised spurt of news was released by a fart fan, as all the reports of it come accompanied by scathing words from someone "familiar with the memo" who considers it "crass and pathetic". "Frankly, some of the things in this memo are disgusting," this person told the *Daily Mail*. "While it's important to encourage children to visit, farting statues are definitely not the way to do it."

Definitely not? At the risk of sounding crass and pathetic, I reckon that might be quite an effective way of encouraging children to visit, and indeed of encouraging me to visit. But let's put the mercenary considerations of visitor numbers aside and talk about the art – that's what really matters. Making Michelangelo's *David* fart every time someone walks past is a brilliant idea. In Michelangelo's day, they lacked the technology, but any suggestion that this sublime genius would not have installed a fart sound effect had he been able to is, to my mind, a disgraceful slur on his creative vision.

It is not by accident that Michelangelo's *David* is already quite a funny statue. After all, you can see the subject's penis and testicles. They are not mentioned in the Bible and must have been fiddly to carve. It is then made even funnier by the fact that, if you walk round the back of the statue, you can see its bottom. But, as Michelangelo surely understood, comedy has a rule of three and, ultimately, it is only a fart noise that can resolve this masterful comic triptych. We have been waiting more than half a millennium for that bum to fart, and we are privileged to live in an age when it's finally possible.

It is to be hoped that a range of fart noises will be available. A sculptor of Michelangelo's technical genius, who can get nipples just right, would not be satisfied with a standard sound-effects-library fart. We're not talking about a mere raspberry here. A range of different guffs should be sampled and played on shuffle so that, even though a passer-by might be expecting a fart, they won't be ready for the kind of fart they hear: loud and fulsome, short and wet, or mosquito-like and meandering, the specificity of the trump can add so much to the realisation of what art historians must surely accept was the great man's original concept.

For me, this joke can never get tired, simply because people who dislike it will never stop disliking it. That's what will ensure the rest of us keep finding it funny. And it raises the question: why don't we fit every public statue with the capability to make a fart noise whenever anyone walks past? Statues of people on horseback could be made to issue two farts, which is even funnier. Would that not be a wonderful thing?

It's divisive in a way – but it would be a new division and so, paradoxically, a unifying one. There's no way the pro- and anti-fart factions would correlate with the pro- and anti-Brexit groupings, meaning that Leavers and Remainers can find common ground over liking or hating the humour of flatulence.

It also might help resolve controversies over whether to take down statues of discredited figures like Cecil Rhodes. A farting statue won't seem to carry the same implication of veneration by the society it stands in. It just says: "Here was some guy, full of gas like the rest of us. He's dead now."

If the government really wants to tackle Britain's current crisis of confidence and identity, this is what it must do. This is its last chance, after all the recent accidents, mistakes and humiliations, to take a great British idea, commit to it and, in the full gaze of the world's media, really follow through.

* * *

In April 2016, I was struck by a weird anomaly in the British property market . . .

East Barsham Manor in Norfolk doesn't seem to be selling. Its owner has just dropped the asking price from £4m to just under £3m. That's 25% off. It's reduced to clear.

Let me start by saying that £3m is still a lot of money. Though not as much as when the manor was built in 1520. At that point, £3m would probably have bought you the whole of England, which in those days came with a fair bit of Ireland thrown in, as a sort of granny flat.

But I want to make sure I clearly say that, even today, £3m really is a lot of money. I want to do so mainly in order not to be hated. If you start saying millions of pounds isn't much money – even in contexts like "It isn't much money to renew a nation's nuclear deterrent" – you're immediately basking in other people's dislike. Just the phrase "not much" in close proximity to the word "million" raises the hackles of those for whom hackle-raising is a major form of exercise.

In fact, there's really nothing to be gained from asserting that *any* sum isn't "still a lot of money". No one makes friends by denigrating any amount of money greater than a pound. And I reckon there'll be those who'd seize on the slightest disregard for 90p. "It's all very well for you, happily leaving 90p in coppers down the back of your sofa – 1.2 billion people live on less than that a day!" "Sorry, I just thought it was quite cheap for a tea."

So I'm sincerely of the opinion that absolutely any quantity of money, no matter how small, is in fact a huge and ridiculous fortune. I totally don't want you to go away with the idea that I'm one of those TV lefties, so massively enriched by institutions perversely constituted for the sole purpose of turning a blind eye to paedophilia that they think £3m is roughly what you tip a pizza delivery man. I don't want anyone thinking that about me. Because that, my management team tells me, is no way to sell DVDs.

Nevertheless, in the context of Britain's current absurd property market, £3m doesn't always buy you much: a flat in central London, a small house in not-quite-central London, a large house in outer London. It certainly wouldn't purchase central London's equivalent of East Barsham Manor, because that's St James's Palace.

But I'm being naive. It's "location, location, location", isn't it? Rural Norfolk's rubbish for the tube. The surprisingly large number of people fortunate enough to earn enough to raise a mortgage big enough to buy somewhere that costs £3m couldn't still earn that in the Norfolk countryside. They need to service those vast debts, and the immense political pressure keeping interest rates tiny is only half the battle. They've got to keep trousering the kind of salary you get by working in the City or practising law, rather than farming or running an antiques shop.

What's more, if you bought East Barsham Manor, you wouldn't just have the mortgage to worry about. It's a Grade I-listed 16th-century mansion set in ornamental gardens. It costs nearly two grand a week to stop it falling down. So it's not a viable option for most of those who could just about afford the price tag.

In fact, the more I thought about it, the more it totally made sense that this unique jewel of Tudor architecture – where Henry VIII reputedly stayed on his pilgrimage to Walsingham, with seven reception rooms, eight bedrooms, a great hall with minstrels' gallery and five acres of grounds, on which there's also a three-bedroom cottage – is roughly equated under our modern value system with a three-bedroom flat in a modern block in Pimlico.

Then suddenly it stopped making sense again. Hang on, I thought. High earners servicing seven-figure debts to sustain modest accommodation aren't the main force inflating the property bubble. It's the billionaires who have chosen London as a place to shop, and its property market as a money laundry. They don't have to worry about mortgages and the tube. They're looking to buy palaces to hang out in for brief periods between superyacht rides. A Norfolk manor house would be fine for them – they could helicopter to Harrods in under an hour. The yacht could drop them off at King's Lynn or Cromer.

But that lot don't want houses like East Barsham Manor, I concluded bitterly. They want Belgravia townhouses, stripped back, knocked through and ruined with onyx and granite and marble. They want screening rooms and gyms, they want cavernous dugout basements for swimming pools and spa treatment suites and windowless bedrooms for servants. They want glass and steel and air-conditioning and panic rooms.

They don't see the beauty and history, the irreplaceable preciousness of a building like East Barsham Manor, they're just looking for a large dehumidified garage in which to keep their diamante-studded Humvees and leopard-print Bentleys. The comparatively modest price tag on this amazing Tudor mansion is, I realised, a direct consequence of the vulgarity of the rich – of the shocking fact that 99% of the world's money is in the hands of people possessing 0.0001% of the world's taste.

"How odd that that bothers me so much," I reflected as I wrung the snobbish spittle out of my beard. It's not the world's growing inequalities of wealth that rile me, just that our new global economic overlords spend their ill-gotten gains so tackily – and that's not a moral failing. Still, the feeling that these people are vulgar as well as rich makes them, to my British sensibilities, hugely more contemptible.

I think that feeling is pretty common (ironically). As a society, we're more comfortable with our former masters, with "old money". Few of us resent the fact that the dukes of Devonshire still live at Chatsworth – they're just some nice old posh people. It doesn't make us brim with rage, unlike an oligarch's planning application to install a second car lift.

This imbalance of anger makes no logical sense. Whether it's the old aristocracy or the new plutocracy, it's still people who've ended up with unimaginable wealth for reasons that are seldom particularly fair. But the harsh edges of unfairness are softened by time; moss tempers its frowning gables into a smile. After all, when Henry VIII stayed at East Barsham Manor, it was brand new – as gleaming and modern as an internet billionaire's penthouse.

* * *

In January 2018, another very British housing crisis loomed large . . .

The residents of Bell End, like many of us, hope that 2018 will bring a fresh start. To be clear, I mean the residents of Bell End, the street in Rowley Regis, not Bell End, the village in Worcestershire. The latter Bell Enders probably hope it'll be a fresh start too, but not in the same way as the Rowley Regis ones.

The English grammatical convention that names of places seldom take a definite or indefinite article is what prevents me from humorously clarifying that I also don't mean the residents of a bell end – the microbes presaging a venereal disease, perhaps. But let's face facts: there's no way that's what anyone would really think the phrase "the residents of Bell End" could possibly mean. That double entendre simply will not hold together. Not even in a desperate last-minute script gagging-up session for a *Carry On* film would they get away with that.

The new beginning the residents of Bell End, Rowley Regis, are hoping for is the renaming of their street. They're hoping for Twat Close. Of course they're not. They want a normal name that isn't slang for either a section of human genitalia or a person so contemptible as to be likened to one. Some of the residents do anyway: there's a petition, currently signed by 61 people, so they're a long way short of qualifying for a Commons debate (the BBC Parliament channel will be sorry to hear).

I'm afraid I can't tell you what percentage of the people who live there 61 names represent. To do that, I'd have to go there and see how big Bell End is. Once again, if only I could have said "how big *the* Bell End is", that would have been amusing. But, to reiterate, it's suspiciously unusual to use definite articles with street names. You'd spot the trick and hate me.

I wouldn't say, "Let's go shopping on the Oxford Street," would I? "These days, there are no newspapers still based in the Fleet Street"? No. Though, oddly, I might say, "The traffic is often terrible on the Edgware Road." I don't know why, and it seems a waste as "Edgware Road" doesn't mean penis or vagina. Or anus, for that matter. "Taking someone up the Edgware Road" has yet to catch on as an expression, probably because, as I say, the traffic is terrible. You're much better off trying your luck in Lisson Grove.

Anyway, I'm not going to Bell End to see how many people live there because, from the name of the place, I can only assume they're all total bell ends.

That's not what I assume. The name of their street reflects on them neither positively nor negatively, and only a bell end would think it does. Even whoever named the street is blameless, as the name long pre-dates bell end's use as an insult, which only really started in the 1990s. The road was named after the Bell End Colliery to which it used to lead. The namer wasn't to know the British were shortly going to stop mining coal and start calling each other bell ends.

So why does it matter? Why change it? Why reduce the country's quirky texture and spoil the fun of all those who travel to Bell End purely to take pictures of themselves next to the sign?

I mean, what are those guys going to do without it? It really doesn't sound like they've got much else in their lives.

That's certainly the view of some of the residents of Upton-upon-Severn's Minge Lane. "There has been no plan to change the name of our road," explained Stephen Young, a 72-year-old resident. "We have had a problem with people nicking the sign, but nobody is that fussed about the name. It's a bit silly really to start a petition."

A stinging rebuke coming from a resident of another of Britain's most rude-sounding streets. But, in the reluctant Bell Enders' defence, the Minge Lane case is subtly different. Stephen Young does not live on a road simply called "Minge", and he might not be so sanguine if he did. That's what gives Bell End its unrelenting suggestive power: the fact that there are no other words involved. No "Road", "Avenue" or "Street". Bell End's name is 100% bell end, while Minge Lane is less than 56% minge.

But there are still Bell End fans among its residents. Roland Burrows, a curator at the Christian Heritage Centre, located on Bell End, said: "I think it's a great name. I've never thought of any rude connotations at all." And Labour councillor and Bell End householder Chris Tranter also likes it: "I was born here and lived here for 40 years and it doesn't bother me. You get the odd giggle on the phone; it is quite amusing really."

Two odd views. It's unusually innocent not to realise Bell End sounds rude, but it's perhaps even odder to live there for 40 years and still find it amusing. Chris Tranter must get a lot of value out of his fridge magnets. Surely, few long-term residents, even if they don't mind the name, would have the sheer force of impish will to continue to find it funny.

Meanwhile, the name's downsides are more tangible. The petition cites "children being bullied and teased at school", and residents also claim that it has a negative impact on property prices: a Bell End semi would apparently fetch £60,000 less than its equivalent on nearby Uplands Avenue. That's quite an expensive joke. I don't blame them for wanting the council to change it.

But it gives me an idea as to how councils can use their naming powers to alleviate the current housing crisis – in particular, the ridiculous prices in London, which mean that, for most people, the housing ladder is dangling hundreds of feet above their heads from the bottom of an oligarch's money-laundering Zeppelin.

Any political pressure on developers to build affordable housing is outweighed by the economic incentive to flog more luxury flats to the super-rich. But, if councils can name the streets, suddenly they have some power: "If you won't build affordable housing, we have a way of making it affordable. Welcome to Nob-cheese Avenue, adjoining Hitler Lane. Go straight up Jimmy Savile's Passage and you're there."

* * *

The Olympics is a puzzling phenomenon. I came to this conclusion reading a news report about the legacy of the 2012 London games. It said there basically wasn't one. The family gathered nervously to hear the reading of the will, only to learn that the bejewelled old dowager had pissed everything away ante mortem. No urban regeneration for Great Nephew the Lee Valley, no sustained increase in trade for dodgy Uncle Tourism and nothing of any real value for kindly Cousin Shortage of Affordable Housing. No inheritance but debts and a drawer full of useless trinkets (stadiums).

I realise this metaphor is screaming like an Elizabethan Catholic under interrogation, but it wasn't me who coined the phrase "Olympic legacy". I just copied it to try and sound modern. That's what we media types have to do when we enter middle age, as well as pretending we can work our phones and buying fashionable spectacles.

Speaking of fashionable spectacles, the opening and closing ceremonies of the 2012 Olympics did actually have perceptible legacies, or positive consequences, according to the article I read. They caused happiness spikes in the London population – so, in bequest terms, more a round of drinks at the wake than the deeds to a Kensington townhouse, but still worth having.

And with that, I declare the legacy metaphor to have died on the rack without betraying the whereabouts of any fellow Jesuits. And with that, I also announce the passing of the metaphor I've been using to refer to the legacy metaphor. It's been a difficult time, and we need to move on.

These happiness spikes were apparently part of a broader elevation of Londoners' moods caused by the Olympics. This fact has been established by a team of "happiness researchers" led by Paul Dolan, professor of behavioural sciences at the London School of Economics, and Georgios Kavetsos of Queen Mary University of London. They interviewed 9,000 people in London, Berlin and Paris over a three-year period around the London games in an attempt to measure their sense of well-being with and without the Olympian fillip. They found that Londoners became significantly happier from summer/autumn 2012 onwards, though their happiness fell back to normal levels within a year.

The way the researchers quantified this was interesting. They said the rise in people's level of satisfaction was equivalent to the mood improvement caused by an £8,000 pay rise. If that's genuinely true of all 8 million Londoners, then the £8.9bn the games cost is quite an inexpensive way of making the city feel like it's received a £64bn windfall. But the effect is temporary. As Kavetsos put it: "Like any party, you have a great time but the following day you wake up with a hangover."

Which brings us to the billion-dollar question, or rather the £8.9bn question: is hosting the Olympics worth it? "If you want to host a party, host a party and do that. It's fine," says Kavetsos. "The problem with events such as the Olympics is they come with all these claims that they are going to boost jobs and the economy. If you look at the literature, that isn't true."

This is what puzzled me. Our society, most would agree, does not underrate the importance of money. Money is deemed, usually rightly, to be behind everything, to be insidious and pervasive. Even those who lust after power are suspected of secretly lusting after money more. Money is the ultimate ulterior motive.

Yet, according to Kavetsos's persuasive analysis, where the Olympics is concerned, the situation is reversed. Money isn't the ulterior motive for hosting the Olympics, it's the ostensible reason. Money, in the form of economic prosperity and urban regeneration, is what's set out, front and centre, as why a city should hold the games. The evidence shows, however, that this money, this greater long-term prosperity, hardly ever materialises. But people still want to host the games. What, then, is the ulterior motive?

It's partly money too, probably. The Olympics may not make cities wealthier, but any given Olympiad enriches many individuals. A lot of public money always flows into private hands, both legitimately and corruptly. Those people can honestly say, "The Olympics will make us richer," and only have to start lying if pressed for a specific definition of "us".

But my hunch is there's more to it than that. I think a big part of the ulterior motive, the unspoken reason, for wanting to host the games is simply that people really want to host the games. They want to do it because they think it's exciting and fun and good. But those reasons sound feeble or untrue to cynical contemporary ears. On one level, we think avarice is shameful, but on another, we think it's the only sensible or believable reason for doing anything. The apparent absence of avarice, we suspect, is just conclusive proof of the lurking presence of sloth, envy and pride.

"You can't put a price on happiness," we airily say, but we don't mean it. We think you can and, in their study, these happiness researchers actually have. A moderate increase in happiness because of a successful civic event is worth eight grand, they say. I'm sure we could get them to price up some other stuff: falling in love, having a child, a crisp autumn day, a satisfying fart. Or, in the debit column, the death of a grandparent, getting beaten up, an awkward silence in a social situation. It could all be expressed in monetary terms.

Since the dawn of time, humans have wanted to quantify things, so we've invented hundreds of units of measurement – kilograms, pints, amps, miles, hours, miles per hour. But it seems we're now trying to use currency as the overall measurement, the uber-unit, the way of quantifying the whole human experience.

It might have been better for Britain if Shakespeare had died poor. The fact that England's, and the world's, greatest writer was also financially astute skews how we rate those skills. People mention his business acumen as often as his sonnets. It almost makes us forget that the man's only genius was for writing. The big house and the second-best bed and all that are just antiquarian colour. His affluence adds nothing to his contribution.

We might be more willing to put money in its place if something as indisputably worthwhile as Shakespeare's oeuvre hadn't also turned a financial profit. It might allow us to remember the unifying, lovable, slick, magnificent, friendly, joyous, expensive success of London 2012 without forcing ourselves to add a tinge of regret.

* * *

It's 6 August 2017, and the Christmas countdown has already begun . . .

"Any customers that aren't really into Christmas this early can always ignore it," said Eleanor Gregory, Christmas and home buyer at Selfridges, about the opening of its Christmas store last week. Am I wrong to project a slight tartness on to that remark? As if the first draft of "can always ignore it" had been "know where they can stick it"?

I probably am wrong. Eleanor seemed fairly upbeat in her other comments: "This new extension to our usual offer is addressing this growing demand for convenience – domestic customers who love to Christmas shop very early in the year to get it wrapped and taken off their to-do list."

At least, I *think* that was also her. The *Guardian* says it was, but the *Telegraph* attributes the phrase to a "Selfridges spokesperson", as part of a long speech that also includes this sentence: "We've been opening the doors to our Christmas shop during the summer for years now and have become a real destination for fans of Christmas and festive decorations," which both *The Times* and the *Independent* claim was spoken by Geraldine James. Not the actress, but the "Christmas home and decorations buyer at Selfridges".

So the whole thing is a bit of a mystery. Are Eleanor Gregory and Geraldine James the same person? Or deadly rivals? Why are both of their surnames men's first names? And has the fact that Geraldine James's name is the same as Geraldine James's held her back? Or has the actress been unaffected by the rise of the Selfridges buyer?

Whatever the truth, Gregory and James have had a great week. Selfridges opened the fake snow-sprayed doors of its Christmas store on Monday 31 July, and the press has been lapping up the story like alcoholic cats around a splat of eggnog. Because it's so *early*, isn't it?! "147 days early", according to *The Times* and the *Guardian*, which presumably advocate doing your Christmas shopping on Christmas Day itself. It's still summer! It's ridiculous! Whatever next?! Driverless buses? A tweeter laureate? A government using chemical weapons on its own people?

Whoops, I've slipped news genres. Which isn't the point of this at all. You'll have got the wrong sort of tut ready. But please don't worry: you'll only need your "Christmas retail push getting earlier every year" tut from here on, and you can save your chemical weapons tut for another time. Doing the two next to each other never feels great and calls into question the whole efficacy of tutting as a force for positive change, an embarrassing sensation for well-meaning westerners.

So Greg and Jim were happy, and the press was happy, and the Selfridges shoppers whose views were sought out by the press were happy – and enjoyed the affectation of interest on the faces of the reporters, to whom they either said "I think it's silly" or "I think it's fine", with just a smattering of "It seems a bit silly but I suppose it's fine". Bloody Lib Dems.

But I was surprised. All my life, people have bemoaned how retailers start gearing up for Christmas earlier and earlier in the year. In my childhood, adults never missed the chance to spoil the fun of a first glimpse of tinsel on an otherwise joyless trip to buy a duffel coat. So, all these years later, it was a shock to discover that the process has still only got as far as the end of July.

Let's get it over with, I say. The sooner the Christmas retail serpent's ravening fangs make contact with its own juicy tail and we have a year-round, ever more tightly constricting festive embrace, the better. We can then accept the situation and move on, like we've accepted post-office closures and the new KitKat wrapper and Winnie-the-Pooh's American accent and a thousand other small worsenings that powerful people have decided we deserve.

Speaking as a miserable sod, I look forward to it. Instead of lamenting a trend, we can settle down into patronising younger people with anecdotes about how great it was when there were great stretches of the year when you genuinely couldn't buy lametta (except on the internet).

A major reason this seasonal department is such a PR hit is that Christmas is more interesting when it's incongruous. Hence the perennial popularity of those news stories about local odd-balls who never take their decorations down and eat turkey with all the trimmings 365 times a year. Set against a background of everyday life, we can see Christmas's strangeness more clearly: the curious food, the weird music, the garish interior design and the baffling proliferation of apparently unlinked symbols – snowmen, reindeer, Middle Eastern shepherds, parcels, stars, bells, bearded geriatrics dressed in red, triangular trees, babies and holly.

Christmas is like our whole culture putting on a disguise – different customs, music, cuisine, symbolism, way of life. If aliens observed us throughout December, they might think they'd got a handle on what we're like, but then, suddenly, it would all change. "What's happened to the jingly, present-giving, arguing, snow-obsessed overeaters?" they'd ask in January. "Suddenly they seem depressed – which is odd because it's finally started to snow."

When I was at university, we nearly put on a Christmas-themed summer revue. We were planning a sketch show to tour the country in July and August and were racking our brains for a theme, when we got very excited about making it a Christmas show, with all the sketches about Christmas and a festively deco-rated set (this was pre-internet, so I don't know how we'd have got hold of lametta). The show was to be called *Deep and Crisp and Even*, with a big picture of a snow-topped pizza on the posters. But none of our usual touring venues would take it. So we did one about the seven deadly sins instead, which sounded much more original to unoriginal people.

But if, like the small touring theatres of the mid-90s, you're not amused by incongruous yuletide references, be of good cheer: despite what the papers implied, the festive retail push isn't actually starting earlier. In 2016, the Selfridges Christmas store opened on 1 August. So just a day later than this year (and the equivalent Monday). Back in 2011, it opened in late July. The trend is at a standstill.

Perhaps Christmas has hit maximum commercialisation, or perhaps our economic system is dying. Let's hope it recovers in the spring. In the meantime, we could drag some greenery indoors and pray.

* * *

For some reason, Samsung has commissioned a study into what people think are the worst interior decoration fads of the last 50 years. I say "for some reason" because, at heart, I'm an optimist. I try to believe there's a good reason or, failing that, some sort of reason, for most of the things people do. But I must admit, in this instance, I'm struggling to think of one.

Raising brand awareness perhaps? It certainly will do that, to a modest extent. Articles mentioning the study will probably mention Samsung, so it's getting more mentions. But are they apposite mentions? It's not as if Samsung makes interior-designy things – or, if it does, there's still a lot more brand awareness work to be done where I'm concerned. Can you get Samsung sofas, or curtains, or lamps, or wallpaper? Why didn't Dulux or Laura Ashley or Ikea pay for this survey? I thought Samsung made mobile phones?

To give Samsung's marketing team credit, they have managed to corner me into mentioning that the firm makes mobile phones. So is that the strategy? To associate the brand with such weirdly unconnected areas of commerce that it forces people to contemplate the fact that it makes phones and puzzle over what links there might be between those phones and whatever interior design study or real ale festival or turbot-breeding initiative the logo is randomly stuck on?

How tortuously cunning! It makes me feel like a dupe for having repeatedly written the word "Samsung" in the last few paragraphs, and moves me to say that I once owned a Samsung mobile phone and, in all honesty, I thought it was crap. Much worse than a Nokia or an iPhone, in my view. And if I was ever interviewed by someone doing a survey into mobile phone use, perhaps sponsored by Robinsons Barley Water or Stanley Gibbons, that's what I'd tell them.

I suppose you can probably get Samsung TVs and surround-sound clobber, which are vaguely to do with interior design and may explain why "situation room levels of audio-visual equipment in what is supposed to be a lounge" isn't one of the study's top 10 most derided trends. Personally, I hate surround sound when I'm watching television. I want the sound to be made by what I'm looking at – and the pictures don't surround you, so it's just distracting when the noises do.

Sometimes it literally makes me turn away from the TV to see what's happening behind me. Which obviously turns out to be nothing. But then, by the time I turn back to the screen, I've potentially missed a key bit of whatever's going on. I mean, I hardly ever have missed anything, but you can't be sure until you've rewound and checked. Otherwise, later on, when you inevitably find some element of the plot totally baffling, you become convinced that it would all be clear if you hadn't missed that crucial instant of screen time. That's my strong view. It's not always the view of the person or people I'm watching TV with. So, all in all, surround sound is a disaster.

But it's not something the 2,000 respondents to the survey were bothered by. When asked to rank their least favourite of the last half-century's home decor ideas, from a list of suggestions drawn up by design writers, their collated responses produced the following top five: first, furry lavatory rugs and loo seat covers; second, stuffed animals; third, avocado bathrooms; fourth, chintzy furniture; and fifth equal, waterbeds, Artex and carpeted bathrooms.

So what do we learn from this list? On the plus side, it shows a timely rejection of trends for absorbent surfaces in the rooms most prone to stray excreta. Anyone who's ever lived in a shared house will have come to view any little pink rug clinging round the communal lavatory pedestal with the sort of awed respect for extreme toxicity usually reserved for a nerve agent.

But, on the minus, it's a lamentable reflection of how susceptible people are to fashion, not just in what is popular, but also in what is unfashionable. It's long established that fashion can make people think they adore the daft and hideous. But this list suggests it can also make them dutifully loathe the completely inoffensive.

I'm talking about avocado bathrooms. A decade ago, I co-wrote a TV sketch about how our culture has completely lost its sense of perspective about avocado bathrooms. And, as further proof of the complete impotence of satire, the situation has only worsened in the intervening years.

It's just green. An avocado bathroom is just green. All that's happened is that a thing, the colour of which can be dictated in the manufacturing process – as it can with clothes, cars, crockery, carpets, toothbrushes and many, many other items – has been made green. An extremely normal colour. It is one of the main colours for things to be. Many things are naturally green, but many others are deliberately rendered green, or partly green, in order to look nice.

But people behave, and are being encouraged by designers to behave, as if having a loo, sink and bath that are coloured green, or indeed any colour other than white, is hideous and insane; as if it shows the worst excesses of "What were we thinking?!" fashion craziness – kipper ties, mullets, puffball skirts and bound feet all rolled into one; as if some final epiphany about the wrongness of baths being any colour apart from white has been reached.

It's not that green sinks aren't currently fashionable; the implication is that it's been decided they never will be again. It's something society has permanently moved on from, like slavery. This reeks of the arrogance of the contemporary: we are the era that's got it right, that finally understands. We will never look daft again.

Well, anyone who observes the world as it currently is and seriously believes this is the age that's definitely cracked it about anything at all, even bathroom design, is an idiot.

* * *

The hull of the ship they're not actually going to call *Boaty McBoatface* is complete. By the time you read this, it will probably have already slid into the River Mersey, bobbed along massively for a bit and then been tugged off into a harbour. It won't be the first time that's happened.

It's going to be called the RRS *Sir David Attenborough* instead of *Boaty McBoatface*, despite the fact that *Boaty McBoatface* won an online poll to decide its name. I think we can all agree, though, that RRS *Sir David Attenborough* is a *much* more sensible name. Then again, to put the contrary point of view, RRS *Sir David Attenborough* is a much more *sensible* name.

We can't know why all the people who voted for *Boaty McBoatface* did so, but it's a reasonable guess that very few of them thought it was a sensible name. It's a silly name, a funny name. They voted for it because they wanted this big, sensible, expensive boat to be called something daft and trivialising.

Perhaps some of them thought it should have a funny name because they believe that, in general, more things should have funny names – that it would add to the gaiety of nations, to the sum of human happiness, if London were called Big-Botty-Town or the UN was renamed the U-Smell-of-Poo. And perhaps some of them thought it should have a funny name to take those self-important polar scientists down a peg or two: "They needn't think they're all that as they take all their measurements in the freezing cold, because they live and work in a thing called *Boaty McBoatface*! Idiots!"

I genuinely think it's a very funny name – I've thought about it many times and it continues to amuse me. Not because it sounds inherently hilarious, like a fart or a burp or a well-timed honk, but because it seems to come from such a dismissive and flippant point of view. "Who cares what the sodding boat is called?" it proclaims. It's so disdainful of the patronising condescension that the whole notion of asking the public what a boat should be called, as if they're children and it's a *Blue Peter* hamster, absolutely reeks of.

It's a sign, incidentally, of Sir David Attenborough's colossal, ocean-going credibility that his name was the one chosen to supplant such a good joke. Jo Johnson, the then minister for universities and science who overruled the *Boaty McBoatface* vote, must have instinctively sensed that people would go along with it being named after Attenborough. Nobody resents Attenborough. Anyone would feel churlish objecting to its being named after him.

In other humourless name-changing news, I learned last week that the Tricycle theatre in Kilburn, just round the corner from where I lived for 10 years, has been renamed the Kiln theatre. This sounds like Prince Charles saying "the Kilburn theatre". Perhaps they're hoping he'll come and cut the ribbon when it reopens after its £7m refurbishment, make the whole place feel a bit more royal and posh. It would be a surprising change of direction for an edgy off-West-End arts venue, but then *The Crown* has been huge for Netflix and that whole post-war meritocracy drive seems to have pretty much petered out, so perhaps we'd all better get back to social climbing.

On reflection, I don't think it's meant to sound posh. The theatre's artistic director, Indhu Rubasingham, explained that "we felt the name reflected our home in Kilburn. And a kiln is also a space for transformation, so we felt it fitted in with our ideas of what we should be all about." A kiln is a space for a pretty predictable sort of transformation, not the sort you'd want to sit and watch. More akin to paint drying than a butterfly emerging from its chrysalis, but I accept that the word shares four of the seven letters of its location's name, and maybe that's good.

You can probably tell that I'm not 100% supportive of this rebranding. Partly, I feel possessive of the place because I used to live nearby. Admittedly, I never actually went to the theatre part of it, but I saw *Quantum of Solace* in its cinema, so you can't say I haven't suffered in its interests. But mainly I can't see the point in the change. It will have cost money and has merely turned a theatre that quite a few people had heard of into one that virtually no one has.

I'm not the only naysayer. Rubasingham's direct predecessor, Nicolas Kent, who ran the Tricycle from 1984 to 2012, described the decision as "tragic" and "a commercial misstep". There's also a protest group calling for it to be reversed and an online petition signed by over 1,400 people.

I haven't signed the petition. I don't like the decision – I can't see any reason for it other than a self-important instinct to tamper with things – but it's not up to me, or to any random online signatories. The naming of theatres is not a democratic process but the decision of the people running them. It's a tiny part of the venue's artistic offering, a creative choice. The rest of us can slag it off, just like we can slag off any shows we didn't enjoy, but we cross a line when we dispute their right to make it. If you want to decide what a theatre is called, get yourself a job running a theatre. A few thousand votes from people who don't know what they're talking about are no reason to change course.

As the *Boaty McBoatface* saga shows, you can't always bow to a snapshot of popular opinion. Who knows why people voted as they did – in what spirit of lashing out against the establishment, of tweaking the nose of the ruling class – without having fully thought through, or been properly informed of, the long-term implications. Sometimes someone has to step in to stop something crazy happening – something terrible that does lasting damage. But only if it's a really important issue, like a boat being given a silly name.

8

Brexit: Snapshots of a Festering, Self-inflicted Wound

There is a chance that, in choosing the title "Snapshots of a Festering, Self-Inflicted Wound" for the chapter focusing on Brexit, I may have betrayed a tiny bit of bias. So I'd better come clean: I am not in favour of it. I've probably already let that slip with all the snide references earlier in the book, but I might as well make it clear.

So if you're in favour of Brexit, or are happy with the way it's been handled, you may not enjoy this chapter. And if you're both in favour of Brexit and happy with the way it's been handled, then all I can say is: thank you for reading my book, Mr Putin.

We don't know how well, or indeed whether, this festering wound will heal. At time of writing, the infection has already seen off two prime ministers, and still nothing is settled. Here are my thoughts on it at various points in the currently-still-endless process.

29 May 2016 – 25 days before the referendum

When lost, baffled and afraid, I yearn for guidance from an outside power. But is there a God? I hope so. It's hard to be sure, though. If there is, He doesn't seem to pipe up that often with concrete advice. The same cannot be said for the man some consider His slayer, Richard Dawkins. He is possessed of all the certainty I look for in the Almighty, and his truth is a lot more effable. God is dead, long live God. In the apparent absence of omniscience, I'll settle for a know-all.

So I was glad to hear that the revered professor had spoken out about the forthcoming EU referendum, a subject that has made me feel particularly lost, baffled and afraid lately. Don't misunderstand me, I know how I'm going to vote – I'm for Remain. I'm unshakeable on that. I just don't know if I'm right. And I also don't know if the side I'm going to vote for will win. I fear the consequences of its defeat and, to a lesser but still significant extent, I fear the consequences of its victory. I'm not finding any of this much fun.

But Dawkins's words gave me solace. He said: "It is an outrage that people as ignorant as me are being asked to vote. This is a complicated matter of economics, politics, history, and we live in a representative democracy not a plebiscite democracy. You could make a case for having plebiscites on certain issues – I could imagine somebody arguing for one on fox hunting, for example – but not on something as involved as the European Union. This should be a matter for parliament."

Goal! Hear, hear! Amen. That is so totally what I think, but I didn't realise until I heard it. It was a wondrous epiphany. If the man can work such miracles, maybe there is no God. And I was comforted by the thought that Dawkins too longs for the intercession of a greater power: not God, but government. In Britain we get to choose our leaders, and dismiss them if we're disappointed by the direction they've led us in. But we must surely reserve our bitterest disappointment for leaders who refuse to lead us anywhere at all.

Calling this referendum is the worst thing Cameron has done to Britain. It's such a hugely selfish and irresponsible act that I can hardly believe we've wasted so long talking about how he's eviscerating the NHS, attacking the BBC and slashing disability benefits when, horrendous though those developments are, this crime is much greater because its consequences could be irreversible.

The issues surrounding Britain's membership of the EU are complicated. The EU's problems, its waste and questionable democratic accountability, are clear. So are its trade advantages and the transformation of Europe under its influence from the world's most murderous war zone, in which each generation strove to slaughter in greater numbers than its predecessor, to a largely peaceful continent. Crucially, the EU has made the prospect of a war between France and Germany unthinkable. The world of 1945 would be amazed and overjoyed by such an achievement.

Maybe the EU's flaws are leading inexorably to tyranny. Or maybe imperialist and xenophobic emotions within Britain are luring us into a self-defeating isolation that will insult our neighbours and make us poorer. These are just the quandaries that come up when you think about it for five minutes. The deeper you get into it, the more terrifying questions arise.

What is the point in politicians if it isn't to give clear answers to those questions? To understand the broad truth that this country wants to continue to exist independently, but also wants to accept global realities enough to protect its prosperity, and then to make a bloody decision? Yet both major parties are, to a certain extent, divided on the issue – the party of government disastrously so.

Cameron has structured his whole career around avoiding this question – around continuing to lead a party that's divided on the most important decision about the country's future. All because he worked out that, if the subject of the EU was properly debated by the Tories, the party would split, and it would be harder for him to become prime minister.

So he has conspired in the absurd scenario where successive general elections have been fought on other issues – where Britain's future in Europe has not really been addressed by the Tories, and instead this bunch of aspiring leaders who can't agree on this vital issue of leadership have brushed it aside, saying: "We'll hold a referendum"; "We'll let you decide"; "Let us be captain of the ship, but we'll negotiate the most lethal reefs by holding a steering vote among the passengers." I don't think a political party has any business existing if it can't agree a policy on this.

Cameron's policy-avoidance policy was deftly done, mind you. It plays well, rhetorically – telling people they'll get to decide, flattering the public's estimation of its collective wisdom. It's a rhetoric politicians have increasingly used of late: "We're just normal, decent people who listen"; "We're like an unthreatening mate whose heart's in the right place"; "By putting us in power you haven't committed to anything except fair and sensible niceness for hard-working people who do the right thing."

"Make the public think that all a leader needs to be is normal and inoffensive, and then maybe I've got a chance!" is the modern politician's motto. We've stopped looking to MPs to display great intelligence, insight, fortitude or a cool head in a crisis. Now they just get to shrug and say, "It's tricky, isn't it?" "Vote for me, I think it's tricky too!"

They won't step up and lead. They won't say they know. Expertise is dismissed as elitist. It's worse to be "out of touch" with the price of milk than to misunderstand the consequences of Britain suddenly severing all its trade deals. They're happy for that decision to be made by random vote after a frenzied few months of both sides trying to make the other seem the more apocalyptic or Hitlerian, each suddenly so certain in its hyperbole.

Except perhaps David Cameron himself. He's campaigning for Remain but, according to his long-time political ally Steve Hilton, Cameron's "instinct" is for Brexit: "If he were a member of the public . . . I'm certain that he would be for Leave." So perhaps he can't decide. Our leader doesn't know which way to go. I'm not just sorry he's prime minister; I'm sorry he gets a vote.

2 April 2017 – three days after the triggering of Article 50

A dramatic photo-essay played out on the front pages of the newspapers last week. On Tuesday: a snap of Theresa May solemnly signing a letter. On Wednesday: one of Sir Tim Barrow solemnly handing it over to the disapproving president of the European council, Donald "Tsk" Tusk. I didn't buy a paper on Thursday as I didn't have the stomach for the inevitable picture of Tusk solemnly wiping his arse with it. I'd already got the gist.

Please excuse the remoaning. I know it's frowned upon. It wasn't for this that all those elderly Leave supporters dragged themselves out to vote! This isn't what they fought a war for! Though not many of them actually did that. Those guys are mainly dead. The Few are now the Fewer, soon to be the None. So I should say: this isn't what they, in many cases, lived through a bit of the war for (but often as infants, so they can't really remember it)!

If they can't remember it, perhaps that explains why they're so sanguine about renouncing an institution that's done more than any other in history to preserve peace between the major nations of Europe. I wonder if their parents would have been so hasty. The demobbed Tommies who voted for Attlee over Churchill might not have been as easily convinced as their children have been that youngsters with foreign accents working in coffee shops is such a diabolical threat to Britain's values and existence. They'd probably seen worse.

Anyway, this kind of remoaning isn't what members of the luckiest generation ever born betrayed the sacrifices of their parents for! I'm sure that's a form of words we can all agree on. What it feels like they actually did it for, and the clamour against remoaning has contributed hugely to this feeling, is for the Remainers to shut up. That seems to have been an outcome that was confidently expected among Leavers, and nobody even painted it on a bus.

"Come on, you lost – you have to shut up now! For years you've been going on and on and on about multiculturalism and fair trade and equal marriage, and how foreigners are lovely and we're nasty, and chickens get treated terribly, and recycling and rape and pitta bread and how nothing is quite as it seems, and now you've got to stop or it's not fair. Everyone voted to say they were sick of it, and that's that!"

That would explain why, as the consequences of last year's referendum grind remorselessly on, there's so much anger and bitterness on both sides. Surely the winning side should be chipper, at least for the moment. This is the honeymoon period – if a divorce can have a honeymoon period. Which I imagine it can: this is the leave your socks on the floor, get drunk and piss in the sink bit. The bleak contemplation of a vast acreage of solitude stretching ahead towards a cold grave is still to come.

So come on, Ukip, put on your favourite pants and order another takeaway, safe in the knowledge that there's a growing chance the bloke who brings it won't be able to live here soon. "Sergei, Sergei, you know me – it's nothing personal! There is just, quite simply, not enough room, yeah? Capeesh? Now what do I owe you, my friend?"

But the Ukippers, even in their hour of victory, don't appear to be very happy. They seem baffled and in disarray, even by their own bickering standards. I suppose they've been going through a bumpy patch: it took them a long time to find a leader who could pull off the elusive double of both being able to stomach the job for more than 18 days and not being Nigel Farage; they've just lost their only MP (not in an election – there was some sort of falling out, as usual); and nobody seems very optimistic about their prospects in the local elections in May.

It's not just that, though. I think the party's Brexit spokesman, Gerard Batten, really got to the heart of the malaise when he said last week: "We don't want Article 50 to be triggered." Wow. My daughter is 23 months old, so never in my life have I been more aware of what Farage would probably describe as "a woman's pre-rogative". Still, was ever such an energetically campaigned-for rice cake so rebuffed? "You what now?!" is the only response.

Contextualised, Batten's statement is marginally less mad. He reckons the whole Article 50 process is "a trap" and we should just leave. Don't get sucked into all that metropolitan liberal elite article-triggering claptrap, he reckons; instead, we just go. Brick up the Channel tunnel, throw a lasso around Rockall and then pull ourselves off into the sea – like the good old days, eh Gerard? The whole complex negotiation of Britain's departure is something he says we could "do in an afternoon". And he's Ukip's Brexit spokesman, so it's definitely his area of expertise.

The party's new leader, Paul Nuttall, was slightly less down on Article 50, but promised that Ukip would be the "guard dogs of Brexit". He also set out "six key tests" for Brexit that he'll definitely be able to say aren't met.

So it's all happening like they wanted it to – like they'd barely have dreamed of 15 years ago – but they're still cross, still picking holes, still cueing up the future rhetoric of betrayal. Meanwhile, Nuttall is promising a huge shake-up of the party, its structure and its policies. "The name will stay, that's the one thing I'll guarantee," he says.

On one level, this is a response to a practical problem: Ukip was established as a one-issue party, and that issue has been resolved in its favour. It's lost its ostensible reason to exist, but it still exists. New issues to bang on about must be found.

But my instinct is that their crisis runs deeper than this. The leading Ukippers have spent decades convinced that the anger and dissatisfaction they felt, with which their lives were infused, was caused by one thing. And now the thing has gone. What if they feel the same? A crushing realisation for them, but also for the rest of us. Their misdirected zeal could easily have tipped the balance in the referendum.

So excuse the compl(rem)aining, but we really must stop people self-medicating their undiagnosed psychological problems by causing huge, ill-conceived geopolitical shifts. First the Iraq war and now this. I blame social services.

29 July 2018

Who would have thought Jeremy Hunt was such a massive nostalgic? I mean, he's not called Jeremy Hostalgic! Seriously though, it turns out he's a real old softie, and I fancy there must have been a tear in his eye on his visit to Berlin last week.

I'm not saying he misses the Nazis! Honestly! I know hyperbole is fashionable at the moment, so it's probably worth making clear that I don't think Jeremy Hunt is a Nazi. I mean, he's not called Jeremy Hazi! Seriously though, the man's not a fascist, even if I don't much like his politics. Having said that, English is all about usage, and I reckon the word "fascist" is regularly used online to mean "someone whose politics you don't much like". Which, oddly, makes it a synonym for communist.

The foreign secretary betrayed this sense of nostalgia when criticising Brussels's conduct over Brexit. "Without a real change in approach from the EU negotiators we do now face a real risk of a no deal by accident, and that would be incredibly challenging economically," he warned, adding that the British people would blame the EU for this and it "would change [their] attitudes to Europe for a generation". So there he is, a Tory cabinet minister, saying that British problems are the EU's fault. Just once more, for old times' sake?

Bless you, but you can't do that any more, Jeremy. Those days are gone. When we chose to leave, the EU's duty of care over our country came to an end. It isn't supposed to look out for our interests any more; it's not accountable to the people you say will blame it. You might as well say that Sainsbury's shareholders will blame the CEO of Tesco if their investment loses value. So what.

I understand how he must feel. For his whole political career, the EU has been there for him. Despite favouring Remain in the referendum, Hunt subsequently told LBC that he'd changed his mind due to the "arrogance of the EU". But in Berlin the other day, he said that, if Brussels allowed a no-deal Brexit, "it would lead to a fissure in relations which would be highly damaging for that great partnership we have had for so many years, which has been so important in sustaining the international order".

He doesn't seem to realise that that's all happening anyway. The "fissure in relations", the complete ending, not just damaging, of the "great partnership" is what we as a nation have decided to do. Which means that's all good, isn't it? It's the will of the people, Jeremy, it's lovely! The poor man is so confused and emotional, he's started talking Britain down.

We're witnessing the end of a way of life. For decades our political leaders, both Tory and Labour, have been able to blame things that went wrong, things they failed to do, anything that seemed unfairly constraining, or frighteningly liberating, on the Brussels bureaucrats. Anything that smacked of globalisation and corporate power, but also anything that seemed overly statist and controlling, anything that was bad for business, and anything that left the individual citizen too exposed. Put simply: anything.

It was a sweet little scam: the people in charge only admitted to being in charge when it suited them. They were good cop. Bad cop was some Belgians you never met. And Brussels is an excellent receptacle for blame. It has an aura of irritating blandness and pedantry, but not of frightening or acquisitive aggression. We could project enmity on to it without getting too scared and, for several decades, without creating the political momentum for anything to be done.

This is why, despite the stratospheric importance of the question of whether or not Britain is in the EU – not just in terms of economics and geopolitics, but of the hearts, minds and self-image of millions of Britons – the two main parties haven't fought a general election on the issue for over 30 years.

They've argued endlessly about privatisation and NHS funding and tuition fees and foxhunting and MPs' expenses, but they've both avoided the main problem, this colossal, festering, unresolved question, and left it as a personal matter for individual members. That's like having decades of religious debate in the 16th century between two groups, both of which refuse to say whether they're Catholic or Protestant.

But it worked well for the politicians. Brussels was there to be slagged off, and there was no threat to party unity. The British people have paid a lot for the unity of their politicians' groupings and, more than anything else, that of the Conservative party, which should perhaps be renamed the "Self-Conservative party", as that appears to be the only political aim on which its MPs are agreed.

The Labour leadership could probably have told its membership years ago, "Look, if you don't like the EU, join another party," and stayed pretty much intact. But the Tories would have split in half and turned from the electoral juggernaut of the first-past-the-post system to two Lib Dem-sized groups with little hope of office without major electoral reform of the sort Tories have been resolutely helping to block ever since the Earth's crust hardened.

So with the rise of Ukip, and the pre-eminent importance of Conservative party unity in mind, David Cameron rolled the referendum dice. It is the most egregious example of putting party before country in British history, and he also screwed it up. It was cynical and it was stupid, the work of a second-rate chancer.

And the long political tradition of Brussels-bashing left him in an awkward position for the campaign. He could hardly say: "You know all that stuff that we've been saying is Brussels's fault for as long as you can remember? Well, it's Westminster's fault, it's my fault." "Your problems are my fault! So do what I suggest!" is a flawed slogan. He'd probably banked on Labour being a bit more effusively pro-EU. Yet another thing that poisonous little prick got wrong.

But when I look at Jeremy Hunt, still trying to blame the EU for everything even now, like an orphaned calf nuzzling the festering corpse of its mother because it's his instinct and that's all he's got, I take some comfort. At least the politicians are losing something too.

23 September 2018

On one of the thousands of occasions I glanced needlessly at my phone last week, it made me notice a news story. Vince Cable, it appeared, had described the hardcore Leavers' delight in Brexit as an "erotic spasm".

I liked that. It's a nicely rude way of describing their irrational excitement at continental division and national isolation, and their inappropriately visceral feelings about the technical details of international trade deals. The whole country is going through a disaster, it is saying, just so a few extremists get to judder with sexual delight.

And it's doubly potent because of who the leading Brexiteers are. Jacob Rees-Mogg, Boris Johnson, Michael Gove and Nigel Farage are people who it is particularly grotesque to imagine having an erotic spasm. In my view, anyway. Yet that grotesqueness has a grim fascination; I can't help thinking about it, about each of them wriggling around, all spermy and thrilled.

Of course, that's not their fault. The fact that they're not conventionally attractive, and so their credibility is unlikely to be enhanced by lots of people imagining them in sexual contexts, is an unfair reason to dismiss their views. And I say that as a thoroughgoing non-oil painting myself. But that's one of the many things about the world that isn't fair, so I have to accept that what I say here is just going to seem less persuasive when I admit that I'm masturbating as I type it.

Then it turned out that Vince Cable hadn't said it after all. The current irritating system whereby the texts of politicians' speeches are circulated to the media before they've been delivered rather relies on our elected representatives being able to spit out the words as planned – which is easier said than done. Or rather said. Certainly easier said than "erotic spasm".

I'm sure Cable knew it was a good line: he paused slightly before trying to pronounce it, indulging no doubt in an instant of self-satisfaction. "This'll get 'em!" he probably thought. I know from my own experience that there's nothing like feeling sure the next line is a zinger to make your teeth, tongue and saliva try to join in with saying it.

So he said "exotic spresm" instead. It's very funny. I recommend watching it. Not the whole speech – that's interminable – but that section. I knew in advance both that he was supposed to say "erotic spasm" and that he'd actually said "exotic spresm", and yet somehow that made it even funnier.

He's standing in a huge room full of people, most of whom presumably know he's about to try to say "erotic spasm" – I mean, I knew in advance and they're Lib Dem members who are attending the Lib Dem conference, so they're bound to. They're all ready, keyed up to laugh approvingly as soon as he says "erotic spasm", and off he goes: "Years of economic pain justified by . . ." little pause – stand by, conference ". . . the exotic spresm of leaving the European Union."

There is a quality to the silence following the remark that is almost magical. It's pure distilled human puzzlement. Hundreds of people simultaneously wondering if they've lost it, if the part of their brain that decodes language has suddenly failed. It's a puzzlement exacerbated by the fact that Cable just ploughs on as if "exotic spresm" means something, or as if the right noise could be dubbed on to the speech in post-production. He doesn't otherwise fluff or stumble, and so it's not even clear that he's aware he's screwed up.

Anyway, it's all good fun, largely because the Lib Dems seem so irrelevant these days. They went back on their tuition fees pledge, and it virtually destroyed them as a political movement. Fair enough: tuition fees are the big issue of our time. That's what all the historians will focus on when they write about this era: the great tuition fees conundrum. How Britain struggled with the huge and painful divisions caused by the towering question of tuition fees.

To be honest, I was pretty pissed off with them when they did that. I don't think they got nearly enough out of the Tories for propping up Cameron's government: basically just a referendum on a half-arsed form of electoral reform, when they might have got a commitment to proper proportional representation. Now that would have been worth betraying the students for. But, as it was, they fell for Cameron's rhetoric about national crisis and used all their power to spare his electoral embarrassment, so that, now the country really is in crisis, they haven't got any left.

That's a much less amusing cock-up than Vince Cable's speech because the consequences are proving disastrous. The Lib Dems are the only political party wholeheartedly representing the 48% of voters who opposed Brexit, yet the chances of them securing those people's support in a general election are vanishingly small.

To my mind, the Lib Dems are right about so much, and yet it does them no good. They consistently opposed the Iraq war, for example, which is now an extremely mainstream view. Obviously, the Labour party is very down on the Iraq war these days but, crucially, that wasn't the case when it was actually happening. At that point, both Labour and the Tories were all for it.

The Lib Dems are also the only political group that's consistently advocated proportional representation, and their failure to gain traction there may be the biggest disaster of the lot. It's because of the first-past-the-post voting system that neither Labour nor the Conservative party can split without facing electoral annihilation. So Cameron called the Brexit referendum to keep the Tories together, and the majority of Labour MPs remain part of an organisation they believe to be ineptly or even malevolently led.

The energy required to keep the Conservative and Labour parties ostensibly united is tearing Britain and Europe apart. Meanwhile, the hapless and laughable irrelevance of the only political movement properly addressing the country's biggest problems is a fascinating manifestation of our looming national disaster.

We get meaningless and useless nonsense from all of our political leaders at the moment. But when Vince Cable does it, at least it's just a slip of the tongue.

7 April 2019

In the quest to understand Theresa May, which capricious fate has imposed on us all, the key is to think of James Cracknell. At time of writing, the 46-year-old is expected to take part in Sunday's Boat Race, and the 62-year-old is expected to be Sunday's prime minister. The former expectation seems marginally more solid than the latter, but both are likelier than not.

Before then, of course, Theresa May may announce – or should that be "might"? Theresa Might may announce – no.

May may announce her intention to step down. Then again, she's announced her intention to step down a couple of times already. But May may have announced her intention to step down again. Possibly more than once.

This patch of British politics is certainly testing the supposed dramatic power of repetition even more than Boris Johnson's sixth-form rhetoric. The word "again" keeps popping up in BBC News website headlines with, by my reading of it at least, an ever-greater tone of dry contempt: "MPs reject prime minister's deal again"; "MPs fail to back proposals again". Meanwhile, EU leaders warn of the danger of a no-deal Brexit again, and Theresa May announces her intention to step down again. It's the world-weary "again" of "The dog's been sick on the carpet again".

Saying she's going to resign is Theresa May's current technique for keeping her job. She says she's going to resign tomorrow in order to remain prime minister today. What a committed remainer. But she's taking it one day at a time. She's in recovery from not being prime minister and the first step is admitting her powerlessness.

The case of James Cracknell will help us. The double Olympic-gold-winning rower cuts an eccentric figure as he strives to compete in the university Boat Race. At his age, he could be most Cambridge students' father and is also older than one of the colleges. He'll never again be as good at rowing as he once was but, unlike the discontinued Quality Street chocolate that shares his name, he's not going down without a fight. He wants one more top(ish)-level race, and he's expending immense effort to claim this comparatively modest prize.

But I get it. All of his other rowing is in the past. In his future, he has only this race, then years of looking back (which is how you sit to row, so at least he's used to it). Similarly, Theresa May, whenever she ceases to be prime minister, will almost certainly never attain the office again. I mean, *surely* not?! I don't want to further tempt capricious fate, but that would be a repetition too soul-destroying even for today's Britain.

So this period of fiasco is the defining, most glorious, most important phase of Theresa May's life. And, as with Cracknell and his rowing, she wants to extend it as far as possible. If she can hang on until mid-July, she'll have been prime minister for three years. Take that, Gordon Brown, the Duke of Wellington and Neville Chamberlain! James Callaghan and the third Duke of Portland will be in her sights!

The difference is that James Cracknell is only rowing a boat, while Theresa May is mismanaging the entire country. So whatever the similarities in their psychological standpoints, it's only Theresa who needs to . . . how best to put it? Is there, I wonder, a more appropriate phrase than "fuck off"? I don't want to swear unnecessarily but, historically, people have found the expression useful. It's certainly earned its place in common usage. And I have to ask myself, if we don't tell Theresa May to fuck off, what on earth are we saving it for?

Whoever comes next, I suppose. Well, I'm going to reserve the right to tell them to fuck off too. That's the kind of consistent political analysis people expect from comedians.

The question of who comes next could well be answered not by a general election, but by the members of the Conservative party. It's the 160,000 or so party faithful and recent defectors from Ukip who, in a leadership election, choose between the two candidates put forward by Tory members of the House of Commons. This is the new, "more democratic" way of doing things, favoured by both main parties, in which a few hundred thousand party members get to overrule the elected representatives of many millions.

The power that our two-party state puts in the hands of the roughly 670,000-strong membership of those parties is vast. And the rate at which ex-Ukippers and radical leftwingers have flocked to join up is a sign that the adherents of extreme political views have cottoned on to this. These partisans are weird radical middlemen getting in between the British people and its elected representatives.

Many Tory and Labour MPs live in fear of deselection by their constituency parties. In general, we only hear about the ones who resist that pressure, either because they are openly disowned, like Dominic Grieve, or jump ship, like Nick Boles. But how many more must be tailoring their parliamentary activities not to the national interest, nor even to cynical electoral efficacy, but to local hardliners' extreme interpretation of party values?

More than half of the constituencies of the UK are either safe Labour or safe Tory seats and, in effect, those places in parliament are in the gift of local constituency parties, just as, in the 18th century, most Commons seats were in the gift of local aristocrats. So, instead of a few hundred lords, it's now hundreds of thousands of activists. That's an improvement, but it's still a screwed system, not a functioning democracy – and the supposed democratisation of how both parties choose their leaders has, ironically, made them less accountable to the wider electorate.

This is not serving Britain well. This isn't about the 52% or the 48%. It's about the 1.4%: that 670,000 who, by energy rather than wisdom, and with the intensity rather than the popularity of their views, foist them on the moderate majority. Theresa May is a creature of this corrupted system and, whether Tory or Labour, her successor will be too.

In the end, Theresa May was prime minister for three years and 11 days, just overtaking Neville Chamberlain but falling short of James Callaghan. In a funny sort of way, that feels about right.

7 July 2019

Have you heard of the uncanny valley? If not, let me say straight away, before you get at all excited, that it's an IT thing. It's a theory in robotics that just happens to have an evocative name. The valley it refers to, far from being a magical land between Narnia and the Big Rock Candy Mountain where everything's a bit weird and the fish fly and the bees swim, is actually just a valley shape on a graph. A flattish asymmetrical U. Specifically, a dip in how positive people's reaction to a robot tends to be as its appearance becomes more human.

The theory is that, in general, as robots look more human, we self-obsessed humans like it more and more, so the line of the graph goes up. Until, that is, the robots are nearly identical to humans. Then our approval dips into the uncanny valley because we suddenly find it creepy, like watching a bee swim. Until, again, the robots become even more humanlike, and indistinguishable from real people, when our approval rises once more at the comforting sight of what we mistake for our own kind. This makes up the other side of the metaphorical valley.

This notion has been knocking around since the late 70s, but is now backed up by scientific evidence. Some neuroscientists and psychologists in Britain and Germany have been doing fMRI scans of people's brains while they reacted to images of robots and, according to Dr Fabian Grabenhorst of the University of Cambridge, "We were surprised to see that the ventromedial prefrontal cortex responded to artificial agents precisely in the manner predicted by the uncanny valley hypothesis."

That's good enough for me. Instinctively, I thought the theory sounded true. In fact, the only thing that surprises me about this outcome is that Grabenhorst says they were surprised. Then again, we don't know that he was really surprised. I'd be surprised if they were surprised, but perhaps I shouldn't be surprised that they said they were surprised. It wasn't Grabenhorst's brain activity that was being scanned, so he could be faking his surprise to make the findings seem more interesting. Confirming what everyone is already convinced is true is probably an area of research that finds it hard to attract funding.

The uncanny valley has got me thinking about the Tory leadership contest and why it is that I hope Jeremy Hunt becomes the next prime minister. I mean, that's quite a thing. I can't say I ever envisaged hoping that, but I do hope it. I hope it, I hasten to add, merely because it's the only alternative to Boris Johnson becoming the next prime minister, but it absolutely is the only alternative to that, and hence I hope it. Genuinely. Put me in an fMRI scanner and you'll see. It's slightly put me off the whole idea of hope, to be honest. If this is the hope, God save me from the glory.

But why do I hope it? Is it because Jeremy Hunt is the marginally more moderate of the two candidates? I don't think so. They're both at pains to prove their extreme Brexiteer no-deal-embracing credentials with every utterance, now that the hardcore leavers dominating their party have decided that anything less than catastrophically crashing out of the EU is a betrayal of 52% of voters who requested an ordered withdrawal. They're desperate to be seen to respect what most of the 160,000 Tory members have decided that all 17 million leave voters really meant. Being more moderate in that frothing context profanes the very concept of moderation.

Is it because Jeremy Hunt is more honest? I'd say he is undoubtedly more honest than Boris Johnson. But if faint praise can be damning, that's faint enough to consign him to an eternity in the lowest circle of hell. It means virtually nothing. And, bearing in mind that what Boris Johnson says he's going to do if he wins is so nonsensical and destructive, the thought that he may be lying is relatively comforting.

Is it for sadistic reasons of my own? Partly, yes, I must admit. There's no doubt that, if Johnson were somehow to lose the leadership election from here, it would be a hilarious pratfall in public life that would dwarf his previous attempts to amuse. After all his careless, self-interested opportunism, the pain and embarrassment that he'd feel would be a balm to soothe me through the first disastrous months of the Hunt administration.

Still, I don't think that's the main reason. My hunch is that this election will cause Johnson pain either way. He won't be a good or happy prime minister because he doesn't really want to do anything except show off. He's pathologically dishonest and unfaithful, which is fine in show business, but it's going to screw up his premiership, which will make him very angry because, at heart, he doesn't believe anyone has the right to question his desires.

And look at the state of his life: professionally it's going OK, but personally, he's a middle-aged divorcé, living apart from all of his many children, shouting and spilling wine on the sofa in his girlfriend's south London flat. It conjures up images of his socks over the radiator and his tablets and foot powder jostling for bathroom shelf space with a young woman's cosmetics. It's a bit grim. So I reckon I'll get to watch him suffer either way.

Fundamentally, I think I hope Hunt wins because Johnson is in the uncanny valley. Hunt is the robot-like creature of politics. With no discernible charm or charisma, he's the typical forgettable figure by which Westminster has been dominated in recent decades: Andy Burnham, the Milibands, Nick Clegg, Jeremy Hunt. The plausible men in plausible suits; platitude-spouting mediocrities, not real people.

Johnson has always seemed different – more fun, more charming, more human. To many – to me, for a while – this was preferable, more like recognisable flesh and blood. But then at some point, perhaps when he was blathering on about painting cardboard buses, something changed. Like a twinkle of LED behind the automaton's human face, I glimpsed the icy contempt. The human warmth is fake, and its very similarity to the real thing is offensive and revolting.

On the 24 July 2019, Boris Johnson became prime minister.

9

Civilisation May Go Down As Well As Up

When the clocks went back, a joke was doing the rounds in various forms. They all went something like: "Don't forget to turn the clocks back this weekend. Unless you voted for Brexit, in which case you've already turned them back 30 years."

These obviously weren't pro-Brexit jokes. The notion of turning the clock back is not supposed to connote a return to the good old days or a restoration of youth; it signifies regression, progress reversed, a deliberate worsening. So an obvious implication is that their writers think, and think that most people think, that in general things get better over time.

Well, milk doesn't. And look at the natural world: things age and die and rot. Or grow and infest and destroy. And sometimes they germinate and bloom. They don't necessarily get worse, I'm not saying that; but they don't always improve either.

Technology confuses this, because that seems to be on a pretty steady upward graph, though it has its blips: in Europe, central heating had a chilly hiatus between the fourth and the 19th centuries. And this whole technological up-graph, from the discovery of fire onwards, may get retrospectively flipped into a huge down-blip in overall human fortunes if it transpires we were gradually making the planet uninhabitable. It's possible that everything any of us has done since we first started scrabbling around for flint has been a mistake.

You may sense from the last sentence that I'm in a bad mood. When I recently expressed disquiet on Twitter at Donald Trump's election victory, one respondent said: "You should have been afraid months ago, by now [you should be] slipping into misanthropic apathy." It seemed like an excellent suggestion.

I'd been hoping Hillary Clinton would win, as you probably were, unless my evaluation of my readership has descended to pollster levels of accuracy. Though, for me, it was mainly a hope that Donald Trump would lose. I didn't have strong feelings about his opponent. She seemed OK, but then people would darkly say things that began "Of course you realise . . .", the end of which I never properly heard, focused as I was on avoiding the social embarrassment of looking like I didn't realise whatever it was.

It's like when I'm introduced to people – I never catch their name because I'm so anxious not to screw up the handshake. "Just look like you realise, for God's sake!" my brain always hissed over the details. "Everyone else here seems to have realised. You're an educated person who realises all the complicated stuff that needs to be realised. You can Google it later."

I never Googled it later, which turns out to have been an efficient non-use of time. Nevertheless, I assembled a vague sense that Hillary wasn't all that, but at least she hadn't said that Mexicans are rapists. If there were terrible things about her, she had the grace to keep them secret rather than proclaim them from a podium. Which, under the circumstances, seemed to me a good enough reason to make her the most powerful person on Earth. Then I went back to watching Trump.

Trump is so watchable – that's surely something his supporters and detractors can agree on. It's not the hair, it's not the extremist rhetoric; it's the sheer magnetism of his self-satisfaction. The density of his self-joy is so great it drags your eyes towards it, like galactic debris to a black hole. When he puts on a statesmanlike face, you just know his inner monologue is delightedly singing, "My amazing face looks so statesmanlike right now!" This is what

Ed Miliband never grasped: it's not about being convincing, it's about relishing the role.

If politics were just a reality-TV show (rather than *mainly* a reality-TV show), Trump would never get voted out. So perhaps it's surprising that he polled fewer votes than Clinton – though not quite as surprising as the fact that he becomes president despite this.

Trump's win hit me in several ways. First, it denied me his defeat scene. I wanted to see that. His character seemed designed expressly for that sort of comeuppance, as surely as the diner redneck in *Superman II*. I was desperate to see him spun round on his bar stool, all scared. It really feels like a missed opportunity, for him as much as everyone else.

Second, it robbed me of a comforting certainty: he can't win – he's too awful. That's the sentiment I've been vacuously exchanging with people for months. "Surely he can't win," one of us says. "I know," says the other. I'll miss that, even though I now regret every time it happened. "It would be a disaster," was the consensus among me and other out-of-touch liberals, even more than over Brexit.

And third, I've started to look on the bright side, and it makes me despise myself. Because, frankly, "It would be a disaster" is much easier to live with than "It *will* be a disaster" or "This is a disaster". So I fail to follow through on my certainty. A mixture of apathy and fear-avoidance extorts a sickly optimism from my brain.

Maybe he didn't mean what he said; maybe the Republican party will restrain him; politicians never get much done anyway; maybe it'll all be fine. This either makes me an overdramatising hypocrite a few days ago or a reality-denying fool now. So I feel lazy, stupid and humiliated by the disturbance to my complacency, as if someone had burst in while I was eating a cream cake in the bath.

I am bewildered by everyone's conviction that anyone who disagrees with them has been misinformed. Another response to my worried tweet mentioned an article about Trump in the *New Yorker* that I'd linked to: "That's like reading about Obama on the KKK newsletter," they told me.

Is it? I really don't think it is. But they seemed so much surer that I'm wrong than I am that I'm right. I'm enough of a historian to understand the insecurity of the lines of communication between what I read has happened and what actually has, but not enough to know what to do. Should I go to that place in Kew?

Civilisations, like investments, can go down as well as up – that's never been clearer. Trump has routed the Whig interpretation of history, along with the metropolitan liberal elite. Things don't always get better over time. But I'm grateful to have lived through an era when it was still widely assumed that they did.

* * *

It's counter-terrorism awareness week again. It seems to come round quicker every year. It's not as upbeat as the US's coincident Thanksgiving celebrations, but fear is a trendier emotion than gratitude, so it all leaves the so-called "new world" looking rather last millennium compared to us. In fact, perhaps the week's timing is no coincidence after all? Perhaps the counter-terrorism agencies are using our former colonies as an example of what can happen if insurrection from within goes unchecked: "Be vigilant or someone will chuck all your tea in the sea!"

I wouldn't mind being aware of counter-terrorism for seven days a year if I could forget about it for the other 51 weeks. But I don't think that's the idea at all. I think we're supposed to be perpetually counter-terrorism aware, just like terrorists are. They're the shining exemplars of counter-terrorism awareness – they think about it all the time. "Emulate terrorist levels of counter-terrorism awareness!" is the message. "If you can be as constantly aware of security issues in a public place as you would be if you were plotting to blow it up, then you'll be a good citizen (provided you are not plotting to blow it up)."

But those weren't the slogans the counter-terrorism-week planners went for. Instead, in a police leaflet handed out at transport hubs advising what to do in a "firearms and weapons attack", they've gone with "Run. Hide. Tell." When the blast of war blows in your ears, then imitate the action of the rat.

This is sensible advice if there's an emergency. No one wants ordinary members of the public charging unto breaches without proper training. It could turn a terrorist atrocity into a health-and-safety nightmare, from which we wake to a litigation shitstorm for breakfast. So it's a reasonable thing to say.

It's also an unnecessary thing to say. If people hear gunfire and explosions in a railway station or airport, they don't need to be told to run away, take cover or tell someone about the issue. Anyone who can read a leaflet, and the vast majority of the illiterate, would do those things instinctively. It's like a poster telling people "Remember, if you let go of objects, they will fall to the ground!"

But the leaflet gives more detailed advice: "If you hear gunfire or a weapons attack, leave the area safely if you can. If this puts you in greater danger, find a safe place to take cover." This raises more questions than it answers. How can you tell whether it's safe to leave the area? How do you know when trying to flee would put you in greater danger than hiding? What sort of place would be safe to take cover in? You might say everyone would use their common sense. But the leaflet's target demographic appears to be people who don't have any.

There is nothing helpful about this document; it advocates doing what people would do anyway and provides no tips on how to do so more effectively. Campaigns like this usually make sense because the courses of action being promoted are counterintuitive – "grasp the nettle", "don't pour water on a fat fire", "steer into a skid". The sort of advice holidaymakers are given for encounters with bears, lions or snakes: whatever you do, don't run, but make yourself look big, or back away slowly, or shout, or charge towards it, or get someone to piss on the sting.

I can't actually remember the details of any such tips I've received because I try not to fill my life with anxious contemplation of the ways I could die. I don't believe perpetual nervous anxiety to be a price worth paying for marginally increasing my statistical chances of survival if disaster strikes. How many people, as they expire, think, "If only I'd worried more!"? The tiny handful who have observed the wrong etiquette with an enraged cobra perhaps, but those who succumb to cancer, heart disease or being hit by a falling piano (and between them those three scourges kill most westerners) probably resent the time wasted learning antishark karate.

Which brings me to what I hate most about the leaflet. As well as its inane running and hiding suggestions, it also says: "Make a plan now and stay safe." As in: make a plan for what to do if a terrorist sets off an explosion or goes mad with a gun while you're on your way to work. As in: think about that eventuality in advance. A lot. Starting now.

No thanks. That doesn't sound much fun. The chances of being killed, or nearly killed, in a terrorist outrage are really rather slight. I know home secretary Theresa May says that there could be one any minute – and that 40 have been foiled since 7/7. But even if we trust her – and I don't trust her – that number is definitely a maximum. She's got no incentive to underestimate, so no more than 40 will have been foiled. Even if they had all happened, and were all as bad as 7/7 and each killed 52 people, that's only 2,080 dead in seven years. A tragic state of affairs, no doubt, but it would still leave terrorist attack as a more unusual way to die than falling down stairs. In terms of death-avoidance strategies, I'll probably do myself more good keeping off the fags and trying to relax.

Some people may find it reassuring to plan for the worst – to fill a lock-up with fuel and tinned food, to work out how they'd kill and eat a cat, or burrow out of rubble, or treat radiation sickness, or swim through a tsunami of sewage – in anticipation of an anti-lottery win of bad fortune. Good luck to them. But I reckon they're in the minority and, for most of us, this leaflet's nebulous allusions to our potential demise are injurious to our mental wellbeing.

But this campaign isn't really about doing us any collective good. It's about an institution justifying and aggrandising its position. Those who are planning what they'd do in a firearms and weapons attack are not questioning police powers and funding, and are unlikely to oppose their increase. This superficially fatuous leaflet is, in truth, a political message: terror is lurking everywhere and only powerful, well-funded (and possibly armed) security services can protect you from it. The people behind this campaign are using fear to get what they want. I thought that was the kind of thing we didn't give in to.

* * *

In the run-up to the 2015 general election . . .

When I saw people predicting that George Osborne was planning a giveaway budget – that he was going to fritter away a few billion at the 11th hour to make people vote Tory – I found it rather sweet. It was familiar, you see – like the smell of Vicks. Not actually pleasant, but it brought back memories from my youth. Chancellors probably shouldn't frame last-minute vote-buying policies, but it's happened many times before and we're all still here, so I was comforted. It's a nice, fond old annoyance, like drizzle, litter and the grocer's apostrophe, rather than climate change, trolling and beheadings on YouTube.

Which isn't to say he necessarily *is* planning a giveaway budget. But that doesn't matter – his critics say he is. He will undoubtedly claim he isn't. "Oh yes he is!" the opposition will retort, and this pantomime works both before and after all the tedious details that actually make up a budget have been announced. It's like the Bible – you can infer pretty much whatever you want from something that long. Henry VIII found a bit in Leviticus that led him to conclude that, now his wife had gone all middle-aged and barren, it was probably a lot holier all round if he started fucking someone else.

The prospect of this traditional fiscal quarrel warmed my heart like the sight of British road signs after a holiday abroad. Like many people, I'm frightened by novelty and crave the familiar, particularly in these unsettling times (I'm over 40). I suppose this fearfulness is what drives some voters to Ukip, the rise of which makes me, in turn, more fearful. It's a chain reaction, in which fear of change changes people's behaviour, which engenders more change for people to fear. If you can make fear your business model, then get ready for a boom. (The good sort, partly caused by fear of the bad sort.) Good news if you've got shares in Kevlar or the *Daily Mail*.

I'm particularly susceptible to a reassuring, cynical budget giveaway at the moment because the atmosphere of British politics is changing so fast and so nastily. A fortnight ago, I was really shocked and depressed, not by a slasher film set in a hospice, but by Prime Minister David Cameron. He seemed to be announcing policies that made life harder for the weak (the fat, poor, young or drug-addicted) in an odd spirit of righteous joy.

It's getting worse. In the past few days, the Tories have been gleefully frothing with horrible new plans. On immigration, charities, universities and free speech, they're proudly making clear that their vision of government is about shutting people up, cutting people off and keeping people out.

As ever, Theresa May is in the vanguard, insisting that the government's spectacularly missed immigration target should be readopted after the election. This is clever. As home secretary, it was her responsibility to hit the target. But, by rejecting the suggestions of several senior colleagues to abandon it, she appears hardline and unwavering despite her own failure.

Arguing in favour of immigration control is easier than arguing in favour of immigration, because you get to tell persuasive anecdotes about depressed wages, Britons put out of work and pressure on public services. Whereas if you're trying to emphasise the benefits of immigration (eg on the economy), you're rather stuck with offering statistics – unless your audience likes hearing stories of improved living standards told in a Polish accent, which, the received wisdom seems to be, middle England doesn't. Free movement of people can be an incentive to commerce and self-betterment, and a vital component of free trade, but these macroeconomic factors provide scant comfort to a constituent who's irritated by the number of Bulgarians in her GP's waiting room.

Theresa May is also behind various assaults on universities. So underfunded that they're desperate to attract higher-fee-paying students from abroad, our seats of learning have become magnets for foreigners. This, May believes, must be clamped down on like a scrotum in Guantanamo Bay. As well as closing "bogus colleges" and "satellite campuses", she also insists overseas students should count towards the immigration figures. This means her unrealistic immigration target will continue to exert a huge downward pressure on an important national export: university education.

Freedom of speech is also taking a kicking. I used to think that issue was one of the Tories' saving graces: their commitment to the welfare state and redistributive taxation might have been suspect, but they seemed to believe in liberty. If you can, you let people do and say what they want – that seemed to be their sincere view. Well, that's gone out the window.

Charities that receive public funding, Eric Pickles has announced, will lose it if they use it to campaign against the government. That's potentially hugely restrictive as, in many cases, a charity only exists because of a failure of government. You could argue that the very existence of, say, a food bank is an implied criticism of the state.

Worst of all, the Home Office is planning to force universities to ban "hate preachers" from campuses – even "hate preachers" who don't advocate violence and who have committed no crime. The government absolutely hates hate preachers. It hates what they say but certainly won't defend to the death their right to say it. On the contrary, they are to be silenced. Preferably before they say anything hateful. Although I suppose they'd have to have said at least one hateful thing to justify the presumption that they were hate preachers. But maybe a hateful glance would be enough – a hard stare, a raised eyebrow, an undemocratic beard.

Quite how you define a "hate preacher", if they haven't broken one of the laws about incitement to violence or hatred that exist already, is unclear. But if we say it's someone who uses inflammatory rhetoric to turn different members of the community against one another, then the Oxford Union may run into trouble extending future invitations to David Cameron.

The Tory parts of the government are absolutely fizzing with spite. And this is all in the run-up to an election, let's not forget. These aren't the electorally unpalatable tough measures that ministers feel they have to push through for practical reasons, or a secret malevolent agenda sprung on us after a landslide victory. This is stuff they're proposing in order to win us round. It's as if the latest Lord Ashcroft poll has found that the British are 90% evil. If so, it's no wonder the Tories believe that hate preaching will convince.

* * *

Despite being an enthusiastic consumer of spy films and novels, I've never much fancied being an actual spy. Physical cowardice is part of the reason – I don't like the sound of all the piranha tanks, gunfights, torture by sleep deprivation or polonium-laced sushi (depending on genre) – but that's not the main deterrent. After all, popular culture makes it clear there are plenty of espionage jobs that don't involve anything more challenging than ducking under some police tape in a cashmere overcoat. That's the sort of spy I'd dream of being, if I dreamed of being a spy, which I'm surprised to find I don't. The suit-and-tie, office-with-a-rooftop-view, "How can we stop them realising we've realised that they've realised we realise?" kind.

Which isn't to say I don't want to be George Smiley: I absolutely do want to be George Smiley. I just don't want to be any of the people he's based on. I'd be thrilled to pretend to be a spy, with lots of people watching and applause at the end. What I'm not tempted by is the long career, wrestling with terrible secrets, mind-bending complications and soul-crushing compromises, while not being able to get credit when it went well, sympathy when it went horribly or a huge pile of money if I happened to be good at it.

Call me a showbiz wanker but, to me, that job sounds crap – though recruitment must have been enormously helped by the efforts the film, publishing and TV industries have made to glamorise it. The occasional poolside page-turner or pacey mini-series on the subject of social workers would probably do wonders for the prospects of thousands of drug-addicts' toddlers.

Not that anyone's taking on more welfare providers at the moment. Under our new prime minister, Theresa May, public spending is all about restraint – that is, the state's ability to restrain people. So it's security personnel they're recruiting, according to recent reports, with MI6 looking to hire nearly 1,000 new spies over the next four years, increasing its payroll by almost 40%. This is part of a widely circulated government plan to increase the staff of all three covert security agencies (MI5, MI6 and GCHQ) by a total of about 1,900.

This all has a very different vibe from the cold war, when Britain's secret services were still secret. Or officially secret anyway, which is not quite the same thing. But that's no longer politically viable. In this era of austerity, the public would be more offended by the notion that thousands of government employees were doing nothing than that they were, say, invading the privacy of millions, testing the limits of international law and abetting our allies in systematically committing war crimes. "I don't mind if they're organising rendition flights, as long as they're not just sitting on their arses!"

Since 1986, when the existence of a secret intelligence service was first grudgingly acknowledged, all three institutions have been flirting with the limelight. As the Soviet Union collapsed, they all shyly took a bow and, at some point between the publications of *Spycatcher* and Stella Rimington's autobiography, possibly when the location manager for a Bond film first rang up to inquire about filming outside MI6, they abandoned the shadows for ever.

In some ways, this process was quite fun – almost like a revelation that wizards or dragons really existed. "So there *are* spies, after all! And they do hang out in huge central London buildings, trying to steal secrets from each other. How magical!"

But there's something rum about this openness. To start with, it's not meaningful openness. We know who the heads of these organisations are: we know, for example, that MI6's current "C" is really called Alex Younger, thus reducing the code name to the same trivial ceremonial level as Black Rod and the Stig. But we don't know what they're actually doing.

The openness about their existence and leadership, but not about the activities of their thousands of staff, is rather rubbing the public's nose in the fact that there are things we are forbidden to know, and forbidden to know about people whose salaries we pay. In contrast, the previous policy of keeping the organisations as well as their activities secret shows a certain delicacy, even a fitting shame that such a recourse should be necessary in an ostensibly free country.

This shame is understandable in the context of the cold war, when the Soviet bloc countries, over which the west, with considerable justification, asserted its moral superiority, kept so much secret from their own peoples. In the free world, secrecy smacked of tyranny. It alarmed people, so, ironically, the scale of it was best kept under wraps.

Nowadays, however, our security services *want* us to be alarmed. They want it because it will make us feel we need them, and this is the bigger problem with the current openness. The Soviet Union gave spies an indisputable *raison d'être*. Since its fall, they've felt the need to justify their existence. Obviously, before you can justify your existence, you have to admit it – but that was just the first step. The government proudly letting it be known, at a time of considerable national austerity, that thousands more security officers are to be employed shows how successful that self-justification has been.

The language of it is familiar. We hear of "security threats", "foiled attacks", of the prime minister "chairing an emergency Cobra meeting". At airports we see policemen with guns, while seemingly random prohibitions from our hand luggage are clues from which we attempt to work out the nature of the latest maniacal assault on our way of life. Maybe this time it was something with liquids *and* shoes? A belt shampoo bomb? A mace made out of plastic cutlery embedded in a Frederick Forsyth novel?

I'm not saying this fear of terrorism is unjustified, and I'm not saying it's justified. I'm saying we don't know, and that it's unwise to leave unquestioned the estimation of the problem provided by the people we're paying to solve it.

The widely reported terrorist threat, the stories of "near misses" and "heightened terror alerts" and the announcement of more investment to "keep us safe" create, from the security services' point of view, a virtuous circle of increasing funding. Modern espionage is about what they're seen to do, when it used to be the opposite. It's become my sort of job after all.

* * *

In an otherwise unremarkable article about how a British Airways passenger, barred from the plane's lavatory, had wet herself, I noticed something that chilled me to the bone – even more than sitting in my own urine throughout a transatlantic flight would have done. The airline, it mentioned in passing, while report-ing how some schoolchildren said they'd been refused water (BA seems to be operating a none-in/none-out policy when it comes to fluids), doesn't accept cash for in-flight purchases.

This is a deeply sinister development, made more so by the fact that it hardly seems to have been noticed. "Why's it sinister?" you may be asking. "I'm sure there are sound practical reasons – no one wants airliners struggling through the sky weighed down by thousands of 50ps. And who doesn't have a credit or debit card these days?"

Not many, I admit – just a few parched schoolkids. But cash is money in its most basic form. The airline is effectively saying it doesn't accept or recognise money any more. Coins and notes with the Queen's head on them, endorsed by a sovereign state, are no longer sufficient. It needs to know who we are; it needs to take its payment by tapping into each individual's credit source. The electronic endorsement of a bank, an organisation accountable to no one but its owners, is required.

This isn't primarily BA's fault. I'm sure all big banks and retail-ers want to try it. No dirty cash pushing up insurance and security costs, everything nicely kept track of – where the money came from and where it went. All that data building up so that, as and when the law allows, it can be ruthlessly exploited for marketing purposes.

It's great from the state's point of view too. If anyone it considers dodgy is spending money, it has only to contact the bank and the access to credit can be turned off like a life-support patient's drip. The slow insinuation of the futuristic-sounding concept of a "cashless society", conjuring up the wholesome Californian feel of the "paperless office", is primarily in the interests of large and powerful organisations. One might almost suspect it was no accident the new fiver had animal fat in it. Expect the next £20 to be gummed together with GM crops and foie gras, with a picture of Jimmy Savile on the back.

This may sound paranoid – credit cards are convenient and most people have nothing to hide. Why does it matter if all our payments are traceable? Just because someone is constantly following you around at a slight distance, it doesn't mean they're going to do you harm. But I imagine those who are constantly tailed really value a few hours' break from it now and again. And, if asking for such a break, they'd probably be irritated if the response was: "Why? Looking for the chance to stare at some kiddie porn and plan an act of terrorism, are you?!"

The anonymity of cash has been an integral part of our economy and society for millennia. Getting rid of that is quite a step. Are we definitely going to get properly consulted on it? The government is already introducing an initiative called Making Tax Digital, which will give it unprecedented access to millions of taxpayers' financial information. Who, in the current climate, is going to champion the cause of ordinary people retaining the right to buy stuff anonymously?

The internet makes all of these issues even more fraught. By the accounts of the print media and security services, the virtual world is an amoral anarchy in which super-villain can talk to super-villain and swivel-eyed loners are groomed by terrorist organisations and provided with easy-to-follow atrocity tips. On the other hand, it also has the potential to allow fully cyber-militarised governments to monitor almost all of their citizens' activities and interactions. Sounds lovely either way.

Last week, Sir Tim Berners-Lee, one of this hell-in-the-ether's most well-meaning architects, sharply criticised the British and US governments' moves to undermine privacy and net neutrality, saying the "human right . . . to communicate with people on the web, to go to websites I want without being spied on is really, really crucial".

The home secretary, Amber Rudd, takes a different view: "We need to make sure that organisations like WhatsApp, and there are plenty of others like that, don't provide a secret place for terrorists to communicate with each other."

Seems reasonable. Except, if there's no secrecy for terrorists, there's no secrecy, or privacy, for anyone. Is that a price worth paying to fight Isis? Or is that surrendering our way of life, famously meaning that "they've won"?

But perhaps Isis and the security services can both win. In the first Metropolitan police statement after the Westminster attack, they portentously said they were treating it as a terrorist incident, thus darkly alluding to the Oxford second VIII's nefarious namesake. And it wasn't long before that organisation claimed responsibility, though it didn't seem to know the attacker's name or anything else about the event that it couldn't have got off the TV news.

It struck me then that, on some level, both the Home Office and Isis wanted it to be Isis. They'd found common ground. Neither side wanted it to be a random nutter who'd hired a car – you don't strike fear into the infidel that way, and neither will it make the public acquiesce to greater surveillance powers. The same horrible, murderous event has occurred either way but, if it's Isis, more people get something from it – including the media, which are justified in much more sensationalist rhetoric than if twice the number of people had been mown down by a non-radicalised driver drunkenly fiddling with his satnav.

To the elements of western governments seeking to increase their control over citizens' lives, Isis has provided a wonderful opportunity. It's just so absurdly evil and unsympathetic. This isn't like the communist bloc, which, for all its totalitarian excesses, had a humane underlying philosophy. These guys actually make videos of themselves chopping people's heads off. So, if presented with a choice between Isis and the Tories, or even Trump, or even Ukip, we're all going to plump for the latter.

But it's a false dichotomy. That's not the choice. It would not be safe to give Isis the power of almost infinite surveillance over everything we say or do online, who we talk to, what we like and every penny we spend. But Isis isn't demanding that. The only issue is whether it's safe to give it to those who are.

* * *

What is the advantage of letting sitting MPs work for lobbying firms? What are the pluses of that for the country? Because we do allow it, so I'm assuming there must be some upside.

After all, there are clear advantages to many things we *don't* allow: smoking on petrol station forecourts, for example. Allowing that would mean, if you're addicted to smoking, or enjoy smoking, or think smoking makes you look cool, you could do it while filling your car with petrol, polishing its bonnet, going to buy snacks, checking the tyres and so on. You wouldn't be inconvenienced by either the discomfort of nicotine withdrawal or a hiatus in the image of nonchalant suavity that having a fag in your mouth invariably projects.

And the same goes for those essaying auras of Churchillian defiance and grit or Hannibal from *The A-Team*-style twinkly maverick leadership, for which a lit cigar clamped between the teeth can be vital, particularly if you've got a weak chin.

Similarly, if you're a pipe-smoking detective of the Sherlock

Holmes mould and are, perhaps, investigating a crime on a petrol station forecourt, or merely passing across one while contemplating the intricacies of a non-forecourt-related mystery, you wouldn't have to suffer a lapse in the heightened analytical brain function that you've found smoking a pipe crucial to attaining. Interrupting such processes to buy petrol may cause murderers to walk free.

And then there's the possibility that allowing smoking at petrol stations will marginally increase overall consumption, and therefore sales, of tobacco products – all the Holmeses and Churchills and Bonds will be able to get a few more smokes in before they die of cancer – which would slightly improve trade and GDP, and so create jobs.

Nevertheless, I am not, on balance, in favour of allowing smoking on petrol station forecourts. The manifold advantages are, in my view, outweighed by the several disadvantages: passive smoking for non-smoking users of the forecourt, nicotine-staining of the underside of the canopy, and various others I can't currently bring to mind.

But you'd think, in a system that flattered itself as non-mad, as I believe the British one still does, practices that are legal would be bristling with more boons for the community than those that aren't. That's got to be the vague rule of thumb, right? So, then, what are the good things about allowing sitting MPs to take paid work from lobbying firms? What are the upsides to that?

The downsides are as hard to miss as a few hundred thousand litres of subterranean petrol suddenly exploding. Let's take an example from the news. It was recently reported that James Duddridge, a Tory MP who was minister for Africa from 2014 to 2016, is being paid £3,300 for eight hours work a month by a lobbying company called Brand Communications. It's one of the few lobbying companies not to have signed up to the industry's code of conduct, which prohibits the employment of sitting MPs. You may say that makes it a nasty firm, but I don't blame it. Why would it sign up to extra rules if it doesn't have to? That's like volunteering to observe a lower speed limit than the one prescribed by law.

The law is absolutely fine with Duddridge's little earner. Former ministers' jobs just have to be approved by the Advisory Committee on Business Appointments, itself described by the Commons Public Administration and Constitutional Affairs Committee as a "toothless regulator" (these committees are so bitchy!), since it has no statutory powers of redress. Then again, as its rulings are almost invariably "That's fine", what powers does it really need?

Duddridge himself says it's all legit because Brand Communications is "not a public affairs company", but the company's website says "James will bring his deep knowledge of Africa, experience of operating at the highest levels of government and extensive networks to Brand Communications", which sounds a bit public affairsy to me.

But I don't know. Maybe it's fine. We can't know it's definitely not fine. Admittedly, according to *The Times*, the head of one of Britain's leading lobbying firms called it "an appalling example of bad practice", and the chairman of the Association of Professional Political Consultants said, "MPs should not be lobbyists. It is wrong to be a lobbyist and make the law at the same time," but maybe it's still fine.

Maybe James just pops in once a month and is incredibly helpful in ways that don't conflict with his public duties. Maybe he's full of creative ideas, a huge boost to office morale and a master of clearing photocopier jams. And then he pops back to parliament and doesn't think about Brand Communications until the next month, no matter what issues concerning their interests cross his desk as an MP and member of the Commons International Development Committee. Yes, maybe it's fine.

Is that the main plus of letting sitting MPs work for lobbying firms: in any given instance, it might be fine? Because most people have got some sort of conscience, haven't they? So fingers crossed!

Another advantage is that it allows MPs to earn extra money, which is nice for them and reduces pressure on the taxpayer to give them more. If we prohibited them from lobbying work and "non-executive directorships" without also increasing their salaries, the job of MP would become even less attractive than it already is, which would inevitably exert downward pressure on the calibre of applicants. A sobering thought. We're in enough trouble as it is – I'm not sure the country could survive our politicians getting any shitter.

So those are the advantages. And the disadvantage is that, as a nation, we could be outbid for the loyalty of every single one of our legislators. I think it's time to extinguish our cigarettes in the nearest sand bucket.

We can't know exactly how much MPs' availability for lobbying work costs the country, financially and morally. But anyone can see that many laws favour powerful interest groups rather than ordinary people, so we can guess it's a lot. Potentially, it runs to billions and our souls. But if we banned MPs from working for anyone else at all and – let's go crazy – *doubled* their salaries, we know pretty precisely what that would cost: it would be £49m a year. That's a lot of money, in a sense. In another sense, it's 1.4p a week each.

So we have an answer: the advantage of letting MPs work for lobbying firms is an extra penny a week each. Just a smidge over. We're even cheaper than they are.

* * *

The 2017 Conservative party conference did not go well for the prime minister . . .

The aspect of Theresa May's calamitous conference speech that worried me most was the letters falling off the wall. For most viewers, that was just the amusing punchline to the sketch. The main bits were the comedian with the spoof P45, the coughing, the water, the throat sweet from Philip Hammond, the throat-sweet joke from Theresa May and, of course, Amber Rudd bullying Boris Johnson into helping her elicit a standing ovation to buy time for their leader to hawk something meaningful up in the hope of restoring medium-term vocal competence.

Summarised like that, it sounds like a brilliantly entertaining speech. But one must remember that these titbits of non-tedium were spread out over an entire hour. It's a gag rate that even the least sparky series of *Last of the Summer Wine* never stooped to. Which is why, even though I am writing an article all about the speech, I have not watched it. I absolutely refuse to watch it. Nothing on Earth is worth that.

For me, it was all about the letters. Everything else is excusable. It's certainly not the first time a prankster with a prepared joke has disturbed the mood of such an occasion. I imagine Simon Brodkin was rather hoping he'd be the main, if not the only, disruption to the speech. So, in a way, it was wise of May to cough her guts up to draw attention away from him. If she could have managed a full Hugh Bonneville in *Downton Abbey*-style blood puke, Brodkin would probably have been completely forgotten.

She's got a nasty cold – that doesn't make her a bad prime minister. Obviously, she *is* a bad prime minister, but not because she's got a cold. Some would argue the cold makes her a worse prime minister – and, as giving speeches without croaking and phlegming is part of the job, it's a persuasive point. Personally, though, I think the cold, by inhibiting how effectively she can put her ideas into practice, will have marginally improved her performance in the post. If she lost her voice completely, she might rise to the dizzy heights of only as crap as Eden.

The issue is moot anyway, because she will almost certainly recover from the cold. It's not going to kill her, is it? Though, if it does, I think I'd still rather see her rotting remains propped against the dispatch box until the next election than let Boris Johnson form a government. But recovery is almost certain.

I suppose, if you press me, there's a tiny chance she neither recovers nor dies. She could become like one of those children you hear about who've been sneezing solidly for years in defiance of global specialists. Theresa could become a late-middle-aged version of that, with coughing and spluttering thrown in – someone just unstoppably sneezing and hacking and croaking and spitting for decades and decades. I think I'm getting a sense of what it felt like to watch the whole speech.

If that does happen, I think the country can use it. Keep her in office, in Downing Street, but knock down the front wall and replace it with a glass screen and let tourists go and watch. For practical reasons, she'd only really be the titular head of the government, but I think, for Britain going forward, the freak-show element is something we can exploit. Particularly once all that PC nonsense from Brussels has been swept aside. We'll be free to reopen the viewing gallery at Bedlam, shove all the animals from London Zoo back into their Tower of London dungeon, from which the bleeding-heart liberal elite unaccountably released them in 1831, and decriminalise pickpocketing and child prostitution.

The whole of London could become a dark, Dickensian theme park, like something Scrooge would dream after a trip to Disneyland and a whole Brie. Lawless, colourful and festive. An impenetrable smog-filled labyrinth of unaffordable street food and random acid attacks. Weave your way via unlicensed minicab between the diesel particulate-smeared glass head offices of accountancy firms and blocks of flats evacuated because of fire-safety concerns. The haunting sight of Theresa May pacing the cabinet room, features ravaged by the effort of constant expectoration, desperately trying to say something audible about council houses, energy suppliers or not giving up, while Japanese tourists tempt her with Strepsils, would fit perfectly into this grisly aesthetic. As a nation, we could really double down on decline.

Sorry for the emphasis on decline, but those letters falling off really got to me. How did that happen? The specific practical answer we were given was that the magnets holding them up were loosened by the audience's repeated standing up, sitting down and clapping. It's an answer that raises more questions: were they not expecting lots of standing up, sitting down and clapping? Perhaps there was slightly more than average because of the need to give the PM extra coughing time, but there was always a chance that there'd be ovations because the speech was really good. Was that a possibility the organisers had ruled out?

And why were they held on by magnets? Is that how signs are usually made? Are the "M" and "S" on an M&S held up by magnets in case they need to be quickly reversed should the company decide on an overnight kinky rebrand? Why not print the letters on the backdrop? The slogan in question – "Building a country that works for everyone" – is so banal as to insult the intelligence of everyone who sees it but, if it's about anything, it's about solidity and competence. Keeping the letters loose, in case of a last-minute central office command to anagrammatise it, is the wrong risk to take.

Others blamed the fact (which was news to most of us) that the Conservatives took their events management back in-house two years ago to cut costs. That's quite the metaphor for Brexit. They stopped sending money away to outsiders, took control themselves, and everything fell to bits.

This was an extremely easy cock-up to avoid and, from some very important people's point of view, it was very important to avoid it. So the fact that it happened anyway makes me queasy. This bad sign is an incredibly bad sign – about the Tories and possibly the whole country. Led by Theresa May, we're turning into a place where the absurd and lamentable are commonplace. What an inauspicious moment in our history to become risible.

* * *

People don't want to be rich any more. It's a world turned upside down. Genies are having to completely rethink their planning strategies in anticipation of an era of altruistic lamp-rubbers. Suddenly they've got to find a way to make wishing for world peace turn round and bite you on the arse.

"I'm thinking maybe an all-life-destroying pestilence, so that the 'world peace' is the silence that follows the death of every living thing," a genie who refused to be named told me. "But I'm just talking off the top of my turban."

"It's actually a fez."

"Sorry – I haven't looked in a mirror for two millennia. Genies can't see their own reflection."

"That's vampires."

After that, the interview turned a bit sour and he refused to be drawn on whether Donald Trump has got any wishes left. "It's genie–client confidentiality. But I will say I've been reading a hell of a lot of books about golf."

What I actually mean is that people don't want to be *called* rich. They still want the trappings of wealth, I imagine. Big houses, big baths, big dinners, legroom, gold, a willingness to use the sort of cash machine that charges you £1.50. Everyone wants all that. They just don't want it to be known that they're getting any of it, if indeed they are – or for the amount of it they're getting to qualify them for that unfortunate section of society, the fortunate.

This notion that there's something unlucky about being called lucky occurred to me in the wake of John McDonnell's controversial definition of the rich as those earning "above £70,000 to £80,000 a year". A lot of people objected to that, and even more objected to those objections. The first group pointed out that £70k a year is far from unimaginable wealth, PIYLIL (particularly if you live in London). So, if your image of a rich person is someone in a gold hat lighting a cigar with a £50 note, then the adjective is unfairly applied to a demographic of dutiful mortgage-paying graduates who occasionally go to Carluccio's.

These complainants' detractors, pausing only to mime playing the world's smallest violin, countered with the undeniable statistical fact that earning £70k puts you in the richest 6% of the British workforce, and the richest 0.09% of the global population. In this row, comparatives and superlatives are oddly less controversial than the terms from which they're derived. Richest doesn't necessarily mean rich, any more than poorest means poor. Tony Blair must have been the poorest man at many plutocratic dinners he's attended around the world, but that doesn't mean he needs to argue over who ordered extra chips.

It's easy to define who's richer than whom, but at what point do you become actually rich? Are you rich if you're richer than average? If so, the £70k bunch might qualify as "very rich". Are you tall if you're taller than average? Possibly. I reckon many who are only marginally taller than the mean would consent to the adjective "tall" (which is not to imply that mean people are short). But then a lot of us want to be considered tall, while we don't seem to want to be considered rich.

Maybe it's always been like that. Wealth generates hostility, so there's nothing to be gained from drawing attention to it. "Get it quietly," as they say in poker. But I don't think that's the whole story. What happened to "greed is good", to conspicuous consumption, to Labour grandees being "intensely relaxed about people getting filthy rich", to the whole Thatcherite dream of the promise of wealth driving ambition, invention and hard work, to Britain's entrepreneurs being lured forward in slavering pursuit of commerce's golden bra, and the whole of society benefiting from any consequent trickle down?

I'm not saying I miss all that bombast, but there was something coherent about it. It was a bold rebuke to the Communist bloc, an explicit elevation of liberty over equality. In a free society, the idea goes, people must be able to improve their circumstances, they must be offered the potential reward of riches. Which unfortunately means you have to have rich and poor. But rich and poor beats poor and poor and, in a land of capitalist opportunity, at least the poor have hope.

In that world, there's no shame in being called rich. Many would be proud of it and, as with tallness, lay claim to it when it's only marginally justified. In the society Thatcher was supposed to have ushered in, "rich" and "successful" would be synonyms, and the phrase "well-deserved success" a tautology.

That's why last week's scuffle to pin on others, or tear off oneself, the label "rich" is interesting. It's become a term of abuse, like "aristocrat" in the French Revolution. Far from assuming the rich deserve their wealth, we're now assuming the contrary. The rich are the bad guys – so, being called rich, whether or not you are, is to be called bad. "Society's all wrong, and you're why!" is what it means. This is unfair because it's a generalisation. But that doesn't make it an unfair generalisation.

I suspect very few people feel rich, either in the neutral sense of having lots of money or the contemporary one of being a profiteer of injustice. All of us, except Bill Gates on the one hand and some poor sod whose name posterity will never record, and who'll be dead by the time you read this, on the other, are aware of people richer and people poorer than we are. So, subjectively, we're all the squeezed middle. And, in these unnerving times, even if you know you're loaded, you probably still won't feel particularly safe or lucky. Hardly any of us think we're part of the problem, which is part of the problem.

For Thatcher's divisive concept to work even on its own terms, it required Britain to continue to become more meritocratic. Not fairer necessarily – because there's nothing inherently fair about the distribution of merit – but a country where success is based on what you do, not the circumstances you were born in. If you're holding a rat race, the prize must go to the fastest rat.

No ideological alternative has really caught on enough to sweep aside Thatcher's vision of Britain, but the fact that high earnings are now a source of social shame demonstrates how tawdry and discredited it has become. Let's bear that in mind as our current prime minister exhorts us to vote for it again.

* * *

When I read that a group of Eton schoolboys had organised their own trip to meet President Putin and exchange portentous remarks in a big, posh Russian room, I could sense an expression crossing my face that I'm glad no one had to see. It must have been a kind of frowning, closed-eyed, open-mouthed, nauseated sneer.

I could feel my jowls attempt to detach themselves from my head. My nostrils seemed to be trying to put some distance between one another, while my eyebrows were huddling together for comfort. Of the words that escaped the weird-shaped hole my mouth had become, "oh" and "those" were the only ones you'd hear on Radio 4, unless Jeremy Hunt was about to be interviewed.

I did not rejoice in the young people's adventure. The pictures of them smartly greeting Russia's puffy little tyrant and lounging across the floor of an anteroom making wacky hand gestures didn't make me think, "Good on them!" Instead, I was filled with loathing, which isn't very nice of me because they're basically children and they haven't really done any harm.

That's not to say they did any good. Putin will feel his regime came out of it well. One of the boys was reportedly quoted in a pro-Putin newspaper (how accurately, we can't know) saying: "Personally, I think that Putin is right to continue defending Assad in his role as president." Meanwhile, on Facebook, Trenton

Bricken, a member of the group, described Russia's leader as "small in person but not in presence", and David Wei, who seems to have been the jaunt's chief organiser, wrote: "Guys, we truly gave Putin a deep impression of us and he responded by showing us his human face." So rumours the president carries the severed face of a rival are true, then.

They obviously think he's great. But that's hardly surprising: they're teenagers and he's the president of Russia, and he was nice to them. They're not in the business of speaking truth to power, but of getting amazing selfies. I'd be the same at their age – I'd probably be the same now. I refuse to think more of them for all this, but I'm going to really try not to think less, particularly as public schoolboys are endlessly encouraged to show this sort of vacuous initiative.

Which is why Eton College's response is suspect. "This was a private visit by a small group of boys organised entirely at their own initiative and independently of the college," it said. I'm not saying that's a lie – I'm sure the school didn't set up the trip – but Eton has a tradition of encouraging pupils to organise societies and events, and this must be exactly the kind of stunt it dreams of its charges getting up to.

"Wow! They met the PRESIDENT OF RUSSIA?! How the hell did they do that?!" would be a more natural response. Instead, the college's line is so dry and dignified as to be a parody of dry dignity. "We can't be expected to keep track of *every single time* our boys meet up with the leader of a superpower," is the tone, and it's disingenuous. It's all a bit "Fog in channel, continent isolated." Stiff-upper-lipped establishment reserve masking feverish excitement at its own coolness.

And it suits Eton very well for people to think that this trip is the kind of dynamic thing that Etonians just do. It subtly reinforces the notion that Eton's pupils are made of more enterprising stuff than normal schoolchildren; that there's something special about them apart from their parents' money and connections, and their own consequent sense of entitlement. The college couldn't possibly assert this view openly – it would be met with ridicule and offence in equal measure – but its over-understated response to the boys' headline-grabbing antics is a clear invitation for us to infer it.

I used to like Eton. As a pupil at a minor public school, I admired it as the independent sector's market leader. I didn't think private education was evil – I still don't – and Eton's continued prominence felt picturesque and reassuring.

Then suddenly, a couple of years ago, I noticed my feelings had changed. My wife and I were driving through the town of Eton, just sightseeing – we'd spent the morning wandering round Windsor – and, as I looked at the beautiful buildings, the inextricability of town and school, the royal castle in the background, the heady mixture of history, wealth and confidence, my face started imitating the gargoyles.

As my sneer of envy, disdain and rage subsided, I realised there'd been a much more significant alteration in my outlook than losing my taste for one public school. It had crept up on me over the previous decade. It struck me that, when I was growing up, when I looked fondly on institutions like Eton, it was on the basis that they were ultimately doomed. They were relics of a more spacious age, an aesthetically attractive one, also an unjust one, but crucially one that was over. For better or worse, and largely for better, history was leaving them behind.

I was brought up with the general post-war assumption that Britain was getting fairer. It was taken for granted – by parents and teachers alike. There might be a nuclear war, oil might run out but, failing that, moral progress was assured. In the old days, the elderly didn't have pensions, now they did; women didn't have careers, now they did; poor people didn't have access to healthcare, now they did; etc, etc, etc. Change might be happening too slowly, but it was happening inexorably and exclusively in the right direction.

I didn't notice the moment when I lost that assumption – it was probably between the Iraq war and the credit crunch – but when we were driving through Eton, it hit me hard. I remembered the complacent feeling of advancing justice with which I'd once looked fondly on the crumbling beauty of institutions like Eton, and I felt tricked.

The British are a nostalgic people: we love costume drama, ancient buildings, stories of kings, tradition. But I realised in Eton that there was a context for these fond backward glances, and that context was progress. Progress towards a fairer society.

Who still believes that fairness is advancing? Britain's period of greatest social justice is probably already over. The sun isn't setting on the lichen-pocked crenellations of Eton, but on the NHS and the BBC. And they won't be remembered in a spirit of bittersweet, misty-eyed nostalgia, but with straightforward grief.

* * *

Birds are probably screwed anyway. Their numbers are falling, their habitats being destroyed. I hope that comes as some comfort to any builders annoyed that it's illegal to cut down trees containing active nests: you can console yourselves with the thought that, in the long term, those flappy little shits have had it.

So, as you resentfully eye up some apparently cosy blackbird that is delaying construction of luxury flats for months and months, causing costs to spiral and profits to dwindle, don't project too much smugness on to the poor thing. Don't think of it like it's Sir Philip Green straddling a branch in the nude, biting into a chicken leg Henry VIII-style and laughing. In reality, it's going through hell. And blackbirds don't eat chicken anyway. Though they are nude – but it somehow seems different because of the feathers. The Windmill theatre probably tried that one on the lord chamberlain.

But what I'm saying is that, annoying though all those obstructive, squeaking egg baskets may be, and challenging though the commercial conditions in which you're operating undoubtedly are, the birds are much more definitely doomed than you. If they're your adversary, you've won. Take that, garden birds! That'll teach them not to contribute to the GDP, apart from via, I don't know, binocular sales and RSPB membership and the odd sack of seed. They're commercially unviable and they're getting out-tweeted by social media.

My awareness that some builders find birds' nesting habits frustrating has risen because of the news that developers in Guildford have been ordered to remove netting from 11 trees on the banks of the River Wey. Apparently, it is not uncommon, during nesting season, for builders to put nets around any trees they might want to chop down to prevent any avian construction from delaying their own. How mean! Just imagine a plucky little sparrow turning up hopefully with a twig.

Obviously, I appreciate that the fact this is mean is absolutely no reason not to do it. It's important to do mean things a lot of the time – that's life, commerce, war, the wild, etc. Birds are mean to worms, and it does wonders for their punctuality. It's a cruel world. I totally get it, and I'm part of it. I've literally just eaten a sausage sandwich and, albeit only as a passenger, I've been an unflinching apologist for some pretty aggressive parking over the years. So, you know, go for it, "Timber!", you've got to build bypasses and so forth.

What made the Guildford case a bit different was that construction wasn't planned to take place on the site until after nesting season – December probably – and, according to the leader of the borough council, the developer, Sladen Estates, doesn't even yet have "active planning permission". So it seemed a bit *too* mean, and one thing led to another, the author Sir Philip Pullman got wind of it online, and now the netting has been removed.

Do try, though, Sladen Estates, not to blame the birds or imagine a naked Sir Philip Green doing a poo on your car and make that a reason to hate chaffinches. It's mainly Sir Philip Pullman's fault – a very different Sir Philip altogether. It's confusing, and I regret bringing Sir Philip Green into it, though it would certainly help matters if he had his knighthood removed, and possibly his Philip as well, just as a precaution, so that everything's clear.

To be fair, Nick Sladen, chief executive of Sladen Estates, seems pretty sanguine. He denied that the nets' removal was prompted by public pressure, claiming it was just because the construction schedule had changed, and said that netting trees was "a positive ecological thing – the alternatives are the development carries on and the nests are disturbed or development is delayed".

I'm not sure why that makes it "a positive ecological thing". The first alternative he suggests to netting is certainly less ecological, but also less legal. The only lawful alternative he gives – delaying construction until the nests have been vacated – is surely a much more "positive ecological" option than forcing birds elsewhere with nets. So it seems quite a stupid thing to say. Of course, he may simply be trying to deceive people.

It's lazy, sly behaviour: let's stick nets over all the trees so that, the moment we've got permission, we can chop them down, safe in the knowledge that there'll be nothing alive in them. It's like people who register patents for theoretical computing innovations that haven't actually been invented, on the off-chance that, one day, someone will – and will then be forced to pay to license their own idea. It's low, parasitic commerce – the business equivalent of goal-hanging.

The news that Severn Trent water is trialling the use of Uber drivers instead of engineers when someone reports a leak feels similarly seedy. "All we're asking them to do," explained a spokesman, "is hold a phone up and respond to the engineer as he makes an assessment."

This idea has the obvious flaw that a minicab driver isn't going to be any better at video-phoning a leak than the customer who reported it in the first place, rendering this whole taxi stage of the leak-triage process completely superfluous. And, frankly, if your solution to the problem of maintaining a vast water supply infrastructure is to send taxi drivers round making videos on their phones, then you should go back and check your working – because that solution doesn't make any sense outside the context of the single line in the budget you're trying to cut.

This is the wrong use of the human brain's innovative powers, more like planning a murder than devising a recipe. It's the product of someone looking to take shortcuts, find loopholes, game the system.

Well, the system can't cope. Our society isn't resilient enough to function if people focus only on the tiny problem in front of them: how to reduce leak-repair costs, how to get those trees chopped down, how to force the deal through the Commons. Our laws and leadership are too feeble to protect it, let alone make it better. We need to lift our heads. The birds are dying.

POST-SCRIPT

The use of Sod's Law as a force for positive change.

That last bit, I'm aware, was a bit of a downer. Quite depressing. And all that depressing talk, you may be thinking, is a bit rich coming from . . . well, someone a bit rich. An affluent, fortunate person. You didn't open a TV comedian's book for that kind of chat. This isn't supposed to be harrowing.

After all, there are shelves and shelves of harrowing books you could have chosen, written by people who've seen harrowing things or had harrowing things done to them. Some readers love all that. It's a huge publishing genre, but one which, as someone who's selected this book, you have studiously avoided. So I have no right to suddenly come over all harrowing, as someone who's got a mortgage and had all his childhood jabs.

So, apologies. I've checked my privilege, and it's cheered me up no end. And, obviously, I might be wrong about society's inexorable decline. I'm just an ant floating on a leaf saying we're about to go over a waterfall. For all I know, we might be about to fetch up at an abandoned picnic, a sort of *Marie Celeste* chequered rug covered in leftover lemon drizzle cake. (That's what I imagine ants would like.)

Here's my excuse: as someone who isn't sure whether there's a God or not, I'm in search of solace. I haven't rejected the idea, but I can't be sure. But there is something I do believe in: Sod's Law. There is clear evidence of Sod's Law in my life that could only be refuted if physicists proved that kitchen floors and the butter-side of toast possessed a mutually attractive magnetism. Until that day dawns, I will believe in Sod's Law.

So think of the conclusion to this book as my attempt to harness Sod's Law in defence of civilisation and progress. This is how my thinking goes: if I publish a big book saying that Britain is just going to get worse and worse, then I bet it won't. I bet it'll suddenly improve. It's bound to. That would be typical. That's Sod's Law.

ACKNOWLEDGMENTS

I would like to thank:

Rowan Cope, Laura Hassan, Alex Bowler, John Grindrod, Lauren Nicoll, Paul Baillie-Lane and Stephen Page at Faber & Faber.

Ursula Kenny and Jane Ferguson at the *Observer*.

My agents Ivan Mulcahy and Michele Milburn.

My friends Robert Hudson, Jonathan Dryden Taylor, Toby Davies and Tom Hilton, who read many of these columns in advance and gave invaluable advice.

And my beloved wife, Victoria Coren Mitchell, whose brilliant, funny brain has hugely improved this book, as well as my whole life.

LIST OF COLUMNS

INDEX

(the initials DM refer to David Mitchell)

Index

Index

Index

Index